DOCTOR FEELGOOD

DOCTOR FEELGOOD

PAUL NEWMAN

JOHN BLAKE

Published by John Blake Publishing Ltd,
3 Bramber Court, 2 Bramber Road,
London W14 9PB, England

www.blake.co.uk

First published in paperback in 2007

ISBN: 978-1-84454-412-7

British Library Cataloguing-in-Publication Data:

A catalogue record for this book is available from the British Library.

Design by www.envydesign.co.uk

Printed and bound in Great Britain by William Clowes Ltd, Beccles, Suffolk

1 3 5 7 9 10 8 6 4 2

Papers used by John Blake Publishing are natural, recyclable products made from wood grown in sustainable forests. The manufacturing processes conform to the environmental regulations of the country of origin.

All photographs from the author's collection

Paul Newman is a bass-baritone singer. He has been a racing driver, a developer, a woodsman, a poker player, a clothing exporter and a glass and furniture designer.

Paul Newman was introduced to me by a mutual friend. He was in the early stages of writing this book and I saw straight away that he had a fascinating story to tell. From Bob Marley's funeral in Jamaica to importing 18 tonnes of cannabis from Africa followed by imprisonment as a maximum security prisoner. His story is full of action.

Paul sang spirituals to me on my birthday, he is a man of many surprises. His book is an adventure from cover to cover.

Martina Cole, June 2007

I first met Paul Newman 18 years ago in Winchester. We met again a few months later at Brixton. He is a very interesting man and has a fascinating story to tell.

We have had the opportunity to renew our friendship more recently. Paul sang at a charity event I am involved with in Greenwich.

This book tells an exciting story. Read it.

Eddie Richardson, June 2007

'Paul Newman obviously enjoyed his "life of crime" and you will enjoy reading about it.'

Clive A Stafford Smith
Legal Director, Reprieve

I dedicate this book to my grandchildren,
Fifi, Jasper, Joseph and Emma.

ACKNOWLEDGEMENTS

I would like to thank Martina Cole for her advice and encouragement, my friend Richard Honour for his help and perseverance and Lucian Randall for his support and input.

PREFACE

I knew from the way that I could get close enough to the ship to watch it unload that security was tipped in our favour. There was a tonne of the best African grass hidden inside those giant bales of timber and we had worked so hard to ensure it was perfectly concealed. Customs would surely not imagine that anybody would send such a precious consignment as deck cargo.

I was close enough to recognise our timber – rough-sawn African iroko hardwood. I knew every single bale and had blisters to prove it. The dockside crane swung into position and the workers on deck hooked the two slings which secured each end of the bale on to the crane's massive hook. The first bale was expertly lowered on to the dock below and the second was placed gently alongside.

The third, at the halfway point on its journey down, jerked to a halt in mid-air. Momentarily, it dipped down at one end. To my horror, the sling at one end began to slip towards the middle of the bale. It swung drunkenly downwards, halted briefly as the other sling took a brief hold, slipped from its grasp and crashed end-on on to the concrete below.

The upper metal banding snapped apart and the planks of wood, like a massive fan, splayed out sideways before falling open on to the dock.

I hardly dared look. It was one of the 50 per cent extra bales of untouched timber I had insisted on adding as insurance on to every consignment.

Someone was smiling down on me that day.

CONTENTS

INTRODUCTION

Bob Marley didn't make it back to Jamaica. Reduced to half his body weight and ravaged by cancer, he lost his fight for life in Miami. This was to be his final journey back from Ethiopia where he had elected to cure his originally operable illness with traditional Rasta medicine.

Two days before he died on 11 May 1981, the Prime Minister, Eddie Seaga, his once sworn enemy and political adversary, had flown to his bedside to bestow his country's highest honour upon the great man. He personally thanked him for publicly reconciling Seaga and Michael Manley at the concert which marked Marley's comeback from being shot in one of the bloodiest and dirtiest election campaigns in the island's history. Where had the guns come from to fuel all this political acrimony? Well, the good old Land of the Free, that's where.

I was staying in Kingston during the short lying in state. On the morning of his funeral, I watched from my balcony as the kites wheeled high over Sabina Park, the site of another of Jamaica's great passions. I dressed for the funeral in a bush suit so much favoured by the less formal Manley regime, in contrast to the suits and ties of the New Order. I was seated at the front beside Eddie Seaga's sister and daughters. The service was a celebration of Bob's life. The music, provided by his mother, wife and young son, Ziggy, along with many more Jamaican stars, set a sweet and sour scene to the final farewell to a man who had lived only 36 years. It was a day of great sadness for me and, as the coffin was carried past to be taken on its final journey in the back of a pick-up truck in accordance with Bob Marley's wishes, I knew that my episode in Jamaica, too, was coming to a close.

Jamaica had drawn me like the Sirens of Ancient Greece. It had seductively enveloped me and appealed to my strong sense of adventure and excitement. I felt at home there. Even during the run-up to elections, hearing the gunfire from the safety of my friend Bolivar's house in the hills high above the city, I never felt threatened. I had come close to settling in Montego Bay and moving my young family out to join me. I often wondered how my children would fare, brown as berries, healthy from a diet of food that was touched by the sun and converted to the delightful patois that was spoken by Jamaicans black and white alike.

I loved the music of Jamaica and was pleased to meet so many of the best performers the island had ever produced. I remember most of these meetings clouded by a warm confusion of fine sensemilla (marijuana). I often wondered how Bob and the others succeeded in achieving anything, constantly drawing lungfuls of ganja from spliffs which resembled ice-cream cornets. I was a child of the Sixties when only the good parties ended in police raids. I had smoked dope recreationally ever since, but, compared to these guys, I was a lightweight.

I went to a good few street parties with sound systems which took your breath away and was always made welcome. I saw a lot of firearms which seemed to be brought along to be used by way of celebration rather than for more sinister purposes. The biggest *gangstas*, like alpha-male lions, spread their seed copiously amongst the female population but seemed happy to share with favoured friends who posed no territorial threat.

After Eddie Seaga had been elected, I was asked by my friend Dr Marco Brown, the Minister of Tourism, to take a look at the resort situation in Jamaica. During Michael Manley's regime, the larger hotels had been nationalised and it had not been a success. Although tourism had been flourishing and occupation rates had been high, government control had resulted in dubious management and the bigger hotels had been haemorrhaging profits. The decision had been taken to reverse the situation and re-privatise every single government-owned hotel. I was invited to register my interest.

My trips became more and more frequent and lengthy. I looked at many a project, before finally deciding to concentrate on one of the larger hotels in Negril and an entirely new development project at Black River. I began to meet and know more and more people and I spent much time travelling the island. The journey by car from Negril to Mandeville was one that I loved, following the coast for the most part. The narrow and often dangerous road passed by secluded bays; small and often temporary roadside rum bars dotted the route. Local people waved you down to try to tempt you with a variety of produce from gynneps, a kind of fruit much like lychee, to pepper shrimps, irresistible prawns boiled with hot chilli peppers and served in paper bags, certain to stain whatever you were wearing, but worth it.

I was accompanied on one of these trips by a friend who had a successful antique business and wrote songs. He deserved to have done better with his music but his irreverent sense of humour did not endear him to everyone. He was being targeted by the Inland Revenue who found it difficult to see his annual returns for some years as anything other than works of fiction and he readily agreed to spend a couple of weeks in Jamaica. Before leaving for our trip, he left a musical message on his answerphone, a merry song beginning with the words '*I'm going to Jamaica... care of Freddie Laker...*'

One night, we were playing pool in a local bar in Montego Bay and a couple of girls approached us. 'Hello, boys, is there anything we can do for you?'

'You could wash the car,' replied Neil.

'And you can go and suck your cock...' was the reply as they left to hoots of laughter from the locals.

There followed a party with Neil performing his entire repertoire to an appreciative and increasingly rowdy audience. We left some time after breakfast.

Neil's return to England was not one he will want to remember. One of the messages on his answerphone went: 'Don't worry about missing your appointment at the tax office, we'll come to you next time...' and they did.

To add to his misery, among the other gifts he brought back to his girlfriend was a virulent case of crabs.

One of my favourite places on the island was Rick's Café situated in Negril just before the lighthouse and set in rocks from which locals would dive into the deep pools below. I jumped a couple of times but never head first; it was necessary to launch yourself a good way outwards to avoid being filleted by lethally sharp outcrops on the way down. The sunsets at Rick's were spectacular. It was here that I met an English artist ten years my junior who had come to Jamaica on holiday with a friend. I was instantly attracted to her and had a strong feeling of warmth in her company.

I had to travel to Kingston two days later and did not know when I would finish my business there. I missed her straight away and called her more or less as soon as I arrived. She flew in to Kingston the next day to join me. She brought sunshine into my life and I adored her. We continued our relationship both in London and Jamaica for some time afterwards.

I had made quite a bit of money in London during the previous few years and with a secure relationship with my bank manager, who dubbed me 'Wonder Boy', I had a high degree of financial security. However, negotiations in Jamaica were becoming increasingly protracted, and every time I seemed to be getting close to finalising a deal I was referred to yet another property.

Eventually, it became clear that I was not destined to get the best hotels. They were secured by prominent local business people. I had spent a lot of time and money and, although I could have stayed to pursue some of the shorter- and longer-term deals available to me, I felt that the time had come to move on.

Around the corner from the New Kingston Hotel, squashed between two modern office buildings, Give Thanks McDonald ran his oyster bar. Seated on home-made brightly painted benches, customers would be served with an endless succession of fresh-water oysters, deftly opened by the big man and washed down with cold Red Stripe. He kept them coming 'til you held up a hand in defeat. It was to be my last meal in Jamaica. My bag was packed ready for the early-morning flight home. I don't think I shall ever return, knowing somehow that I would never be able to rekindle the affection I have in my heart for Jamaica.

Back in London in the early Eighties, Thatcherism had taken hold and greed and selfishness were the order of the day. The property market was spiralling upwards and everybody with any unborrowed equity in their houses was become a property developer. I hated the new regime and did not feel comfortable climbing on to a bandwagon I despised. But money was dwindling and I had to find a means of earning a living. I had a large house and a big family to support.

One Sunday afternoon, I was mowing the front lawn. And it was then that fate determined the path I was to take.

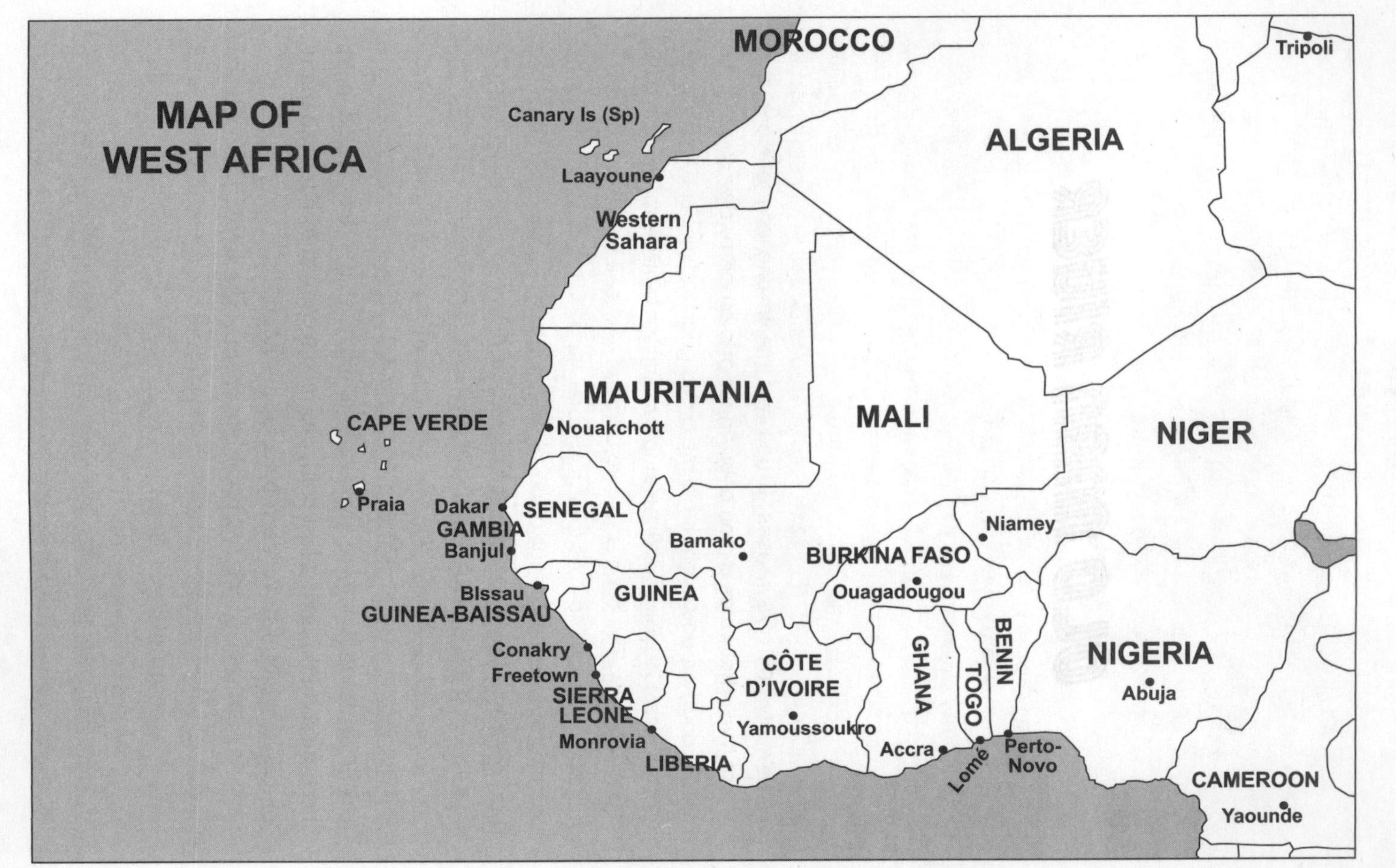
MAP OF
WEST AFRICA
MOROCCO
Tripoli
Canary Is (Sp)
ALGERIA
Laayoune
Western
Sahara
MAURITANIA
MALI
NIGER
CAPE VERDE
Nouakchott
Praia
Dakar
SENEGAL
GAMBIA
Banjul
Niamey
Bamako
BURKINA FASO
Ouagadougou
Bissau
GUINEA
GUINEA-BAISSAU
BENIN
GHANA
TOGO
NIGERIA
Conakry
CÔTE
D'IVOIRE
Freetown
Abuja
SIERRA
LEONE
Yamoussoukro
Monrovia
Accra
Perto-
Novo
LIBERIA
Lomé
CAMEROON
Yaounde

1

OLD MAN RIVER

People are full of surprises. If you met me in one environment, you might think that I was a man of business or a property developer. If we met in another, you might label me a designer and maker of glassware and furniture. If you heard me sing, you might believe me to be a full-time musician. The truth is, I have been all of these things. In addition, I have been an international smuggler. In 1990, I was convicted of masterminding the importation of 18 tonnes of cannabis from Africa and sentenced to ten-and-a-half years in prison; designated a high-risk, Category A prisoner, a 'threat to national security'.

It has been difficult to know where to start this story. Most of my life has been an adventure. I have a short attention span and am easily distracted. I have travelled so much that I feel that I have become something of a lost soul, destined to return to haunt so many places in which I have left a piece of my heart.

It is now several years since I left prison. The human mind has a knack of softening pain in the fullness of time, but I regularly remind myself of the futility of incarceration and the consumption of time never to be returned to me.

Since my release, I have enjoyed many more adventures, but it is as a singer that I have found peace and fulfilment. I am a bass-baritone and I love to sing the repertoire of the great Paul Robeson. We share an affinity in socialism and I suppose his 'Roots' are my 'Holocaust'. He is my spiritual brother; we share a love of humankind and weep at its tragedies.

During a visit to Iran where I was designing and making glass, two poor souls were publicly executed for adultery. It sent a shiver down my spine and I reflected that I had been lucky to be free to get stoned in a very different way. Some of my wanderings have caused pain and for that I am sorry. I have no religion and yet feel a strong sense of Judaic tradition from the kosher blood coursing through my veins. This I inherited from my father who managed to escape from Vienna in 1939 at the age of 16.

When I was a child, I remember he spoke little of what he had experienced but often expressed regret that he had never found peace with his own father, whom he left behind and never saw again. I adored this little bearded man with his strong Austrian accent whose hackles would rise like a Semitic Jack Russell every time he was faced with a uniform or authority of any kind. I loved to go with him to the sweat shop that he owned in Fournier Street, in the middle of what was then the London Jewish ghetto around Brick Lane. The little synagogue on the corner, now a mosque, epitomises the permanent state of flux in the city which I love. I remember some of the rich characters, many scarred by their experiences but in too much of a hurry rebuilding their lives to permit the luxury of self-pity. All was conducted in a madness of desperate energy and high volume in a world where nobody 'paid retail'.

The combination of my mother's fashion-design skills and my father's dogged industry enabled him to sell up and take early retirement at 40 to enter the life of academia for which he had been originally destined. My parents also introduced me to classical music at an early age. It has been a life force for me ever since and always a companion at times of great loneliness.

I was sent away to boarding school. There I had elitism and Christianity stuffed down my throat like a Strasbourg goose. Intent upon resistance, I squandered my education and thence began an alienation from my father, to whom I had become a disappointment.

From the age of ten, I began to spend much of my school holidays with my maternal grandparents and was the apple of my grandfather's eye. He was a tyrant and a drunkard and his politics were somewhere to the right of Attila the Hun. He was also an engineering genius and had a factory, which designed and made parts for passenger aircraft. I spent many a happy day with him at London Airport where he would toss me the keys to his car, allowing me to drive for hours around the perimeter track at breakneck speed.

Later, at the local pub, at closing time, he was more often than not carried out to his car by his friends and laid on the back seat. Seated on a cushion, with his hat on my head, I would drive him the 30-odd miles home. Not once was I stopped.

I was lucky to be taken on many European trips and holidays. I have a natural gift with languages and, combined with my love of life and people, can recall many an adventure and an early thirst to find the heart of every new place.

On one such trip motoring through France in my father's brand-new Citroën, we happened upon Les Collombes. This grand château belonged to Josephine Baker, the black American 1930s star of stage, screen and record. She was also a human rights activist and decorated for her undercover work with the French Resistance during the Second World War.

We booked in to stay for a few days and were joined by an uncle and aunt from America on a grand tour of Europe. At the age of 11, I could not understand why my father and uncle were so besotted by this – to me – somewhat elderly but nice lady.

I willingly accepted when my father bet me my holiday pocket money of 10 shillings, against his new car, that I could not spend the night with her.

I explained the situation to Ms Baker, who, much amused, cuddled me goodnight in her baronial four-poster bed. My father still owes me a Citroën.

The relationship between my father and I became increasingly strained and we had many periods of extended silence, the last of which was broken some eight years ago. I had been travelling to

Poland regularly for quite a long time before finally finding enough courage to go to Auschwitz to visit the relatives I had never known. Afterwards, I wrote to him reminding him of his regrets of a generation before. Within days, he had flown to London from America where he now lives. We have been close friends ever since.

We still argue, sometimes late into the night. At his request, I took him to Poland where we tried to find some trace of our ancestors with small success. Many of the records were destroyed by the fleeing Germans before the camps were liberated.

My father's two sisters were the only others to escape Vienna. Erika married Seymour who, along with his two brothers Cyril and Norman Beech, qualified as a solicitor. Each had his own practice, and all three were struck off by the Law Society for separate misdemeanours. Norman was the first to go. Having stated in a television interview that, in his opinion, London would be a safer place with fewer police, he finally lost his certificate after dressing a client, in court on a burglary charge, in a wig and moustache. In this guise, the client was 'identified' by three policemen who had 'verballed him up' – i.e. falsified his statement – so that he appeared to admit to a crime which he had not committed. It's one thing to expose corruption, but quite another to breach protocol.

On a family holiday in Italy, Seymour borrowed a screwdriver to mend something on the car. Afterwards, he put the tool in the boot. Shocked, I asked him, 'Are you honestly going to steal that screwdriver?'

'No', he replied, 'dishonestly.'

Where did I get my sense of adventure, rebelliousness and naughtiness?

Who knows?

2

TULCHAN

In 1969, along with a business partner, I had raised the money to buy three terraced cottages in Greenwich, none of which had bathrooms and one had no electric light. I had a flair for renovation design and, although we went through the usual delays finding and keeping a good builder, we came out with a fair profit and a bank happy to continue to back us. At around this time, secondary banks had begun to emerge awash with money and keen to lend. They were much less hidebound in their approach to business.

Both of us were keen on shooting and we heard that Tulchan, one of the Earl of Seafield's grouse moors near Grantown-on-Spey in the Highlands, was up for lease for the 1970 season – 22,000 acres of grouse, pheasant and wildfowl shooting with deer stalking, salmon and capercaillie (a large turkey-like bird which lives on pine needles and tastes of turpentine). Neither of us could afford to pay for our shooting but we calculated that we might show a small profit at the end of the season by selling all-inclusive sporting breaks by the week with accommodation in the large and impressive lodge. I remember our game dealer was called Archie Grice and our telephone number was Advie 200, with all our calls being filtered through a very nosey operator.

We set about advertising and the response was better than our wildest dreams. Our activities at Tulchan attracted quite a lot of interest and I still have an original cartoon by Martin which accompanied an article in the *Sunday Express*. I got a call one day asking me to meet a prospective guest at The Ritz. I arrived to be ushered to a table where I was met by the owner of Weetabix, Tony George. He explained that the family had a suite permanently reserved along with a regular table in the dining room and their own wine cellar. The service was deferential in the extreme and, when we'd finished, the head waiter was informed by my host that he ran 'a good pub'. He had recently paid £1 million for a stretch of salmon fishing, a fabulous sum in those days by any standards.

He duly arrived in a new Rolls with butler, Labrador and wife. She was sent out daily, having to drive the car herself, while the butler was needed on loading duties with his master on the moor. She was instructed to do the rounds of all the little local shops and introduce them to their new product, Alpen, packets of which were stacked in the boot.

We had some wonderful characters staying at the lodge. I remember one, Graham Horne, heir to the men's clothing business. He arrived with a newly tailored outfit for each day of the week and seemed to spend more than half of his life shooting all over the world. Apparently, the family had their own grouse moor and he recounted the days of his grandfather when, at the beginning of the season, the family's own railway coach would be attached to the night train and the boys of the family would amuse themselves taking pot shots at sheep with rifles on the journey north.

The moor was beautiful and much of it was so isolated that one could see no sign of life for miles around. Unlike pheasants, grouse cannot be bred for shooting, encouraged in numbers only by the keepers providing them with as good a habitat as possible. The old heather is burned in order to make way for new growth on which the birds can feed. This results in the hillsides looking like patchwork quilts. Grouse are territorial and, if allowed to overpopulate, they are prone to a disease which decimates their numbers. Often, the journey, in sure-footed, four-wheel-drive vehicles, up the hills to the first shooting drive of the day, took nearly an hour. A previous tenant, the Duke of Gloucester, a peppery old boy by all accounts, insisted that lunch was served on the moor daily for all his guests by his butler and staff in full livery.

Apparently, one morning, as he was sitting on his shooting stick out of sight from the grouse, his loader informed him that the birds were coming. Seeing the Duke immobile, he moved closer to wake him. He had died leaning against the side of his grouse butt.

We had a delightful party of Austrian aristocrats, one of whom, Countess Seilern, recounted stories of her family shooting estates in Hungary before the war. Her father, apparently very popular among his employees, introduced a system of compensation for those estate workers who were shot while beating pheasants towards the guns, at the rate of one gold coin for every piece of lead. The rule was overturned a week later when the injury rate multiplied tenfold with poor workers throwing themselves into salvoes of shot at any given opportunity.

We closed the lodge at the end of December and, just as we had done so, we received a booking for a week's pheasant shooting in mid-January for a party of Germans. They booked into a local hotel and we met them on the first morning. We were somewhat surprised that all of them looked as if they had just parachuted in. Most of them sported items of wartime German military uniform and some rather disturbing badges. My partner and I, both German speakers, decided not to let on that we could understand them and we were shocked during the day to hear comments and conversations distinctly Nazi in nature.

We were also booked in at the same hotel that night and, at dinner, we elected to take a table by ourselves away from the main party. After the first course, the man at the head of the table, referred to by his military rank, stood and gave a rousing speech. The only difference between what he had to say and a Nuremberg rally was that it was the pheasants who were to be exterminated. I stood to attention, clicked my heels and delivered my own speech to my friend sitting opposite me and, before he could stand to reply, our message had been understood. The following morning, we reimbursed them for the week's shooting and drove off in the snow, leaving them to make their own travel plans.

We had a few catering problems which we overcame but we always had trouble finding local staff. The lodge had a reputation for being haunted and many potential employees who could have done with the money were too scared even to approach the place from the long drive. One of the bedrooms was particularly unpopular and at least three of the guests mentioned strange noises and things being moved during the night. One of the guests had a Springer Spaniel which would occasionally chase an invisible 'enemy', snapping at its heels as it moved at walking pace across the hallway. A friend who came to stay one night flew down the staircase hysterically shouting, 'Dracula, Dracula.' He had left his window open while dressing for dinner and returned somewhat the worse for wear to find three large bats circling the bedroom light.

We had a couple of New Zealand girls working in the kitchen along with whatever extra help we could find but never had anybody to look after the bar. Instead, we left a stock of drink in the library and an honesty book; everyone thought this very stylish but there were a few drunken nights when memories were somewhat hazy. One guest who flew from Sydney for two weeks' shooting drank every single bottle of champagne in the house and did not once make it on to the moor.

Many of our guests wanted to do the triple, which involved shooting a stag and then a grouse and catching a salmon all in one day. I did it once and immediately regretted killing the beautiful stag. I never shot another and, since leaving prison, have had no desire to shoot living creatures ever again.

3

PRISON VISITING

The property business continued to flourish. I moved into a small farmhouse near Faversham with my growing family and saw immediately the potential for conversion of farm buildings; most especially timber-framed barns and oast houses. We also built a close relationship with the Historic Buildings Division of the Greater London Council and worked hand in hand with them to save several historic buildings.

Many of these wonderful properties found themselves in areas very much less grand than when they were originally built. Most were in a state of sad dereliction and renovation costs were almost certain to exceed those of more modern buildings. The key was to find a use that compensated the high costs involved. This side of the business earned us two prized awards.

I busied myself locating suitable conversion properties in Kent and Sussex for which I would negotiate a price without planning consent. We had a great solicitor who often would follow with a contract less than a week later. We began to get a reputation and received several approaches by word of mouth. Our conversions were always imaginative and popular and, by early 1972, I began to look for a somewhat grander property in which to house my family. I eventually bought an ancient manor house in Biddenden at auction for £70,000 with 24 acres of land and a garden which the previous owners opened to the public. I loved the place and set about a restoration project which took about six months to complete.

I learned to fly in the summer of 1972 at an airfield in Headcorn, Kent. It was just a grass airfield in the middle of the countryside and difficult to find. I used to hire aeroplanes to spot suitable prospective buildings from the air and mark them on a map.

The life of the village squire at the age of 25 went to my head and I must have been a bit of an arse. However, I still remained true to my political beliefs, a solitary socialist in a sea of rural blue.

Some years before, I had met a friend of my father who told me about his work as a prison visitor. He explained that a large proportion of the prison population received no visits from family or friends and were in need of outside contact. A small number of men and women regularly visit prisons all over the country, usually spending one evening a week behind bars. My father's friend was, I remember, very religious and I had a strong impression that there was a strong evangelical element to this humanitarian activity. The late Lord Longford devoted much of his life unselfishly bringing comfort to many forgotten souls and spent a good deal of time with my friend Eddie Richardson while he was 'away'. Eddie, an accomplished artist, painted a portrait of Longford and captured his likeness exceptionally well.

I made contact with Maidstone Prison and was not surprised to learn that prison visiting was handled by the chaplain. He was more than willing to take me on, despite the fact that I made it clear that I had no personal religious agenda. We had a glass of sherry with the Governor who could not quite grasp why a young agnostic would want to do such a thing but, within a week, the formalities had been concluded. Very soon, I was given a list of those who would appreciate some outside contact.

I spent one evening a week at Maidstone and had a pigeon hole where the chaplain would leave requests from inmates, usually with a short outline of why they were locked up and for how long. I was initially assigned to a murderer coming to the end of his sentence. His mother, the only remaining member of his family, had died while he was in prison. After a couple of visits, he was moved to an open prison in preparation for his release on licence.

At the request of the chaplain, I also saw a convicted rapist but could not overcome my feelings of revulsion at his crime. The chaplain told me that he was not surprised at my reaction, after which I began to be allocated young prisoners on the main wings.

There is a section called Rule 43 in most prisons which separates sex offenders and grasses from the rest of the prison population for their own protection. If they ever find themselves exposed in the prison mainstream, particularly in long-term establishments, their life expectancy can be measured in minutes.

After some months, I received a request to visit a young chap inside for armed robbery. I went to see him on the wing during evening association, when everybody's cells were open. We immediately got on well and had a game of snooker, during which I was introduced to quite a few of his mates. Afterwards, I was invited into his cell for a coffee, during which several of his mates popped in to say hello. The next week, I was introduced to John and we immediately hit it off, sharing a passion for motor racing. John was a highly respected 'wheel man' and much in demand for 'that perfect getaway'.

In order for me to continue to visit John on a regular basis, he had to register for prison visits. It was unusual for prisoners receiving regular visits from family to request to see a prison visitor, but John's application was granted. Before long, I was holding a weekly party with half-a-dozen regulars, which was totally unorthodox but strongly supported by the chaplain. I was often fed by my hosts who had an Indian chef 'on the firm' and I would usually bring a flask of brandy with which we would lace the coffee.

John was unexpectedly granted parole in 1974 and he came to stay in Biddenden with his family during his pre-release home leave. After his release, we tried to get some business going together but things were getting hard and we agreed to go our separate ways. We kept in touch for a while but he moved house. We were not to meet again until that fateful day after my return from Jamaica many years later.

4

BLACK... RED... AND BACK TO BLACK

By 1974, we were riding high. We had acquired a local building company and managed our own developments. With money still freely available, we were able to expand our holdings at breakneck pace. Our accountant estimated that we were worth over £2 million and rising steadily. Around this time, I began to get a feeling that it would be a good idea to hold an auction to sell off most of our property portfolio. It would have enabled us to pay off all our bank borrowings and slow down the mad spiral of expansion. My business partner agreed reluctantly and I set about planning the sale with a local estate agent. For some reason, it never went ahead. Within a month, we were caught in the vortex of a property crash from which there was no escape.

The secondary banks were tumbling just as quickly as they had sprung up and every financial institution ran for cover. Our assets soon became liabilities and our net worth slid from plus £2 million to minus £1 million. There was no money to complete work in progress and we had to lay off our workforce.

We had, of course, personally guaranteed our borrowings and it was not long before the Official Receiver came knocking on the door. In those days, one had to attend a public examination in court as part of the bankruptcy proceedings. I remember being harangued by a barrister for two hours about my extravagant lifestyle, while the local reporters took hurried notes. The story hit the headlines in the local papers and, feeling tainted, I was reluctant to go out and face the world. I felt a sense of failure and responsibility for those employees who, only weeks before, were able to work as much overtime as they wanted. I remember the local tradesmen being much more sympathetic and discreet than the wealthier locals who would rather cross the road than face their erstwhile friend with a case of financial leprosy. After my bankruptcy, the local butcher, with whom we had always run an account, would always ask in a loud voice, 'Cash or account, sir?' I could have kissed him in front of all his customers as I pulled the money out of my pocket to pay him.

I lost my beautiful house. We were permitted three months in which to find alternative accommodation and, by the time most of the contents were sold, we had little to take with us. The gardener, Bunny Monday, who had worked at the house since long before we had bought it, refused to leave. He was by then well over retirement age and argued that he had little need of money.

On one occasion, my grandfather drove to visit us at the house. When my mother was a child, the whole family had come to Biddenden hop picking and he had brought some photographs taken at the time. When Bunny looked at them, he immediately recognised himself as a young man with an arm over my grandfather's shoulder in front of a local pub. I occasionally drive past Biddenden Place and feel a tug at my heart strings.

Fortunately, we were able to keep our heads above water. My wife was able to benefit from a share of the proceeds of a joint venture with the Historic Buildings Division of the GLC which came to fruition six months later. With it, she bought a big sprawling, tumbledown Victorian pile on the main road in a neighbouring village. The vendor was a strange man called Lord Haliburton, who was emigrating to Australia. It had oil-fired central heating which we could seldom afford to run and patches of dry rot which we dealt with piecemeal.

A friend of mine who farmed locally was telling me one day that he was grubbing a 20-acre wood. He explained that he was offering the wood and trees in exchange for digging up and burning the larger roots and I immediately put up my hand. My Bristol car had been repossessed some months before and I drove around in an old Mark 1 Land Rover which I had bought for £50. My farmer friend gave me a small trailer and I bought a chain saw. I put an advertisement in the local paper offering logs at £10 a load and I was inundated with calls. I was in business. Within a short time, I was able to cut and deliver 30 loads of logs a week all on my own. I supplemented my income with a weekly local game of poker which usually paid dividends.

Twenty acres was a lot of wood and I soon realised that I could not clear it alone. I took on some experienced and tough locals and began to cut wood for pulp. This was collected by local contractors on large lorries which we had to load at the end of the day. The lorries would drive to paper mills in Sittingbourne where they would be given a weighbridge ticket which I was handed the next day. The woodmen worked on piece rates and each would pile their own work separately. I paid them in cash against the weighbridge tickets and was paid myself by the contractor at the end of the week.

The contractor and I established a good rapport. He, too, had been bankrupted many years before. He had built up a very successful business with his own yard and several lorries on the road. One year, he took his family on holiday to France. He got into conversation with a local one night in a bar, who told the contractor that he knew of a large wood of mature and straight walnut trees which were up for sale. He inspected the forest the next day and found the trees to be of fine veneer quality. The price was so low as to make the deal irresistible. He found a lawyer and returned to England to raise the capital to buy the forest. The deal went according to plan and he returned with his team of woodsmen. A few days later, the first trees were delivered to the sawmill and, at the first cut, sparks flew from the blade which was rendered useless by a large piece of metal. It turned out that the forest had been in the middle of a First World War battlefield and every single tree had been peppered with shrapnel.

I continued with the log business but gradually found myself playing more and more poker. Now travelling twice a week to London, I often would not return home until after the day began in the woods. I appointed a foreman for the wood pulp and subcontracted the log business to a couple of lads whom I knew from the local pub. I still went to the woods whenever I could and paid the men every week at the house. And it wasn't long before another project presented itself.

5

CARE

Before leaving Biddenden, we met some local people who had joined a project jointly promoted by Kent County Council and the university in Canterbury. The project had identified a problem in placing older children in care for fostering or adoption. Many children by their early teens had already acquired quite lengthy criminal records and knew how to be disruptive. We had plenty of room and, in 1975, we decided to join.

Shortly after we moved to our new house in Bethersden, our new guests began to arrive. They were all damaged to some degree, were reluctant or refused to go to school and all smoked heavily. Some had been in care for most of their lives and others for a short time only, either by order of a court or rejected by parents who could not or would not cope. The police became frequent visitors to the house in a quest to clear up local petty crime and some of the kids had developed an intimate knowledge of the British criminal system. One boy who lived with us for about six months had on his record one offence of 'taking and driving away a train'.

He had been with a friend at a Medway station when the driver got off to take a pee. They jumped in and drove the train full of commuters to the next station where they were arrested. Many had done a spell or two at 'DC', a kind of institutional boot camp, and all were case-hardened. The woodcutting business provided an opportunity to earn money for cigarettes and had the attraction of being close to dangerous machinery. Besides which, there were tractors and Land Rovers to be driven. Some of the boys became very adept at things mechanical and found a level of self-discipline. Others could not resist pushing the self-destruct button when just on the verge of a positive breakthrough.

One 14-year-old girl – whom I shall call Jane – came to stay after spending most of her life in care. Her mother, a mad bag lady, lived in a hole in the wall in Whitstable. Occasionally, I would go and collect her and take her home for a bath and to be fed. She would ramble on incoherently but had occasional moments of lucidity. We found out that Jane's uncle was in reality also her father and Jane was conceived in the waiting room at Whitstable Station. Jane's mother would occasionally launch into a tirade of abuse at the 'uncle' who, it transpired, had been taking Jane out from the homes she was in since she was 12.

Since she had been with us, she used to go out for an hour or two in the evenings and I often noticed the same little sports car parked up the road. One day, I lay in wait and brought the man in the car to the house. I was not surprised when he announced that he was in fact her 'uncle' and I demanded to know why he chose to meet furtively rather than coming to the house. I kept him there and called Jane's social worker, who rushed out from Ashford. It came to light that for two years the social services knew that this man had been having sex with his then 12-year-old daughter in his car on a regular basis. The authorities had chosen to do nothing other than move Jane to another home.

I hit the roof. I physically dragged the man to the kitchen and, before throwing him out, told him that, if I ever caught him hanging around Jane again, I would make sure that he would regret it.

I returned to the living room to find Jane being forcibly restrained by her social worker who rounded on me for having upset the poor girl who wanted to be with her father/uncle/lover. Once more, I went nuts. Poor Jane, who was in love with this monster, announced that she was going to run away at the earliest opportunity. Later, while she was taking a bath, I ensured that she had nothing more than slippers and a dressing gown to change into in the hope that she would calm down and see sense.

A few days before, I had received a call from somebody called Lucy Hogg. She announced that she was a TV producer and, along with a famous director, wanted to come to meet us with a view to making a film about our fostering activities. The next morning, she arrived at the front door. Very well spoken and a little nervous, she referred to the famous director a couple of times before announcing that it was in fact Lord Snowdon and he was sitting outside in the car. She brought him in and it soon transpired that Lucy was the new woman in his life.

I took to him instantly. We had been chatting easily for quite some while when I saw Jane in her dressing gown jump out of the bathroom window and run through the garden into a ploughed field beyond. The scene that followed would have made a great silent movie. Jane, closely pursued by Tony Snowdon across the wet field, eventually came to a breathless halt weighed down by heavy clay. They looked at each other for a while and both burst out laughing.

Later in the day, Jane made another escape, leaving behind a note calling us 'all bardits'. She returned for a while and was there during the filming, which took about a week. I remember little about that week, apart from Tony being recognised by an old boy in the local pub. 'I knows you, don't I?' he said. 'You be Wally... you're a mate of my brother-in-law.'

We called him Wally for the rest of the week. One scene from the film which sticks particularly in my mind showed my youngest daughter, then still very small, climbing through a cat flap to open the back door.

6

THE ROAD BACK

Poker continued to provide well and I spent up to five nights a week playing in private games, casinos and illegal spielers, often ending up around breakfast time in one of several establishments open early for the night people of London – cabbies, gamblers and prostitutes all with tired eyes and a tale to tell. I had become a night-shift worker and I felt in need of a change.

I can't remember where I had heard that the clothing business was booming in Holland, but around 1976 I bought some American baseball clothing from an importer and made my way by car to Amsterdam. I sold what I had with me to a guy who had three boutiques, and the next day, he called me with a big order. I spent a week researching the market and discovered that almost anything different or innovative sold like hot cakes.

When I got back to London, I scoured the wholesalers. In a store specialising in army surplus and work wear, I found a one-piece plastic disposable overall on sale at 50p. I discovered that they had a consignment of 4,000 pieces and I did a deal for the lot. They took my cheque but I knew there was not enough money in the bank to cover it. I had to move quickly. That night, I was on the overnight ferry to Vlissingen with a newly acquired Australian estate car stuffed to the brim with overalls.

I managed to drive through Dutch Customs without a declaration and made my way to Amsterdam. By lunchtime, I had sold them all for £5 each and was on the ferry back later that day with the cash. The cheque had not even been presented for payment by the time I paid in the proceeds of sale.

I was back in Holland a week later. Disco was big at that time and I saw several girls dancing in my overalls. The bravest wore nothing underneath to show just a sexy dark hint of nipple and pubic hair through the opaque plastic.

During the following two years, I could do no wrong. I had thousands of Hawaiian shirts made by Ronnie Stirling and all sorts of other clothing items for which there was a ready market in Holland. I often travelled there twice a week, always delivering personally and never once being asked for credit. This time, I got out at the right time and earned enough to finance a return to London and the first step back on to the bottom rung of the property ladder.

In 1977, the house in Bethersden was sold and I bought a big house in Greenwich which had been converted into two maisonettes. It did not take long to return the house into a single unit. The week that we moved in with the help of my new bank manager, I bought another two houses in the area in need of renovation. The property market was on the up again and, after three months, I sold the house we were living in for almost double what we had paid.

My children acclimatised to town life quickly enough and soon made friends. It was a great relief when we no longer had to ferry them all over the countryside in order to maintain a social life.

During the following two years, I bought, renovated and sold a large quantity of houses in Blackheath and Greenwich and had a team of builders who really could be relied upon to turn a job around within weeks.

I first met Jools Holland around this time who lived with the girl who cut my hair. Julian was still playing with Squeeze and, although the band seemed to be busy and had a loyal following, there never seemed to be much spare money to fund a decent lifestyle. We became very close and Julian could always be relied upon to play the piano at any occasion. He never tired of finding new recordings and musicians and his infectious passion for music set the foundations for his rise to becoming the world's foremost musician's musician.

I was keeping fit playing squash whenever I could, partying hard and chasing pretty girls. I was able to pay the bills when they came in, drive fast cars and live life to the full. I sold the house in Greenwich when parking became too difficult and began to look for something larger. After some searching, we were given details of a big Victorian house in Mottingham with some 22 rooms and its own coach house set in three acres of garden. It was on the market for about £50,000 and had an unexpired Crown lease of about 19 years. The big wrought-iron gates opening to a sweep-around drive were both emblazoned with the name Norlesden House.

The vendors were three publicans – Nora, Les and Dennis – and the estimate of £5,000 for new gates told me that Norlesden House was what it would remain. It was love at first sight and we moved in within a month. There was a certain amount of dry rot, which had to be dealt with, and a large amount of flock wallpaper which had to be removed. The neighbouring house had been occupied by the cricketer WG Grace, who also ran his doctor's surgery there alongside an illustrious sporting career. I was told that he died rising from his sick bed to see the first Zeppelin airship on its way to bomb London during the First World War.

Julian left Squeeze around this time and needed somewhere to audition and rehearse his new band, Jools Holland and his Millionaires, with vocal backing from The Wealthy Tarts. He took over our coach house which became ever full of music.

I had bought another very big house in Blackheath, which was destined to be converted into four flats. It provided the perfect venue for our ever-popular annual New Year's Eve party which each year had a different theme. This year was to be 'Bring a Gnome', and those who did not have immediate access to a gnome were given a list of addresses where one could be found.

Music that night was a wonderful jamming session provided by members of Squeeze and Police, with several other well-known and not-so-well-known musicians joining in. Close to 800 people came to the party and, in the morning, we had a collection of over 300 gnomes. Julian made sure that whenever he was abroad during the next few years the gnome would send a card to its parents.

7

TROUBLE

Things were going rather well... rather too well. I was about to experience an encounter with the law, which dispelled any remnants of respect I had for British justice for ever.

One evening late in 1979, I answered an impatient ringing at the front door. I opened it to two men who identified themselves as plain-clothes police officers. They told me that they were making enquiries about the alleged theft of clothing from Stirling Cooper nearly two years before and asked me if I had any documents relating to my dealings with the company. I was shocked. They barged inside the house and I was told that it would make things much easier all round if I co-operated and gave them all the paperwork I had. I led them to my desk where I located various receipts and invoices which they took from me.

I was then told that I was being arrested on suspicion of the theft of goods from Stirling Cooper and was led outside to their waiting unmarked car. It was an alarming experience. My wife, wanting to know what was going on, was told that I was being taken to West End Central Police Station for questioning. I told her to call my solicitor Chris Johnson at home and to get him to do something.

As soon as I arrived at the station, the officers began to pressure me to answer questions. I insisted on calling my solicitor and was told that he had already called and was due to call again in a few minutes. I refused to answer any questions until I had spoken to him. The phone rang.

'Chris, help me, I don't know what the hell is going on.'

Chris tried to explain what was happening. 'The copper told me that he is making enquiries about some goods that Stirling Cooper say you stole from them.'

'I can't believe it. There's an outstanding bill that I refused to pay because the goods were late. I lost more money than the value of the invoice. But that's a civil matter, isn't it?'

'Of course it is. Listen, Paul, if you need me there, I should be able to make it in an hour-and-a-half but, if you've got nothing to hide, the policeman told me that all you need to do is answer his questions and he'll let you go.'

'Are you sure?'

'Let me speak to him again.'

I passed the policeman the telephone. He spoke to Chris for a couple of minutes and passed the phone back to me.

'Paul, he assures me that he'll let you go after you have answered his questions. If you're worried about any of the answers, just say so now and I'll get in my car.'

I told him that I would do as he suggested and, unless there were any problems, I would go to see him at his office the following day.

The policeman asked me over and over again about the jeans which I had ordered. Stirling Cooper had made me some samples earlier in the year and I had taken substantial orders for June delivery. In the end, after several delays and excuses, they were ready in late September. I was very unhappy about the situation but eventually agreed to try to offload them. In the end, I had to sell them at a knock-down price. In all, I had lost a lot of money because of the delay and I refused to pay for them. I eventually fell out with Stirling Cooper over the transaction and invited them to sue me but warned them to be ready for a large counter-claim for my loss of profits. I heard no more from them and assumed that that was the end of the matter.

I continually answered the policeman's questions by answering that it was a civil matter. I pointed out repeatedly that I had always paid for all the other goods that the company had supplied me. The laborious task of checking and correcting my written statement took until 2.00am when, true to his word, the policeman took me to collect my property from the charge room and bailed me to return at some time in the future. My father was there to meet me. During the journey home and still in a state of shock, I related the story to him.

The next day, I drove to Sevenoaks to see Chris and, after a leisurely liquid lunch, he succeeded in reassuring me that I would probably hear no more about it. How wrong he was.

A week later, Chris called me. He told me that the policeman wanted to see me again to answer some more questions. We arranged to go together and made an appointment for the beginning of the following week. Chris told me that the case would probably be dropped there and that I would be formally released from bail.

Once seated, the policeman passed me some invoices and asked me why some were for one sum of money and others for a different sum for the same goods. Chris asked for some time alone with me before I answered. I told Chris that, in order to pay less import duty in Holland where I sold the goods, I was always given a second invoice made out for a lower sum. I said that sometimes I was also given blank invoices which I could fill in myself. He advised me to refuse to answer any further questions.

Back in the interview room, I was passed the invoices again. I did not answer. He then passed me two blank invoices and asked how I had obtained them. I did not answer. I was charged with the theft of the jeans and six further charges of theft of invoices. I was bailed to appear the next day at court to answer the charges. I was devastated.

After the hearing, Chris made an appointment with a leading counsel whom we went to see together. It was a formal affair with junior counsel present, too. Despite the usual warning to say nothing that might be incriminating, I decided to tell the story exactly as it was. The barrister was not encouraging. He told us that, in addition to having no corroborative evidence to support my explanation, I would do myself no favours in court by admitting to the dishonesty of evading Dutch import duty. In his opinion, even taking into consideration strong character evidence, I was facing a possible custodial sentence of up to three years. He recommended I consider a plea bargain against my admission of guilt on all counts and thought that I might get away with a year in an open prison.

I was in a dilemma and did not know what to do. Chris, ever sympathetic, offered to do anything he could. He was not a specialist and offered me the services of a newly appointed young partner, Stuart Nicholson. He ran the partnership's criminal department and we had always got on well together.

I decided to fight. I was innocent. I spent a long time with Stuart trying to work out my strategy and, in the end, I knew that I needed to get some supportive evidence.

The young Indonesian chap I had employed in Amsterdam two years before, called Mando, would not be difficult to find. He was a real ladies' man and not an evening went by without him making an appearance at the discos around the Leidseplein.

Stuart and I went to Holland together and, sure enough, we caught up with Mando before the end of our first day away. He willingly gave Stuart a statement, as did the shopkeeper who had been let down by late delivery of the summer jeans.

Back in London, we went to see the barrister again. I suggested that we go back to the police with the statements from Holland, which clearly showed that this was not a criminal matter. Once again, he was doom and gloom personified. He was of the opinion that it would be unwise to show them our defence at this stage and most unlikely that they would drop any charges.

During my dealings with Stirling Cooper, I had got on very well with the export manager who was familiar with the invoicing procedure. He had left the company to set up a business of his own and I had no forwarding address. It took me some weeks but, eventually, I tracked him down through a shop where his wife worked. We met one evening. He confirmed that it was common practice to provide export customers with reduced invoices.

I had been made to feel like a criminal. During the year that the case against me was prepared, I was, at best, unsettled and, at worst, panic-stricken. Like the sword of Damocles, it hung over me, waking me, haunting me and tormenting me. Apart from the ongoing expense of it all, I had difficulty in concentrating on work and I lost the drive to push forward with the advantages I had gained in the property market. I could not erase from my mind the vision of spending the next Christmas in prison. I was depressed and disillusioned.

Just before the trial, I could no longer stand the negativity of my barrister and I sacked him. We took on a young enthusiastic junior and I spent hours with him until I was satisfied that he had the whole case clearly set in his mind. A week had been set aside for the trial and, each morning, I would meet Stuart at Waterloo Station, to travel together on to Knightsbridge.

The prosecution presented their case. The manager of Stirling Cooper was called to give evidence but my barrister omitted to ask him if he had ever authorised the issue of extra invoices in a lower sum than the value of the goods. I called forward from the dock and the judge permitted us a few seconds' discussion before my barrister returned to ask the question.

'We are a reputable company,' replied the manager. 'I would never sanction such a thing.'

My barrister, now on a roll, repeated the question, reminding him that he was under oath.

'Never,' he replied.

Prosecution over, I took the stand as the first witness for the defence. I related the history of my business with Stirling Cooper and explained the story of the summer jeans.

The next day, both of our Dutch witnesses gave their evidence. That afternoon, we called the former export manager of Stirling Cooper. My young barrister was quickly into his stride.

'Would you take a close look at Exhibit 6 please?' Pause for business. 'Can you tell me if you recognise the signature on those three invoices?'

'Yes, it's mine.'

'Are you sure?'

'It's my signature.'

'And how did your signature come to get on the invoices?'

'Because the manager told me to write and sign them.'

He confirmed that this was not unusual practice for export customers. He reiterated that I had stolen nothing and that anything I had in my possession by way of blank or written invoices had been given to me. Unexpectedly, he also confirmed that he clearly remembered the history of the jeans and was present when I invited the company to sue me.

Like a good game-show host, the judge took the opportunity at that juncture to adjourn early until the following morning when he would sum up.

I still took some toiletries with me to court the next day. The year's wait had so darkened my optimism that I was still not confident of the outcome. The judge summed up fairly and sent the members of the jury to consider their verdicts. I was permitted to sit in the court canteen to await the verdict.

The jury was out for an hour. Eventually, they returned their unanimous verdict of not guilty on all counts. The angry judge gave instructions for the police to investigate the question of perjury of some of the witnesses. On my way out of the court, I walked past the outstretched hand of the senior policeman.

I was free, but the year had taken a severe toll. I was disillusioned and exhausted. Somehow, I knew that it would have been much easier to tolerate if I had indeed been guilty. In due course, I was to find out whether that was true.

I had a Jamaican friend in London, called Alden Powell, with whom I had done a couple of property deals. My daughter Emily's Jack Russell, Suzie, was, to my eternal shame, a terrible racist, and each time Alden came to the house we had to lock the dog away. The dog had a litter of puppies to whom she had passed all her prejudices, but Alden was determined to take one of them for his children. Within hours of taking it home, it had attached itself devotedly to Alden's doting family. It was a constant source of hilarity to them all that the dog used to go mad whenever any of his Jamaican friends came to visit.

Alden was very active in the Jamaican community. He invited me as his guest to a reception one evening at the Jamaican High Commission where I was introduced to the Minister of Tourism, Dr Marco Brown. Marco and I hit it off immediately and he invited me to come to Jamaica.

After the trial, Alden reminded me of the invitation. The timing was perfect and, the way I felt, I would have been happy to leave England for a life in the Caribbean. My love affair with Jamaica was just what I needed, but I eventually returned to London having spent all my reserve funds and much more besides. I had a good bank manager but his patience would not last for ever and I had a wife and family to support.

After Bob Marley's funeral and still suntanned from Jamaica, I was mowing the front lawn one Sunday afternoon. A passing car hooted and screeched to a halt in the road outside. As the white estate reversed into the drive, I recognised John, his beard and long hair now salt-and-pepper grey. I realised that it had been nine long years since we first met at Maidstone Prison, way back in 1972.

8

INDIA

John and I embraced, happy to have found each other again nine years after those visiting days at Maidstone Prison. I brought him into the house, anxious to hear his news. He was on his way to meet somebody but hurriedly told me that he had been buying and restoring classic cars and was also looking to get something going in Africa. We arranged to meet the next day.

John came to the house the following morning and we spent a long time catching up with each other. I mentioned to him that I had met a chap named Michael looking for finance to go to India, where he had been on the trail of some aeroplanes and vintage cars. Michael told me that he had spent some years on and off in India and, with the help of a Bombay businessman, had discovered a treasure trove from the old Raj.

After partition in 1947, Ghandi had abolished the Indian aristocracy and most of the privileged families had hidden away many of their treasures. India had an embargo against exporting antiques and objects of historical importance but, for years, had been leaking treasure to the West, where it was highly valued.

Michael had spent a lot of money in expenses pursuing the long convoluted process of being passed from one contact to another and had run out of money.

He spoke of Rolls-Royces, Hispano Suizas, English sporting guns, clocks, antiques and, most intriguing of all, the aeroplanes.

Apparently, a Maharaja had gone to England in the 1930s and learned to fly. He was so enthusiastic that he resolved to build an airfield on his estate near Calcutta and form a flying club where other privileged locals could also learn to fly. He bought and paid for 20 Tiger Moth biplanes and returned to India where he built his flying club. By the time the crates arrived from England, the Maharaja had tired of running a flying club, although he still maintained the airfield from where he did his own flying. The crates were put in store.

During the Second World War, the RAF had several training squadrons in India. Apparently, the Maharaja's airfield was used for this purpose and two Spitfires were left behind.

John told me that he had discovered that herbal cannabis could be purchased in Ghana for £5 a pound and he had some good contacts there for supply. He asked me if I wanted to join him in this venture and to think about how best to go about it. I readily agreed. The prospect of making some quick money greatly appealed and, after my recent experiences leading up to my acquittal at Knightsbridge Crown Court, I welcomed the opportunity of getting my own back on the authorities. We arranged to meet Michael that evening.

Michael was ecstatic, having given up on his chances of making his fortune, here at last was a new sponsor keen to finance another treasure hunt. We talked late into the night and agreed to leave for India as soon as possible. After Michael had left, John and I agreed to spend time together in India planning how we were going to progress our decision to import the grass from Africa.

We left a week later and flew Air France via Paris. We smoked a joint on the short hop from Heathrow. Surprisingly, none of the other passengers registered any reaction. The onward trip to Bombay found us arriving very late at night. Michael knew the ropes and we emerged from the airport after passing through the formalities to a prepaid Ambassador taxi. The dust, noise and hubbub that is India, day and night, is something special and wonderfully chaotic.

We checked into the Oberoi Grand. Even in the middle of the night, an army of liveried flunkies was available to us at the clap of hands of the night manager, who welcomed us with an obsequious bow. Hungry after a long journey, we ordered room service and were served a feast by waiters in uniforms of the Raj, who hovered in the room until we were finished.

The next day, rather than book an expensive hotel car, we hailed a taxi on the street and hired it for the day at a cost of about £5. We drove to the house of our Indian contact Bashir and were amused to find the name 'B Dey' inscribed on a plaque outside.

Bashir was charming. Many promises were made to go to see everything in Bombay Michael had told us about. Most of the treasure we wanted to see was in Calcutta and we planned to move on after three or four days but it seemed that there was a lot of local ground to cover first.

Bashir and Michael led in one car and John and I followed behind in the one we had hired that morning. We seemed to take a very tortuous journey via a very poor area. Here we picked up a young chap in a well-laundered but threadbare tropical two-piece and a pair of blue flip-flops.

There followed a tour of antique emporia, some in cellars in side streets, some in 'go-downs' in industrial areas and some in shops. None seemed open for business but, as soon as we arrived, action immediately ensued.

Wherever we went, a small army of employees was kept busy fetching item after item, while an old servant with a tray would appear at regular intervals with tea, water and soft drinks. Initially, it was impossible to get any prices. Eventually, having selected and rejected for a long period, each piece in which we'd shown even a vague interest was labelled and numbered. As each piece was held aloft by the manager, the proprietor apparently plucked a price in sterling out of the air. Throughout the performance, the man we had stopped to pick up said nothing and made no contribution to the proceedings, except to rock his head from side to side each time a price was mentioned.

At some of the establishments, extra people joined the party, again participating no more than our original passenger had. John, I could see, was frustrated by the whole scene and I asked Bashir to identify everybody. He explained that each extra person was responsible for an introduction. It soon became evident that the more participants there were, the higher the quoted prices.

I was no antiques expert, but knew that, considering we also had the job of smuggling whatever we bought out of the country to evade the embargo, the prices were far too high. We decided to buy nothing, leave Bashir to take his own car and return to the hotel to discuss the situation. We agreed that Bashir would come to visit later that evening. I told Michael that I was unimpressed.

John and I decided that our first priority was to get stoned and we determined to find some 'temple ball', the renowned Indian crème de la crème of cannabis. Michael, a non-smoker, was obviously scared to participate so we left him at the hotel to contemplate our disappointment at the day's events.

We headed into town on foot, much to the surprise of the doorman, who was ready to hail any form of transport we fancied. We immediately began to collect a growing posse of poor, bare-footed and often disabled small children. The more change we gave them, the larger the entourage, and dozens of sad little hands pulled at our clothing as we tried to make a getaway.

Low on coins and patience, we eventually shook off the little beggars and found a street vendor selling Pierre Patel copies of every pair of designer sunglasses imaginable. You've guessed it, he knew a man in the marketplace opposite who sold the best dope in the world. We settled for some rather elderly grass sweepings rolled in a twist of brown paper and took a motor rickshaw back to the Oberoi. Our clothes were filthy from so many dirty little fingers pawing at us, so we called the laundry service to take them away before showering and rolling a joint.

We both felt low from becoming angry with the children earlier and were told by Bashir, who arrived early evening, that it was not good to give anybody money on the street. He said that organisers of professional begging rings, many of which inflicted terrible disabilities upon healthy babies, shared little of the pittance the children succeeded in getting.

We made it clear to Bashir that, unless we could deal at the right prices directly with the vendors and principals, there was little point in continuing. We were happy to set aside a percentage of all purchases, by way of a buyer's premium, in order to pay commissions, but insisted on eliminating the string of people in the middle. His sincere and heartfelt assurances inspired little confidence but he announced that the next day we were to see a vintage Rolls-Royce.

In the morning, we were taken to the rather splendid but down-at-heel Art Deco house of a young Maharaja. He had recently inherited from his father and was keen to realise as much capital as possible in order to be free to continue to live a life of luxury. He made us very welcome and introduced us to his beautiful young wife. Indian women have a delicate vulnerability about them, which I find enigmatic and very attractive. The size of the population somewhat belies the impression that sexual emancipation and freedom have not yet arrived on the subcontinent.

It was confirmed that there was an old Rolls-Royce which had been made for the Maharaja's grandfather as a hunting vehicle and we were given photographs of the car in its prime. It was fitted with a high rear seat for two from which tigers could be shot and large running boards on the sides for servants.

John was excited and said that he knew that a few of these cars had been made in the Twenties and only one had so far found its way on to the Western market. We were told that the car was quite a way out of town on the old family hunting estate and, although intact, was in a state of great decay. After some reticence to mention a price, both parties seemed happy to agree a deal at around £10,000. We were promised a call at the hotel when arrangements had been made to view.

We chatted on easily when, unannounced, the Maharaja left the room to return with a box in which was a collection of jewellery, bright and garish in the Indian style and encrusted with rubies and emeralds. He explained that his inheritance included a London house in a square near Harrods. He was looking for help to get the family treasure out of the country to enable him and his young wife to live there. We readily agreed to take the job on and to discuss the details when we returned to view the Rolls.

On the way back to the hotel, we stopped at another emporium where we bought some scrimshaws (carved shells) and bisque dolls to take back in our luggage.

We stayed on for another couple of days only to be told by the Maharaja that he would be unable to show us the car for a while. So we decided to travel to Calcutta as soon as possible and stop off in Bombay on the way back. Internal travel in India is a choice between a very slow train or flying with airlines with dubious safety records. The distance between Bombay and Calcutta is such that the latter is the only realistic alternative.

The first thing that hit us about Calcutta was the smell. The hotel, again super luxurious, was a kind of overprivileged oasis in a desert of noise, rubbish and chaos. We left Michael to get the ball rolling while we relaxed with some beers by the pool.

On the first evening, we were joined before dinner in our room by Ashok, a senior Calcutta police officer. We spent a couple of hours explaining what we wanted to achieve in his city. He impressed us with his precise responses to our questions and readiness to point out any pitfalls.

Ashok personally knew of some English sporting guns which we could see the next day. He confirmed the story about the aeroplanes but warned that a great deal of time would be needed to wade through the chain of people in the middle. We were keen to establish a financial arrangement with Ashok but he refused to discuss it. John then asked him where we could find some pretty girls and he replied that the hotel did not allow Western guests to bring local girls in.

I escorted Ashok to the lobby. There he explained that many local people might be reluctant to deal with us if they knew Michael was involved because he had been arrested the last time he was in Calcutta. Apparently, he had been grassed up by somebody who had been elbowed out of his commission on a deal. Michael and a couple of others had been caught exporting a load of antiques. The goods had been confiscated and Michael put under house arrest in his hotel until Ashok could escort him to the airport.

John was furious. We tackled Michael who tried to make light of the affair. He appeared to be more annoyed that Ashok had told me, rather than the fact that the Indian contacts had experienced serious problems over the incident.

After dinner, John and I retired to our room. We decided to stay on in Calcutta for a few days to see what Ashok and Michael came up with. John was concerned that Ashok had been reluctant to quantify any rewards for himself. John then told me that he had been introduced to a Ghanaian African chief who had been staying in London with friends and was looking for somebody who could find a way to export large quantities of high-quality fresh grass. The black-market rate of exchange was about 50 times more than the official rate and the cannabis could be paid for in local currency. At £5 a pound, the profits were enormous. Good-quality grass made upwards of £500 a pound in London.

Ghana had just been taken over in a military coup by Jerry Rawlings and a regime had been imposed with a curfew from 8.00pm and strict border controls. Not much was going into or coming out of the country but, apparently, the chief was well connected and close to the new regime.

I felt a mixture of excitement and trepidation. Here was a different kind of crime to what we were up to in Calcutta. A few days' house arrest in a five-star hotel was very different to a few years banged up in England if it went wrong. However, I had made my decision and I had a feeling that I would be able to make a valid contribution.

The phone rang at about midnight. It was Ashok. 'How do you like your girls? Slim or with a little meat on?'

We gave him our order. Twenty minutes later, he called again and explained that a hotel employee would escort the girls to our room through the staff entrance and service lift. We were, on no account, to let the reception know we had company and had better order room service before they arrived. He told us not to give them any money 'and, by the way, the girls will do anything except blow-ups'.

We got in a supply of drinks. A little later, there was a soft knock on the door. Three pretty girls stood shyly waiting to be ushered in. We tipped the waiter who was evidently anxious to make his getaway. He told us that he was under orders to return at five the following morning to escort the girls off the premises and was gone.

At the first words we said to the girls, they broke into fits of giggles; they didn't speak a word of English. Because Michael was not exactly flavour of the month and the girls were so pretty, we decided to have a party for five. Sign language was the only means of communication, but we all shared laughter. The girls were obviously pleased that they had not been split up but were strangely shy to be naked in front of each other. After an initial period of awkwardness, everybody relaxed and had a good time. We offered the girls money when it was time to leave, but they looked frightened and refused to accept it.

Earlier, we had found a small ornate box next to a bowl of fruit and an unsigned note saying 'Welcome to Calcutta'. Inside was a generous quantity of temple ball. It was just as well we agreed to delay sampling until the next evening. We were 'nailed' to our beds for the rest of the night.

Ashok came at 8.00am to take us to look at a couple of vintage vehicles. Instead of travelling together, he and I left in one car and John and Michael took another. I was taken to an old house where I spent a couple of hours inspecting a Maharaja's collection of English sporting shotguns and rifles. The Indian climate is not the best in which to look after anything made of metal and the barrels of many of the guns were badly pitted.

I agreed to buy a beautiful pair of Purdey double-barrelled rifles and a set of three cased twelve-bore shotguns along with seven others by Holland & Holland, Rigby and Churchill.

Ashok assured me that there would be no problem with export and he would personally put them on the flight when I left. In order to buy the guns in India, I needed a valid firearms certificate. Ashok and I went together to his place of work.

A young officer was instructed to look after me and we began the process of filling in interminable buff-coloured, badly printed Indian forms.

At one point, three scruffy men in chains were dragged into Ashok's office flanked by two young policemen with their long truncheons drawn. Seated at his desk, Ashok barked questions at the prisoners who were whacked by their escorts if there was any delay or reluctance in their responses. When they had been marched out, I asked what they had done. Ashok told me that they had burned down a building killing about 20 people in a religious dispute. I asked their fate and was told that they would be executed within a week.

John had found a Hispano Suiza and a car called a Prince Henry Vauxhall. Ashok was confident that we could manipulate the paperwork to export the cars but still refused to discuss any personal rewards for his help. I got my firearms certificates and the guns were brought to the hotel where we broke down the ones that were not in cases.

We decided that for a first trip we had done enough buying and spent more time at the hotel pool and bar while awaiting the paperwork to move the cars. Michael made several calls to Bombay to try to make arrangements with the Maharaja and was told that 'he had been called away and may not be back for some time'. Ashok said that the stigma surrounding Michael was bound to be the cause of the disappointment and we decided to put Bombay off for another trip without him.

From time to time, the pool would be brightened up by young Australian girls who were working voluntarily with Mother Teresa during their university holidays. They were billeted at the convent which had rudimentary accommodation and no luxuries. The use of the pool at the Oberoi Hotel did not cost much by Western standards. I made friends with a girl called Karen who had finished university and had been working with the charity for the previous two months. Along with a friend, she planned to go travelling after another month and return to Australia a year later to embark upon a career in film-making. We arranged to take them out to dinner later in the week.

Ashok's plan was to issue new paperwork for the cars identifying them as old Ambassadors and drive the Vauxhall, which could be made roadworthy, to the Nepalese border. The Hispano would be dismantled, crated and exported as spares. Still, he resolutely refused to discuss personal remuneration saying that he would rather call it a favour which he could call in when he visited London. I was convinced that he was genuine but John became ever more uncomfortable. In any event, it was evident that it would be some days before anything more could be done and we were spending a lot of money on expenses.

We were determined to move the African project forward as soon as we possibly could and I suggested that John return to London to set up a meeting with the African chief. John agreed to take Michael back with him. They flew out the next day, taking the small items we had bought in Bombay with them. I felt safe knowing that, if anything happened to me, it would be better to have back-up in London rather than all of us being stranded together in Calcutta. Besides, I now had a date with two pretty Aussie Sheilas the next day.

From time to time, I had trouble sleeping. I normally took an early swim or a sauna in the cellar of the Oberoi but, the following morning, I decided to take a walk just as the dawn was breaking. I emerged to find a lorry driving past at walking pace. There was a water tank on the back of the truck to which two hoses were attached held by men spraying the pavement. While I watched, they laid down their hoses, picked up the limp body of a poor man who had died in the night and threw it unceremoniously into the back of the lorry.

Later that morning, I got a call from Karen who explained that many of the girls were down with a stomach virus. It was chaos at the convent with limited toilet and bathing facilities and the two girls readily accepted my offer to move to the hotel. I collected them and left them to clean up and rest while I went with Ashok who had arrived unexpectedly.

He took me to another house in a side street where the contents of a couple of dozen tea chests were unveiled to reveal the glass fittings from a Maharaja's ballroom. There were mirrors, chandeliers, sconces, lamps and door furniture, all made to order by the Lalique factory in the Twenties and in perfect condition. It could be bought on that day for £2,000. I thought long and hard but turned the offer down, not wanting to delay my return any longer than necessary. I had made my commitment and wanted to go to Africa as soon as possible.

It was another ten days before I could leave. The car was tow-started and could hardly be described as roadworthy. It leaked and misfired, made a thunderous noise from the corroded exhaust and the brakes were something of a lottery. By lunchtime on the first day of my journey and having attracted the attention of half of the people I passed in this ancient contraption, I called it a day. I returned to Calcutta to have it dismantled. We never got our hands on the Hispano, but the Vauxhall was air freighted to England. I believe it now resides in California proudly restored to its original splendour.

After a couple of days, the girls got better and we returned Karen's friend to the convent where I was invited in to join them for the early-evening meal where I was sat beside Mother Teresa. She was exactly as everybody imagined her – saintly. We made some conversation during the meal but she was a woman of few words. Afterwards, Karen returned with me to the hotel, and we remained together until I left a few days later.

It wasn't long before I began to sweat profusely and soon developed a fever more violent than I had ever experienced before. The doctor immediately diagnosed malaria and I was dosed up with heavy medication. I managed to book a direct flight back to London the next day. I said my goodbyes, paid the bill and was put on the flight by Ashok who checked in my bags packed with the guns and personally supervised them being loaded on to the aeroplane. I slept the whole way back and woke to find that I had soaked the first-class seat, leaving most of my fever behind.

On arrival, I got my bags, took a change of clothes to the nearest

Gents, where I did my best to clean up and look presentable, and proceeded to the red channel where I expected a serious delay.

I duly declared my armoury and explained where the guns had come from to a Customs officer who seemed remarkably unmoved. I showed him my shotgun certificate which I had in my wallet and explained to him that I thought this would cover me for the guns. When I asked him what I should do with the rifles, he said that it would be much easier to take them all with me and save a lot of paperwork. I emerged ahead of many other passengers queuing for the green channel.

John met me at the gate and we stopped at Holland & Holland where we left the guns to be included in their next sporting sale. They realised enough profit to pay the expenses of the trip. The scrimshaws turned out to be sophisticated fakes and I still have the bisque dolls.

But the promise of far greater riches preoccupied me, especially when I heard that our African chief was in town.

9

GHANA

After a couple of days' rest, I was feeling fine again. My doctor warned me that I always stood the risk of recurring bouts of malaria from time to time and recommended that I continue to take the novoquine tablets for a while, even though they had failed to do the job in India.

Chief Charlie had arrived from Accra with his wife two days before I got back from India. I went with John to meet them in a semi in Stamford Hill, where they were staying with friends while in London. The house was full of Ghanaians – noisy, laughing, smiling, happy people. The living room was an apparition of expensive bad taste with oversized 'Barney Rubble' wood-and-leather settees, glittering gold-plated and smoked-glass coffee tables. The thick patterned carpet had declared war on the wallpaper. The ensemble was set off by burgundy-and-gold vertical-striped curtains.

Charlie was an imposing figure – big, tall and strong. He smiled at me with his 'pearly-white shark' teeth and grasped my hand with the traditional Ghanaian handshake, which ended with a noisy flick of the fingers. I liked him immediately. His wife, who was called in from the kitchen to meet us, was no less imposing. Not much shorter than Charlie, she was large in the way Ghanaian men like their women.

At an unseen signal, she retired to the kitchen where it was evident that the preparation of food involved a great deal of noise. I was soon to learn that all Ghanaian meals included *fufu*, a thick glutinous substance made from powdered cassava, which lay inert in every bowl of soup and on every plate of food. I must have eaten tonnes of the stuff but never got to like it. I am convinced that all Ghanaian houses suffered from subsidence from the daily preparation of *fufu*, which is pounded with large mortars and pestles in every kitchen in the land.

John had advanced Charlie money some days earlier. It was clear from the carrier bags and boxes in the living room that they had been shopping. We sat discussing for many hours how we could best conceal what we hoped would be one tonne of top-quality pressed cannabis for our first consignment. Charlie had been to the bush and, if we were to get the best-quality grass, we had to move quickly. The cannabis was ready for harvest and we had no more than two weeks.

Charlie knew a factory which made wood-block flooring. The plan was to put pressed blocks of cannabis inside the individual packages and reseal them in polythene. Charlie was keen to take more money with him with which to buy the grass, but we had agreed beforehand that it may be too tempting to trust him with too much at this stage. We promised that we would meet him in Accra in two weeks and gave Charlie just enough with which to pay some deposits.

Later in the evening, we were introduced to Paul, a young Ghana Airways pilot. During the conversation, he innocently told us that Ghana Airways were leasing a DC10 aircraft from KLM at a very high premium. They had paid a deposit for a new aircraft the previous year which had been completed a couple of months earlier, but, as they had been unable to raise the funds to pay the balance, the aeroplane, painted in full Ghana Airways livery, had been parked in the Arizona Desert awaiting the balance of the purchase. I explained that I had some friends who were in finance and knew that they had an associate company specialising in aircraft leasing.

The next day, I contacted my financial friends. I was called back a short time later by their contact in the associate aircraft leasing company. Aircraft finance was a small world and the plight of the Ghana Airways DC10 was common knowledge. There were two problems, one of which was that the airline had acquired a bad reputation internationally for paying their bills. On many occasions at Heathrow, a big tow tug had been parked in front of the aircraft's nose wheel to stop it from moving until an accumulation of landing fees or refuelling bills had been paid.

The other problem was that, only weeks before, Flight Lieutenant Jerry Rawlings had seized power in Ghana after a military coup and the financial stability of the country was very much in question. It was not, however, the end of the line. There were various ways to raise the capital necessary to rescue the aircraft from its sandy parking lot. Any financial institution would need to be satisfied that the revenue created by the sale of seats was sufficient to service the repayments. An independent feasibility study would be an essential prerequisite.

I called my pilot friend Paul and explained the situation. Not long after, I received a call from the Chief of Operations of Ghana Airways in London. He invited me to fly to Accra as their guest and to help plan how to move the purchase of the DC10 further ahead. Unknown to him, I had my perfect cover.

Before leaving for Ghana, we had to set up or find a company to import the wood-block flooring. With that purpose in mind, I bought an off-the-shelf company from an advertisement in *Exchange & Mart* and rented a small serviced office in the City. Using the false names of the directors and the address of the office, I was able to open a bank account and took the opportunity of depositing £1,000 in cash. The cheque book, when ready, would be sent to the office. The office was a small room in a large old Victorian block with a receptionist who answered the phone for any of the tenants who wished to have their calls routed through the main switchboard. Any messages could be picked up remotely from the anonymity of a telephone box. I was beginning to enjoy my new life of crime.

The wood-block flooring would be packed in a container and imported via Tilbury Docks. I had been thinking for some time about whether a method could be found to track the safe passage of our cargo and I went to see an old friend. Ever since I had known him, Max had been an electronics buff. I told him that I needed a means of concealing some valuable paperwork and to find a way of warning me, remotely, if the item it was concealed in had been tampered with.

He asked how much hiding space was needed. Charlie had explained that foreign exchange had to be declared at the airport and Customs would be looking for money. We would need cash and quite a lot of it. We estimated that about £20,000 would be enough. I made a calculation and gave it to Max.

He called me the next day and I went to see him. He came up with the idea of using a portable radio and incorporating a small transmitter connected to a switch activated by a pin. If the pin was removed, it would set off the transmitter which would then send a signal on a given wavelength. Freight containers have two heavy hinged doors which are jammed into place by levers on the outside. They are then sealed by Customs once the container has been cleared for export.

We would carefully place the radio inside the container and attach a string to the transmitter-activating pin, the other end would be tied to the inside of the door closed first. In the event of it being opened for inspection at Tilbury, the pin would be dislodged activating the transmitter. A signal could be picked up on a car radio parked within range near by. Max would also remove one of the speakers from the radio leaving enough room in which to hide our money. We were ready to leave.

The chaos at Heathrow was unbelievable. Every single passenger was laden with bags, boxes, mysterious items sewn in jute sacking and electrical goods. We would need a miracle to take to the air. Nobody appeared to be queuing at check-in and there seemed to be no sense of order whatsoever.

I managed to make eye contact with somebody who looked

official and presented him with our tickets. We were expected. Within five minutes, we had been given our boarding cards along with a compliments slip upgrading us to the first-class cabin and we were relieved of our bags.

We were an hour late taking off, a regular occurrence. Shortly after, Paul, the young pilot we had met before, opened the cockpit door and joined us for a cigarette. Paul had been asked by the airline to look after us and, knowing that I was a private pilot, he invited me to the cockpit. I was allowed to take the controls for a while and stayed strapped into the 'jump seat' for landing. With no other traffic, the approach into Accra was straight in with a gradual descent. The visibility was perfect and, ahead of us, the long runway, shimmering in the afternoon heat, was in sight for a long time.

Some way out, I could see what appeared to be two very large snowploughs parked at the end of the runway. Apparently, the airport had been built by the Russians at a time of close political alliance. During this period, Russia had been busy making friends in the Third World and travelling construction teams built many schools, hospitals, factories and airports. They were all built to identical plans and came complete with the equipment necessary to run them. No consideration had been given for climate, hence the snowploughs and extensive central heating fitted in the tropical terminal building.

We had the advantage of getting off the DC10 first and stood by the door while the aircraft steps were pushed manually into place. The door was opened and a blast of dry, airless, tropical heat drove us back before we made for the descent to the tarmac. The airport terminal was built on two floors and on an upper open viewing platform beneath the sign 'Accra International Airport' thronged hundreds of colourful waving people greeting their loved ones.

The walk to the arrivals door was lined by menacing-looking military personnel each clutching AK47s and dressed in sweaty fatigues. We presented our passports which were scrutinised and checked against a list of names in a well-thumbed book. After showing our inoculation certificates, we were waved to the search area. This consisted of three cubicles with a filthy curtain either side in which you were frisked by another sweating soldier while standing on a plinth. 'Cigarettes?' I handed him a packet of Bensons which he pocketed and he slid aside the curtain to let me into the baggage-claim area. There was no carousel and the bags were pushed into the room by porters through plastic strips hanging from a wide opening to the tarmac outside.

Many packets of cigarettes later, we pushed our way through the crowds of people waiting for the emerging passengers and followed two strong young porters toting our bags on their heads. We refused several offers of taxis and, having no local currency, tipped the happy men a dollar apiece. Charlie was nowhere to be seen and, having given up on any chance of a cold beer at the airport, we stood with our cases outside the terminal feeling hot and vulnerable.

Paul, our pilot, emerged and, just as we were about to accept his offer of a lift, a beaming Charlie pulled up in an old Peugeot 504. He made no attempt at an apology, introduced us to his younger brother Jo, who loaded our bags in the car, and drove us away.

The airport at Accra is very close to the city and, within a few short minutes driving through wide dusty streets, we arrived at a modern-looking single-storey hotel where there was much evidence of abandoned construction work.

A young man in a T-shirt, dirty trousers and flip-flops was outside on his haunches frying an egg on an open fire. When we pulled up, he hurriedly took the pan inside and returned to take our bags to two large rooms, each with adjoining shower.

There was a fridge rattling away in the room allocated to me, and Charlie opened the door to proudly reveal the contents – four beers. A rarity in Ghana. He explained that the hotel had no facilities but he would bring eggs, fruit and more beer later. We would have breakfast cooked al fresco at the hotel and be picked up in the morning.

A curfew had been imposed after the coup from 8.00pm to 5.00am. Patrolling soldiers were under orders to shoot anybody caught on the streets during those hours. We showered and changed and, at 4.00pm, drove off to dinner.

Two streets away, still in the 'Airport Residential Area' where detached houses nestled secretly behind tall walls and sheet-metal gates, we drove into the covered courtyard of the empty restaurant. We were brought menus and told in hushed tones that beer was available. John and I spent some time poring over the extensive choice on offer and were looking forward to a good meal.

The waiter returned to take our order and, after being told 'It finish' in response to our first three selections, we finally established that chicken and sweet potato chips was the only dish available. The waiter arrived holding a chipped white enamel bowl of warm water and a towel over his arm. Each of us washed our hands before the meals arrived – there were no knives or forks.

I was soon to learn that my right hand was for eating and it was considered bad form to use the left, even to hand something to another person. In the course of time, I even got used to eating soup without cutlery. The hand-washing ritual was repeated after the meal and we returned to our hotel.

Charlie explained that he had reserved just over a tonne of best-quality grass and had used all the money we had given him in London to pay deposits. He took a small bag from his pocket and we inspected the fresh green buds which smelled strong and pungent. Charlie asked us to trust him to go to the bush without us where, he argued, we would be very conspicuous and, as a consequence, the prices were sure to rise. We agreed to his request but insisted on being there to supervise the pressing and quality control. I unscrewed the back of the radio and we gave Charlie £5,000 before he rushed off to beat the curfew with ten minutes to spare, promising to return the next afternoon.

There was no breakfast but Charlie sent a man with a carrier bag full of bundles of money each trussed in three rows of rubber bands. There was another bag full of beer which I put in the fridge. He told us that Charlie had left for the bush and would not be back that day. We had an appointment the following day with Ghana Airways and decided to spend the morning looking around. The houseboy got us a car and we set off into the heat of the day.

The roads were terrible, full of deep potholes that would test a tank. Occasionally, the traffic would come to a halt as each obstacle had to be negotiated at less than walking pace. All along the route were broken trucks and lame cars in various stages of roadside repair.

Long queues were evident at any petrol station open for business and Jo explained that rationing was in force everywhere. We headed into town, passing rows of small concrete business units all with rusty roller-shutter fronts. Few were open but we passed some stocked to the brim with cloth, domestic utensils and other essentials.

The car parked at the town square where Jo led us through some randomly planted evergreen trees to a vibrant market of stalls and huts, many selling carvings and a large selection of ivory, ranging from whole carved trunks to bracelets and tiny charms. All sorts of other endangered species were displayed, particularly a selection of skins and furs.

Two hundred years before, this very place was the busiest slave market in the world and the shackles and blocks to which the poor people had been tethered were still very much in evidence.

We walked to Zongo Lane, a short street on each side of which were impromptu set-ups of small tables and chairs. From these, black-market currency dealers openly plied their trade. John and I were conspicuous wherever we went – two white faces in a sea of black – but we did not feel remotely in danger.

Every unstable economy has a trade in hard currency but it was a great surprise that in Zongo Lane it was so public, with thousands of pounds in sterling, dollars, francs and deutschmarks on open display. The trader had to supply a young assistant to help to carry the bundles of local currency we exchanged for £2,000.

We collected our swimming costumes from the hotel and went with Paul to the only squash club in Accra. Along the way, the road was flanked by an avenue of tall trees and from each one hung thousands of large fruit bats. They were to become a familiar sight as they spread their large wings at dusk and took to the sky. The curfew was not for them. Some time later, I was to be introduced to bat soup which is served with the unfortunate creature, head up, floating in the bowl in which it had been cooked and with a generous portion of *fufu* submerged beneath. It is not a culinary experience I want to repeat.

The squash club was a simple concrete set of buildings with four open-top courts and a swimming pool. We sat beneath a large grass parasol and ate falafel cooked by a friendly girl. I had left my racket in London but Paul promised to get one and suggested a game the next morning before my meeting with Ghana Airways. We swam in the clear unchlorinated spring water and spent a happy afternoon chatting.

Paul's brother was a pilot in the Air Force and we were invited to a family gathering, the following Saturday, at the barracks in which he lived. He said that there were many vacant houses in the Airport Residential Area owned by people who, having earned their wealth, somewhat dubiously under the previous regime, were reluctant to return for a while. With the benefit of the black-market rate of exchange, we could rent our own house for very little. On the way back, we stopped at a small shop near the airport where one could spend only foreign exchange. It was somewhat sparsely stocked but we bought some bacon and cheese which we put in the fridge when we got back to the hotel.

Because of the curfew, life in Accra began early and we hurried to our appointment at 8.00am. On the way, Paul told me that a house was available near to where we were staying and we could see it straight away. He was not included in the meeting and left us with the Director of Operations, promising to return for us after checking on his duty roster.

We were joined by the accountant who explained that they were currently negotiating with another source of finance. I gave them my contacts and offered to help in any way possible. It was a short meeting. We agreed that they would make contact through Paul and I said that now that we were in Accra we would probably stay for a few weeks to get to know Ghana.

Paul took us to see the house. It was a white-painted single-storey building with four bedrooms and a large living area leading out to a walled garden with a well-watered, green manicured lawn. We could pay for it in local currency and it was available for the equivalent of £20 a week.

The houseboy and his cousin, who would do odd jobs and errands, were happy to accept double the going rate at another £20 and, in addition, the Peugeot in the garage could be bought for £250. We gave Paul three months' rent and the money for the car.

By curfew, we had returned to the foreign-exchange shop, filled the fridge with what we could find and stocked the bar with duty-free booze. Paul bade us farewell until Saturday when he would return with cigarettes from his next flight from London and to take us to the party.

The houseboy was marvellous. He looked after us with a happy pride. His cousin went early every morning to buy freshly caught fish and lobsters straight from the fishing boats and found a source for the excellent locally brewed beer. Fruit and vegetables were in abundant supply, too. We were in heaven.

Charlie's man arrived the next morning as we were eating breakfast. He was surprised to find that we had settled in so quickly. He explained that it was doubtful that Charlie would return before the weekend and that he would prefer to stay in the bush until our consignment had been cropped. He gave us more fresh buds which were smooth and mellow to smoke. We had brought a generous supply of Rizlas, which I never saw on sale in Africa. We spent a day chilling out in the garden and took the car for a drive, surprised to find it full of petrol.

Putting the car back in the garage, we noticed some girls hanging around on the corner of the street. One came up and introduced herself with a shy smile while her friends watched on giggling. The houseboy told us that they were good local girls and we invited them in. Our radio still worked from its single speaker and we played tapes we had brought with us. After a couple of beers, nobody was sober and the girls danced in the garden to music they had never heard before.

I remember one unusually slender girl, called Alice, who teased me with her eyes. We had some passionate moments in the garden but it was not until a few days later that she spent curfew with me. John disappeared with one of the other girls for an hour or so but they all left before 8.00pm, still laughing as they tripped home. I would make a point to try to establish that girls were old enough to make their own decisions as to who they slept with and always declined in cases of doubt.

We spent quite a lot of time at the squash club before the weekend and I played the young resident professional every day. He was jailed in England a few years later, having been caught trying to smuggle in some grass in his suitcase with which to finance his participation in a squash tournament in London.

Paul arrived to take us to his brother's party still in his Ghana Airways uniform and laden with cigarettes. Everywhere in Accra, there was a strong military presence and we were saluted smartly at the guardhouse of the barbed-wired compound of the officers' quarters.

The party was in full swing at the small but well-kept bungalow, identical in every way to all of its neighbours. Richard, Paul's brother, welcomed us at the open front door. We were handed drinks and introduced to the other guests. The ladies were all dressed for the occasion, some in traditional Ghanaian costume and others in colourful dresses. They all wore wide-brimmed hats. The happy music played loudly and some of the ladies, elbows raised and bottoms out, were dancing back and forth to the infectious rhythm. The men, some in fatigues and the rest casually dressed, lounged about drinking and chatting. None had made an effort to smarten up for the occasion. Most of the Ghanaian Air Force were there and the President came by for a short time to shake everybody's hand; he was a very popular man. We were made welcome by everybody. I had a dancing lesson which caused great hilarity. Nobody seemed particularly curious as to what we were doing in their country.

The party continued until the early hours and we were told not to worry about curfew. Gradually, as the children got tired or fractious, the women began to diminish and, by midnight, it appeared to be a men-only affair. I remember spending some time chatting to a young pilot called Victor who had gained his wings a year before. Richard sent us home in the back of a military Land Rover manned by two soldiers and we drove back through eerily empty streets, as if in the wake of a nuclear war.

Victor died two days later on a training flight up country. They were flying at low altitude in the early morning mist in loose formation and, without warning or distress signal, Victor's plane flew straight into the ground. He was 21.

The Air Force flew Italian trainers made by Aermacchi – pretty single-engine jets with a disastrous safety record. Like the British fighter pilots during the Second World War, more were killed in training than in combat. We were invited to join the mourners at his funeral two days later at the officers' mess.

Charlie reappeared on the morning of the funeral, his black face striped with white lines in tribal fashion and dressed in the robes and hat of a chief. He embraced us both before sitting in an armchair. He refused food and drink, explaining that the witch doctor at his village where he had been for a blessing on our venture had painted his face and imposed a fast until sundown. He explained that more than half our consignment had been harvested and placed in a building for safety. The lorry to transport the grass, to where we were to supervise the pressing, had broken down. He had begun to press into blocks at his village until the lorry jacks they used for the purpose had also broken.

John was angry. We were keen to ensure that the buds of the cannabis were trimmed and very little stick was pressed with it. The only way to do so was to be there to oversee the operation. Charlie said that only a few blocks had been pressed before the jacks broke and promised not to process any more until we were present. He sped off to try to locate some heavier-duty jacks and we agreed to meet later at the officers' mess.

The mess was like something out of the Second World War. A big sparsely furnished room with a large bar, an upright piano, a blackboard and several shields on the walls, each bearing the name of a departed brother. There was a lot of wailing and public displays of grief. Everybody from the party two days earlier was there. The main difference was that all the men were now smartly dressed in their uniforms. In addition, there were some older people and a good turnout of non-commissioned soldiers and airmen.

The President gave a speech, immediately after which the music began and, within minutes, I was at another party. This time, the dancing was in earnest and many women I had seen only a few minutes before collapsing and weeping inconsolably became transformed.

The President thanked us for coming and we were steered towards the older men, all of whom had some important role to play in the new government. This time, there were questions, all of which I was able to answer.

I spotted a very pretty girl who did not appear to be attached to anybody in particular. She returned my smile and I introduced myself. Her name was Elizabeth. She was a final-year medical student and her sister was married to one of the pilots. Her father was a doctor, one of the older men I had met earlier. She had been educated in England where the family also maintained a small home. We got on well and agreed to meet the following week to sample the delights of the only Chinese restaurant in Accra.

Charlie arrived late. He had washed the paint off his face and changed into another set of regal robes, and I was interested to note that he was received with a high level of respect. The sun had gone down and Charlie was wasting no time in putting away a large amount of alcohol in as short a time as possible. He told us that he had found some very powerful bottle jacks that would do the job. We agreed to meet at the house in the morning.

Charlie arrived early, evidently somewhat the worse for wear. His man brought in one of the jacks to show us, which had apparently cost quite a lot of money. We gave him another £5,000 and he promised to return by the weekend, having bought the balance of the crop and transported it to the place where we had a pressing engagement. The Cedi, the Ghanaian currency, had been falling in value and, as a consequence, we were likely to get more grass for our money. We could be returning to England with a tonne of puff and some change.

The grass had to be pressed into a regular and specific shape in order to fit neatly within the packages of wood-block flooring. A sheet of half-inch-thick steel, about 12 inches square, formed a flat base. On to this were welded more steel plates, sideways on, in the shape of the finished block. A steel-plate lid was then cut to the exact shape of the block to fit tightly into the mould. The base of the jack was attached upside down to a gantry overhead and the ram placed on to the lid where it was pumped down on to the contents.

The grass had to be dried in the sun for a few days to reduce its moisture content, after which the buds were trimmed off and placed into the mould. The jack was then pumped to exert enormous force on to the lid of the mould which compressed the contents. Any excess moisture was squeezed out through a half-inch hole drilled in the flat base into which a rod was inserted to push out the finished blocks. The blocks were then wrapped in polythene and swathed in sticky brown tape.

No matter how well this process is performed, it is always impossible to mask the smell completely. I have known blocks to be sprinkled with pepper to put sniffer dogs off the scent. It is a long laborious process and, because of a lack of electricity in the bush, it has to be done manually. I designed a machine with a remotely pumped hydraulic ram but the components were not locally available. We did not want to risk exporting them from England for fear of detection.

We continued our healthy lifestyle – swimming in the sun, playing squash and eating nothing but good fresh food. We held a couple of impromptu parties at the house and, on two occasions, had guests for breakfast.

I took Elizabeth to the Chinese restaurant for Friday lunch, and afterwards she took me to an afternoon disco which closed at 7.00pm in order to give the revellers time to get home. It was fun and we agreed to meet again. There was no telephone at the house and that is how I wanted it. It meant that communication was rather like 18th-century England – if you wanted to get in touch, you sent the houseboy with a handwritten message. Otherwise, you just turned up on the off-chance of meeting the person you came to see. There would always be somebody with whom to leave a note.

Charlie arrived at the weekend triumphant. He had bought just over a tonne of grass. It was all waiting at the farm to be pressed, with the workforce standing by. He wanted to source some more adhesive tape and asked if he could spend the weekend in Accra before we set off on the next phase.

On Monday morning, we drove for about an hour. At the edge of the city was a roadblock manned by the military, checking papers and searching every car. We drove deep into the bush, occasionally passing small villages of mud huts and infrequent signs of cultivation, catching the odd glimpse of African wildlife.

We turned off the road and drove up a long driveway to a series of buildings. There was no sign of life but, as we pulled up in front of the house, a tall thin man of about 40 came to the front door. His name was William and he greeted us warmly. After taking some water, we were led to a large concrete barn with a corrugated roof and heavy iron door. It was opened to reveal a man holding a single-barrelled shotgun, which looked like it might do him more harm than he would inflict on the target, were he ever to pull the trigger.

The barn was full to the brim at one end with fresh cannabis and the pungent smell was almost overwhelming. We inspected some of the plants at random and saw that about a dozen blocks had already been pressed and sealed. With a sharp knife, we opened them one by one to reveal that each one had more sticks in than buds. One look at Charlie told us that he had been nowhere near when they had been pressed.

Charlie told us that he and William were partners in the venture. I got the impression that the man could be trusted and that he understood what was required to satisfy the UK market.

At the other end of the barn, the press had been set up with the jack bolted to a heavy RSJ. This was secured across the corner of the building with each end embedded in the masonry. Within a few minutes, half-a-dozen men appeared and we set to work. Two men were armed with scissors and we showed them where we wanted the buds cut. Another loaded the mould while the strongest two manned the jack and press. Then a young and fit man wrapped the blocks and mummified them in brown tape.

Our production line was slow but we made steady progress and were happy at the quality of our purchase. We estimated that the work would take two weeks at least and agreed that John and I should return to Accra daily in case we were missed at the roadblock.

Charlie had shown us a sample of the wood-block flooring. The pressed blocks of grass fitted perfectly inside with a layer of wood on top and around each side. We needed about 2,000 boxes to fill the 20-foot container and estimated that about a third of them would conceal the grass. Charlie had not told us that he only had about a hundred boxes and was not too certain how many more he could get. We told him to concentrate on solving this problem and agreed to take another worker back with us the following day to continue the work on William's farm.

For five days, Charlie went missing. One of his men said he knew nothing but his loyalties lay with his boss. William was not so blindly loyal; he was angry at his partner, telling us that he had been absent for most of the time the crops were being harvested, leaving him with no explanation and the lion's share of the work. William was thoroughly dependable and we were able to take the odd day off. Nobody knew where the flooring factory was to be found and there was no address on the boxes. We were becoming anxious. The pressing was going well and our estimate of two weeks' work seemed pretty accurate.

John was becoming restless and, when Charlie finally turned up with no apology and again daubed in paint, I had to step in to halt a fight. He never explained where he had been but later I discovered that he had a family at his village and a girlfriend in nearby Tema.

We made him drive us to the flooring factory where we found the machinery idle and unattended. The owner was away and he had left his manager to hold the deserted fort. With the political uncertainty, orders had dried up. A large German company was keen to buy a large slice of the factory and rejuvenate the equipment, but the bosses were frightened to come to Ghana, having been told they might be kidnapped.

We were taken to the stock room and were happy to find about 1,000 cardboard packages. We needed 800–900 more. The flooring blocks were stacked in their thousands but the problem was that the packaging manufacturer had run out of cardboard. We paid the manager for the stock and offered him a nice bonus if he could locate the packaging to do the job. Charlie promised to pick him up the next day and together they would search for a solution. Charlie knew that he had pushed his luck far enough and our added threats hopefully ensured that he would be there.

Charlie and the manager came by the following afternoon with a solution. The factory had enough cardboard to make another 300 boxes and would make thick bases for the remainder, which could be shrink-wrapped as they were. There were already more than enough in which to conceal the pressed cannabis. The flooring factory's vacuum-sealing machine had broken and one had been located at a local food-processing plant and it was available.

By the end of the week, about 1,300 packages had been delivered to William's farm along with the sealing machine. Nearly half of the grass had been pressed.

I told John that I was happy to see the rest of the job through alone and it would be a good idea to set up the distribution network in London in time for the arrival of our container. His relationship with Charlie was strained to say the least, and neither benefited from the other's stubbornness. He agreed to my suggestion and he was set up with a first-class seat a few days later.

I saw Elizabeth again two days before John left and she came to the house for dinner after which I drove her home. She made it clear that the next date would be very much less formal.

I was not needed at the farm and knew exactly how much stick should be left over for burning; everybody was doing their job well. The vacuum-sealer proved troublesome, but I made some adjustments, which seemed to work. After I had spent the day working on the machine, I stayed for a drink. By the time I realised what time it was, I had only 45 minutes to make it back before curfew.

I figured that, if I drove quickly, I could make it. William tried to persuade me to stay the night but I had a squash date early the next morning and did not want to miss it. One of his men had to get more tape in Accra and took a ride with me. There was not enough time to drop him home and he would stay with me 'til the morning.

The soldiers at the roadblock were taking their time. When I remonstrated, they replied that I should have allowed more time for my journey. By the time they let us go, it was clear we were not going to make it. I drove off at breakneck speed.

Just after 8.00pm, a soldier brandishing his gun stepped out in the road to stop us. I sped past him, turned off the lights and accelerated up the road. We could just hear the bark of the rifle above the racing engine as several shots were fired after us.

We made it to the house ten minutes late and the houseboy who was waiting for us quickly closed the gate behind us. My heart was racing but we were soon laughing over a couple of drinks.

I had met a couple of English chaps at the squash club who had lived in Ghana for a few years. One of them had met and married a Ghanaian girl while she was at university in London. He was persuaded to come to live in Africa to look after the family's extensive farming interests. His friend, the Best Man at his wedding, came to visit, met a girl and never left.

We met for the occasional game of squash and got on well. That morning, I was invited to the farm and, after squash, we drove about half-an-hour out of town. They kept polo ponies and we exercised three of them for about an hour. I was OK on a horse but these animals had unbelievable acceleration and could change direction like a Mini Cooper S. We had lunch together with their families and enjoyed a relaxing day.

They were curious as to what I was doing, but seemed to understand why I was in no hurry to return to England after it was evident that Ghana Airways didn't need my help. The men told me that they were planning a trip to Togo to buy some luxuries and have some fun and, if I was still around, I would be welcome to join them.

Occasionally, and with no warning, a Land Rover would arrive after curfew to take us to a party at the officers' mess. A couple of days after my hair-raising drive from William's farm, I had settled in for the night when the houseboy appeared with two soldiers. My immediate thoughts were that my car had been identified, but I recognised one of the men as he casually saluted and invited me to take a ride.

I arrived at the party at about midnight and it was immediately obvious that I was several beers behind my noisy hosts. I told Richard about the breach of curfew and he burst into laughter. He called over a colleague who told us that the incident had been brought to his attention and he had told Richard. There were not too many Peugeot 504s in Accra driven by white men and they had taken bets that it was me. There was much hilarity and I was offered the use of an armoured car the next time I planned a trip out of town.

The container arrived at the farm and I spent time there supervising the loading. The packages which were only sealed in polythene were the last to be put on board. We celebrated in Ghanaian style, sprinkling home-made gin on the ground and blessing the safe arrival of our work. The radio had run out of batteries and there were no replacements to be found, so Max's work had been in vain.

Charlie, whose absences had become less critical, was now needed to get the container to the docks and get me the bills of lading before I could leave. He reported back to say that his shipping agent, who was the only one he trusted, was away for two weeks and could not be contacted. He offered to fly to London with the papers when they were ready, but his performance to date did not inspire confidence in me. I decided to leave only after our baby was on the high seas and with the paperwork safely in my hands.

Only one of my English friends was now going to Togo, and I agreed to go with him the following Friday. We were to go to the border by car, a journey of about four hours, and use taxis while in the capital. I spent a morning getting a visa at the Togo Embassy which took a full page of my passport in the form of a splendid heraldic shield personally signed by the Ambassador. I was told that we would have a lot of fun and would be staying in one of the finest hotels, before returning on the Sunday.

Elizabeth and I spent a couple of days together during the week. She wagged a finger at me as I drove off to meet my friend at the squash club on that Friday morning. At about 10.00am, we set off for Togo in his air-conditioned Land Rover.

10

TOGO

Pete's Land Rover was perfect for the trip through the bush. The terrain was now familiar to me and did not change appreciably along the route. Togo, an ex-French colony to the East of Ghana, had become a kind of trading post for luxury goods and pleasures for those from neighbouring countries who had hard currency. Lome, the capital on the country's narrow coastline, had casinos, hotels and nightclubs and was open 24 hours a day.

Pete's wife tolerated his occasional trips and knew that he would not return from his shopping excursion without sampling the pretty girls for which Togo was renowned. The French had left behind their language and cuisine, and Pete told me that there was a selection of fine restaurants. I had brought along a couple of hundred pounds and he had about double, needing to stock up on household luxuries no longer available at home.

A couple of miles from the border, the route became busier and busier with roadside vendors in abundance trying to flag down passing vehicles to buy their wares. Everything from cigarettes to second-hand fridges seemed to be on offer. Many hopeful travellers were trying to hitch rides in both directions.

The border was like a level crossing with hand-operated barricades which swung vertically either side of a small area of no-man's-land in between. We turned off the road 50 yards before the barrier into a guarded car park, refused the porters who offered to carry our light baggage and walked to join a small queue alongside the road. We were not long at the formalities on the Ghanaian side and walked across the divide to another checkpoint where our passports were stamped and baggage checked before being waved into Togo.

A row of smart Mercedes taxis waited at a rank a few yards away and we climbed in, having handed the driver the bags which he put in the boot. As we drove away, I noticed an open army jeep carrying some soldiers pulling in behind us from the other side of the road.

Within a very short distance, rows of well-stocked shops with big neon signs came into view. Bars and restaurants seemed to be busy and, as we neared the centre of town, bigger and better hotels lined the route. The taxi came to a halt outside The Grand in the busy central square and a liveried doorman with a porter and trolley rushed to greet us.

Pete was already standing on the pavement. The jeep which had followed us lurched to a halt across the front of the taxi. Four soldiers in fatigues and red berets jumped to the ground and ran to surround us, shouting as they pointed their short black Uzis directly at us.

I already had my hands in the air before I made out that they were shouting at us in French to do exactly that. Two of the soldiers who looked a little nervous trained their guns directly at me as I climbed to the pavement. We were handcuffed and bundled into the back of the jeep. Our bags were taken by one of the soldiers from the very frightened taxi driver who did not get paid. We sped off round the square which was now packed with silent onlookers.

I speak French and asked the sergeant beside me what was happening. I had difficulty understanding the strong African patois he barked back at me but I understood enough to tell me that silence was the best course of action. It was evident that we were very much the enemy. Although they were heavily armed and we were helpless, I could see that these soldiers were spooked by us.

The little police station was not far away and we were soon inside a room where our arrival was awaited by two officers. The sergeant and one other soldier remained, as we were subjected to a loud, rapid-fire string of shouted questions and accusations. We were accused of being mercenaries from England arriving in Togo a few days ahead of an imminent military coup. The fact that I spoke French was not necessarily to our advantage and, as a consequence, we were regarded as potentially more senior. One of the interrogators held a stubby swagger stick which he brandished threateningly but neither of us was hit during the questioning. We were ordered to hold our still handcuffed arms in the air while we were searched and our pockets emptied. Our passports were scrutinised and, along with the cash we were carrying, put in a drawer in the desk.

Pete had a multiple visa and I decided to speak out. I was told to shut up but I persisted. I told them that Pete lived in Ghana with his family and the stamps in his passport proved that he was a frequent visitor. The officer shouted that we had been seen arriving in a military vehicle. I offered to take them to see some of the children's toys left inside Pete's Land Rover. They kept repeating that they had intelligence about the coup and that nothing we said would change their minds.

After some time, the volume and urgency of the questioning began to subside but our attempts at reasoning were ignored. We were taken into the next room where, in Wild West style, there were two cells divided by metal bars from a small area with a desk and chair for the jailer. Although it was early evening and the light was fading, the heat was overwhelming. We were together locked inside one of the cells in which there were two wooden beds raised only a couple of inches above the floor. There was a large tin of water with a metal ladle attached by a light chain to the rim and nothing else apart from countless mosquitoes. The other cell was empty.

Before the door was locked, I asked for some fresh water and the young soldier was sent with the tin. We had already been refused a telephone call and when I asked what was to happen to us, we were told that the President would decide our fate in the morning. I asked for food and the sergeant told us that we had to pay if we wanted anything brought in. When I told him that our money was in the desk in the next room, he laughed. He replied that he would pay for our food that evening and possibly the next day we would be dead. Our handcuffs were removed through the bars once we had been locked in our cell.

Our guard that night was the young soldier and, after asking a couple of times, he brought us our cigarettes. We set about killing mosquitoes but could not staunch the flow through the bars of the open window above. Another soldier arrived with food a little later and we were given a fine meal of steak with chips and a big bowl of salad. Halfway through the meal, seated on our beds with the plates on our knees, I looked over at Pete with a smile. 'The prisoners ate a hearty meal...' was all I said and we both began to laugh. The release of tension was instant and, each time one of us said something, we gave way to uncontrollable bouts of giggling.

The young guard began to loosen up later in the evening and accepted cigarettes from us. He refused to allow us to use the telephone and, when I offered him money, he replied that we had none. He often repeated the words in French, 'You are mercenaries.' I tried logic with him but it fell on deaf ears.

The sense of dread when the drone of a mosquito stopped to feed on our blood overcame the fear of our plight many times over that night. I was woken from a fitful sleep some time before dawn with the arrival of the sergeant who called the young soldier out of the room. There was an indistinguishable conversation from the neighbouring room allied with the welcome smell of coffee.

The sergeant came in with two cups, sweet and black, and a couple of bread rolls. He pulled the chair from behind the desk, took a cup from the soldier and joined us on the other side of the bars of our cell. 'You mercenaries... why do you laugh when you may die today?'

I told him calmly that I thought that he knew by now that a mistake had been made and that he should release us. 'We came for shopping and some fun,' I insisted.

He told us that he thought we had been trained very professionally. I told him that we had money and would pay him for our freedom.

'What money?' he said.

I replied that Pete had family in Ghana and, if we could call them, they would bring some to the border. He replied that the decision was out of his hands.

We were brought a bowl of warm water and washed as best we could. We were given our bags. Much of the contents had been taken but both of us found a change of clothes. We were tired and in discomfort from the bites but did our best to keep cheerful and often laughed at the silliest of things.

The sergeant came back around midday and told us that a decision about our fate was not now to be made for another day or two. Once again, I offered him money for our freedom and he began to look interested. He explained that the money, sunglasses and clothing they had already taken were in payment of fines for border irregularities but pressed us to arrive at a hypothetical figure. We finished our theoretical discussion at £200 each, many times the annual salary of a soldier. He left us until the middle of the afternoon.

Pete was taken by the young soldier to the desk and allowed to use the telephone. There were no lines. Eventually, at about six in the evening, he got through to his wife. It was too late to set out for the border with curfew due to begin two hours later. Our Togolese captors were unwilling to do the deal during daylight, and it was eventually agreed that we would be available for the exchange at seven the following evening.

During the intervening period, we were regularly engaged in conversation by the young soldier and the sergeant. Nobody, however, told the mosquitoes that the regime had been relaxed. We were well fed and brought some good French wine. The sergeant drank heavily and, by the time of our rendezvous, he was somewhat the worse for wear from our jolly party.

Pete's friend was waiting for us just inside the border and we shook hands with our captors as an envelope of money was exchanged for our passports. We elected to return to Ghana to stay overnight in a hotel by the border and drove back to Accra the following morning.

It was another week before I could leave with the shipping documents which Charlie, in his casual way, eventually delivered to me after another two-day vanishing act. I spent most of the last night partying in the officers' mess and was placed once again in the first-class section of the aeroplane for the return flight to London.

7

BACK IN FUNDS

I returned to London feeling on top of the world. After weeks of sun, swimming and squash, coupled with a healthy diet, I felt invincible. I was now at the mercy of the bank manager, having slipped dangerously into the red while I was away. I promised him an imminent injection of funds and he agreed to let things ride for the time being. I don't think we considered for a moment the possibility of our importation going wrong, but I was always reluctant to tempt providence and calculate what my share of the spoils might be.

I took the papers to a shipping agent who told me to expect arrival of the container in about three weeks. He calculated the duty and VAT and I gave him a cheque. If we adhered to our plan, it would not be necessary to break cover at all prior to the arrival of our baby. All we needed was to provide the shipper with the delivery address. John went to see the friend who was to accept the consignment at his warehouse and returned with bad news. It was obvious to John that his friend had second thoughts and was making lame excuses to get out of the job. We decided that it would be unwise to try to persuade him and we needed to find another place to accept the load.

The previous year, a great friend called Chris Griffin and I had decided to make some investments in classic cars. We bought an Aston

Martin DB6 Volante in need of restoration and a neighbour of mine introduced us to Roy. He was a big, rough, coarse man who, along with a business partner Martin, ran a car-repair business. He had fallen on hard times and readily took the job on, working from a couple of lock-up garages near the flat in which he lived in Forest Hill.

After we sold the restored Aston for a small profit, Roy asked if we would bankroll him to buy a small workshop in New Cross, for which he and Martin would pay rent. In return, he promised to give our restoration work priority.

We agreed and gave them enough extra money with which to set up the spray booth and buy the tools of their trade. It turned out not to be the best of investments and rent was less than regular. In due course, I bought out Chris's share of the investment and, not needing money urgently, I let things ride.

Roy willingly agreed to our offer of £10,000 to accept delivery of the container. I provided him with a letter from the flooring company I had set up, agreeing the deal at a much lower sum. If the delivery was discovered, this would give him a legitimate excuse. It would also serve as a good way to get the arrears of rent that were owing to me. I informed the shipping agent of the delivery address and he promised to let the office know when the ship was due.

Within a week of my return, Chief Charlie was back in London. We had given him specific instructions to stay away until after we had received the container and had time to sell some of the contents. We went to see him. I was keen to let him know that I was unimpressed with his behaviour, especially in the light of his unreliability in Ghana. We had rustled up a couple of thousand pounds to keep him quiet and he agreed to return on the next flight to Accra.

Everything went according to plan. The container was delivered to New Cross and, in two hours, everything was unloaded and stacked neatly in the workshop. We were not sure exactly how much grass had finally been packed. When the sticks and stalks were trimmed, we expected to be left with less than one tonne.

The day after delivery, we set about opening the flooring packages and, with electronic scales, arrived at a final weight of 860 kilos. I would have preferred to keep the stuff sealed in the flooring packages until we needed it. Out of polythene, the smell was very strong indeed. The consignment appeared to have deteriorated a little in transit and some of the blocks had some mould on the outer surfaces.

Similar to most businesses, there were importers, wholesalers and retailers. We were lucky – the market was virtually dry and word soon got around that a new consignment of 'bush' had arrived in London. In a few days, about a third of the load had been sold and it was not long before we were able to pay off all the expenses and take a handsome dividend for ourselves.

Although at the time there were no restrictions on the amount of cash you were able to pay into the bank without suspicion, I chose to pay off my overdraft in instalments. I explained to the manager that an investment in Jamaica had paid off and, because of foreign-exchange restrictions, the money was being brought in cash in dribs and drabs.

Roy asked if he could sell some of the grass on commission, and we were happy to agree. Within a short while, he was moving big quantities and the money was rolling in fast. Roy used to arrive at my house in Mottingham and up-end carrier bags full of cash to be counted and bundled with elastic bands. Each bundle contained £1,000 made up of ten separately folded £100 sections. I had never handled so much cash before and it became a problem finding hiding places in the house in which to put it.

The poorer-quality grass with too many sticks or tainted with surface mould was kept back until the end. In due course, everything was sold. There was still no competition in the market place where, in those days, there were many smokers with a preference for herbal to resin. I ended up with about £200,000 for my share. It had been easy work and a great deal of fun. I considered myself lucky to have had so many experiences in four new countries in less than a year and felt proud that I had done a good job.

12

JOHN'S RETIREMENT

John was a regular visitor at my house in Mottingham. The back door was always open and anybody willing and able to tackle Suzie and Jasper, my brace of Jack Russells, had free access. This mother-and-son double-act had quite a local reputation. Jasper had homicidal tendencies, verging on psychopathic, and lived by the simple premise 'If you can't fuck it, kill it.' The house had double gates with a sweep-round drive and many a hapless postman was caught in a scissor movement with a Jack Russell attacking from either entrance. One of my friends had a penchant for expensive shoes, and Jasper did not endear himself by perforating several.

I had been out locally and returned one morning to find John sitting alone at the large kitchen table with a cup of coffee. He told me that he had decided to start a Formula Three racing-car team and was retiring from our lucrative business venture.

Both he and I had had successful racing driving careers, cut short for different reasons, and it was too late to start again. He had decided to run a two-car team, one with a paying driver and the other to be driven by Ross Cheever, a young American whose brother Eddie was a Grand Prix driver. Ross had no money but they hoped that they would attract sponsorship along the way.

The team, which was called Valour Racing, emerged on the grid at the beginning of the 1983 season. Both cars, painted in distinctive livery, arrived in an equally well-turned-out transporter and many heads were turned at this obviously well-funded and professional outfit. Nobody except John and I knew where the money had come from.

Anybody wanting to make a small fortune in motor sport should start with a large one. As with most professional sports, only a few people at the stratospheric pinnacle of Formula One earn fabulous sums of money. The rest, bolstered by dreams of success and discovery, pour their hard-earned cash straight down the drain. It is an addiction which spells the ruin of most who take part. Even a long spell in jail does little to dampen the craving. I am still a hopeless victim and take my petrol intravenously, getting my kicks from watching my young grandsons racing schoolboy Moto X.

Ross Cheever turned out to be very quick indeed. In his early inexperienced days, he had a lot of crashes. These cost John dearly but, from the beginning, Ross turned in impressive results. Formula Three cars are very difficult to set up. They have restricted power and, with a myriad of permutations of wing settings, gearing, suspension and tyres, detailed mechanical knowledge is imperative. John had a fine chief engineer in the team, but a never-ending succession of newly discovered tweaks by the competition required the ability to learn quickly and stay on top of the game.

Sometimes, John could not figure out why some cars, driven by slower drivers than Ross, were able to find more straight-line speed or extra grip. After protests by some of the team managers, it soon became evident that by no means everybody was playing with a straight bat. I remember John being horrified that some participants in his beloved sport would resort to cheating in order to gain an advantage.

It was a great source of amusement to me that here was a man ready, willing and able to bend the rules in most other areas but, at the racing track, refused to be anything other than a 'true sportsman'.

Two years later, when my daughter Emily had been selected to drive for the illustrious Club Azzuro Italian karting team, I was taken aside by a well-known sporting figure and told always to remember: 'The best cheat wins.'

My son Oscar, born in 1972, was ten years old when I bought him a 100cc racing kart. I had a lifelong love of fast cars and motor sport. My racing career was cut short for lack of sponsorship and I always hoped that, one day, one of my children would be able to achieve what I had been unable to do. Ever since he was tiny, Oscar was fascinated by anything mechanical. He would play contentedly for hours with his collection of model cars and spent much of his life racing around our large garden on his bicycle.

The day after Oscar got his kart, I tied the machine to the roof rack of my wife's Mini Estate and, with the family, drove to the track in Tilbury. The track, on a piece of wasteground opposite a housing estate, had not changed at all since I had first seen it at the age of 16 when I won my first kart race.

Oscar was not fast enough to keep the spark plug from oiling up. A few other karters had arrived with their machines and I got a willing push start after donning a helmet and gloves. I drove a few laps to clear the engine and reluctantly brought the lively machine back to its owner. Oscar managed one or two laps this time with a succession of tentative stabs at the throttle. When it oiled up again, my daughter Emily, then 12, asked to have a go. She dressed appropriately and put her unimpressed dog Suzie into the car. Having cleaned the spark plug, I push-started her on to the track. Immediately, it was obvious that she was a natural. It was clear that she had the confidence to drive quickly enough to keep the engine running. Emily did not want to come back into the pits. Each lap she got faster and faster and began to find the best cornering lines. Oscar complained that his present had been commandeered and, at that point, Emily obliged by spinning off the track in front of the pits from a little over-exuberance.

Emily's turn of speed gave Oscar the determination to drive faster and the spark plug needed no further maintenance. Before the end of the day, Emily had another go. She was soon overtaking some of the other more experienced drivers. She announced that karting was all she wanted to do.

I wasted no time. I bought everything we needed to go racing and commissioned the making of a trailer into which everything could be loaded. I found out that juniors could hold a competition licence from the age of 11 and set about obtaining one for Emily. Oscar would have to wait for another year before starting to race. I soon learned about where the tracks were and we set about practising as often as we could. I learned quickly and soon was able to maintain the equipment. Everywhere we went, I asked questions and found everybody happy to share their knowledge.

Emily was becoming more and more competent and, together, we decided that she was ready to race only one month and a handful of practice sessions after sitting in a kart for the first time.

Race day dawned. The trailer had not been finished so I borrowed an old Transit pick-up truck from Roy. We arrived at Tilbury that Sunday morning looking more like we were tarmacing drives than going motor racing. To make matters worse, it was pouring with rain. We had not encountered these weather conditions before and someone suggested that I made a 'wet box'. I quickly learned that, if I did not construct something to stop the water getting into the carburettor, Emily would not do much driving that day. With some help and a commandeered sandwich box, we were ready.

For her first six race meetings, Emily would be classified as a novice. Her competition licence had to have six official signatures before she would be able to upgrade to National status.

During practice, just about everybody spun off the slippery track at least once. I had to make some adjustments to my wet box to fix a misfiring engine and, before we knew it, the first of the three heats was lining up on the grid.

Having no clutch, races were from a rolling start after a couple of formation laps. First lap into the hairpin and Emily managed to drive around a pile-up involving most of the leaders. She ended up fifth overall in a field of about 24 and was becoming accustomed to the wet conditions. After the heats, she was placed in sixth for the start of the final and proudly collected her first trophy for being the first novice home, by a mile, and finishing fifth overall on the day.

We raced somewhere every week until Emily made her National licence. Emily won all six novice trophies and, at a track in Norfolk, collected another for third overall.

It was not long before I discovered Sisley Racing near Brands Hatch. Bill Sisley sold me one of his latest racing karts. Sisley had a resident engine tuner called Brian who prepared two quick motors. We got on well and Bill happily gave me a lot of good advice. He had a young man working for him called Johnny Herbert. He was a shy young chap of 17 who would ride to work every day from Romford on a small motorbike. Every day for lunch, he brought a small pack of wafer-thin Spam sandwiches made by his mother Jane. Johnny was a great kart driver and had achieved many successes for the Sisley team. Bob, Johnny's father, had a limited income as an electrician and could not afford the expenses of travelling to all the rounds of the international kart-racing circuit. They used to manage two or three a year, sometimes towing a caravan to Sweden or other distant venues.

Johnny's equipment was never up to date. He had the added disadvantage of having to buy 'over the counter' tyres, not having a manufacturer's contract with the benefit of 'trick' compounds. Nevertheless, this quiet unworldly boy showed a level of aggression and control on the track, which brought results far beyond reasonable expectations.

Bill offered Johnny's services as mechanic and coach to help Emily. He could see the potential in this pretty and talented young girl in a male-dominated sport and suggested a possible inclusion in the Sisley team.

Within three months, I had bought a large slice of Sisley Racing. Bill wisely retained the leisure side of the business. He now owns a very successful track at Rochester which benefits from the rise in recent years in corporate entertainment. Bill's partner in this venture is John Surtees, the only man in history to win motorcycle World Championships and move on to achieve the same in Formula One. He was principal Ferrari works driver for some years and was so much loved and respected by the Italian people that the Vatican made him a Count, the next best thing to being sanctified.

This rare honour had also been conferred on John McCormack, the great Irish tenor who spent much of his working life at La Scala Opera House in Milan. Some years ago, I met his grandson in Dublin. He owns a restaurant there and plays in a jazz band. Also called John, he claims that his grandfather's title is hereditary and uses it unashamedly.

Johnny spent more and more time with us. He accompanied us practising, was mechanic for Emily when racing and stayed at Norlesden House on a regular basis. He had become one of the family. Ever reluctant to try new recipes, he expanded his education in our company but was not much of a conversationalist. Having achieved pretty much all that one could in the British karting scene, he raced in an international class which only existed in Europe. His ambition was to graduate to racing cars and he and his family dreamed of a chance to prove his ability.

Still too young to hold a competition licence, Oscar was getting faster and faster. One day practising at Tilbury, the senior British champion Tony Negal was testing some engines which had been prepared for him by his tuner Dave Evans. Dave was there with his friend Gary Till, both of them looking after Tony and timing each lap with a stopwatch. Tony was a successful businessman and arrived in style, usually in a new Porsche, leaving his mechanic to drive the van with the equipment. Little ten-year-old Oscar, driving much less up-to-date equipment than Tony, was flying. Gary and Dave were increasingly amused as a more and more frustrated Tony Negal tried everything he could to match Oscar's lap times. They tried to explain that Oscar had a substantial weight advantage but Tony was not happy. We all became friends.

Gary, now a chartered accountant, became Emily's mechanic and David our engine tuner. David, keen to pursue a career in motor racing himself, later became my 'middle man' looking after the timber-import company. He received an eight-year sentence for his part in the cannabis conspiracy.

I took on a manager to run Sisley Racing's day-to-day activities and sought ways to make the business pay. I made a direct approach to the number-one European engine manufacturers, IAME based near Milan. The boss of this company wielded great power. He held a senior position in the sport's governing body and, a little like Enzo Ferrari in Formula 1, was central to kart racing internationally. Their in-house tuner, like the Court Alchemist, produced engines that were faster than anything else. His locked workshop, cloaked in secrecy, led one to believe that his was a dark art, practised in churchyards after midnight.

I succeeded in negotiating an exclusive arrangement to import engines into the UK. My buying power enabled me to place and pay for an order for a quantity of racing motors previously unheard of and to secure some 'factory motors' for our own use. I was entertained at lunch by the bosses. The then International Karting World Champion, Mike Wilson, employed by IAME, came along to help with translation. My Italian was passable at that stage but we needed somebody to help with technical terminology. It was becoming clear to me that Italy, the centre of international kart racing, was run by an exclusive club that held all the winning hands. If I was to have access to the inner circle, I would have to nurture these contacts.

Before the end of Emily's first racing season, she was selected to represent the British Junior Team at a track in Holland. There were five other team-mates, including Jason Plato, later to become British Touring Car Champion. The competition was against a six-man team from Holland and another from Germany, which included Michael Schumacher.

There was to be a series of races over two days and the winning team was the one with the highest aggregate finishes. We brought Gary and Johnny Herbert to mechanic and took the night boat from Sheerness to Vlissingen. Much alcohol was consumed during the crossing and our hungover party arrived at a rain-sodden track to discover that the opposing teams had been there already for three days. They were all firmly entrenched and prepared for battle. Everywhere was evidence of heavy expenditure with a pitful of campers and awnings under which was a selection of the very best equipment.

We were outclassed and under-experienced. The racing was very fast and highly aggressive and team orders included dangerous blocking tactics to prevent opposing team members from moving forward. At the end of one of the races, Emily was driven into at high speed by one of the German drivers. Her machine cartwheeled down the track before landing on top of her and breaking her ankle. The local hospital offered to operate and pin the break, but we would have had to stay on for a few days before she was able to be moved. We elected to go for a temporary plaster cast and get back to England. She was out of racing for two months.

On another trip to Italy, I met Antonio Ducati, grandson of the founder of Ducati motorcycles, *bon viveur* and aristocrat. He owned a factory making racing-kart tyres and wanted to introduce them to the UK. We got on very well and I agreed to try to persuade the RAC, who govern British motor sport, to give them a try in a subsidised 'one-make' class. By injecting money into the sport and sponsoring prizes, we finally succeeded in achieving our goal and, to this day, Vega tyres figure prominently in British kart racing.

Sisley Racing was, however, a serious financial burden. It was clear that sales of racing karts were limited. The engine deal from Italy proved to be very successful but they only served to bolster up a business that would always be unprofitable.

Emily made a gradual return to racing, having lost a lot of confidence from the accident so early in her career. We persevered with a weekly programme and, in time, she began winning again.

Before the end of the year, I arranged for Johnny Herbert to test a Formula Ford car at Brands Hatch. He had only recently passed his driving test and I taught him to 'heel and toe' in a little Austin Healey. This involves turning the right foot while braking to 'blip' the throttle with the heel at the same time. It enables engine braking to help slow the car smoothly while at the same time keeping the engine turning at optimum speed. Every racing driver has to master this technique and Johnny learned quickly.

We arrived early on practice day. Johnny was fitted into the car with the seat and pedals set up correctly. His parents were there and it was clear that there was a great deal of tension in the air. Bob, Johnny's father, was clearly agitated and constantly told him that he had to do well that day if he stood a chance of racing cars. I made it clear that there was no pressure and we would see how the day progressed.

On the second lap of the second practice session, Johnny spun. He hit nothing but we called him in to check out the car. As soon as he arrived at the pits, Bob was hovering beside the car and, before Johnny could get out, he was being berated by his father. With a stopwatch around his neck, Bob made it clear just how fast he expected him to drive that day. The situation was intolerable.

Johnny was in tears. I told Bob that, if he did not leave the pit area and watch from a distance, I would put a stop to the session. I put my arm round his son's shoulder and we took a walk to the end of the pits. I explained that, if he crashed early in the day, before he was ready to push the car hard, we had no choice but to pack up and go home. I was sure that he was a talented driver and had every confidence that he would do well. There was a great deal to assimilate and it would take time.

Johnny drove the car for another three or four sessions that day. He became much more confident, spun a few times and became quicker as the day went by. Bob watched from the safe distance of a grandstand and we all got together at the end of the day in the Kentagon, the Brands Hatch bar.

I had expected Johnny to acclimatise sooner. He was very nervous all day, always asking if he had done enough to get another chance. He was a poor communicator and could not give the mechanics any feedback at all. When asked what the car was doing in the corners, he replied, 'I don't know.' We had to resort to guesswork to make any adjustments.

It emerged that this particular make of car was known to be difficult to drive and had a reputation for a tendency to swap ends, or spin. I promised Johnny Herbert another day.

13

BACK TO GHANA

I had been spending money freely. By early 1983, it became clear that I would have to slow down appreciably or go back to work. Roy had been trying to persuade me to make another importation from Ghana and, with the prospects of an expensive season's racing ahead, I was feeling tempted. Charlie worried me, though. I knew that I would never change him. William, his partner in Ghana, had given me his telephone number and I decided to get in touch.

A week later, I collected William from Heathrow and checked him into a comfortable anonymous hotel in Bayswater. It did not come as a surprise to me to learn that Charlie had lied to William about the amount of his remuneration for the last consignment. Furthermore, more than half William's share still remained owing. William was unwilling to work with Charlie again but feared his influence and power in Accra. News of my arrival in Accra would spread within minutes of touching down, but I would not allow an importation to take place without my personal supervision. We resolved to offer Charlie 10 per cent of his previous fee in exchange for calling on his contacts for help should the need arise.

I gave William a tour of the sights of London and a generous amount of money to spend for the few days he stayed before his return to Ghana.

A week later, I was booked to fly back to Accra. I bought another radio, removed a speaker myself and packed the void with money before screwing the back in place. I had left most of my clothes at the house, which I had continued to rent, so, apart from a few bits and pieces and some presents for the boys, I would travel light. I did allow myself the luxury of a couple of good squash rackets and a supply of yellow spot balls.

I had no baggage to check in and found a friendly face at Heathrow to get my boarding pass. Paul was not on duty but I knew the captain, who gave me an invitation on to the flight deck.

African airspace came as an eerie contrast to the heavy traffic of Europe. Unwatched and unheard, often hours would pass in radio silence. The flight to Accra took an extra half-hour as the captain avoided a series of storms. Like a giant slalom in the sky, we slid between great black columns of lightning-illuminated cumulus cloud, taller than the ceiling height of the DC10. The combination of advanced instrumentation and pilot skill brought us to our destination after a turbulent flight, much of which passed with seat-belt signs illuminated.

I was happy to be back. I knew the score by now and, several packets of Bensons lighter, I emerged unscathed at the front of the airport building after only a few minutes. By arrangement, I took a taxi the short drive to the house where my smiling houseboys were outside to welcome me home. I had ensured that the wages were kept up to date and, after a delicious dinner of lobster washed down with a couple of cold beers, I spent a quiet evening alone listening to music.

I had agreed with William that it would be better for him to keep away from Accra as much as possible and that I would drive to his farm, which was both private and inconspicuous. I had a kind of warm and cuddly feeling as I drove out of town early that first morning, enjoying, once again, the familiarity of the journey. The soldiers at the barricade did not delay me unduly and I made the journey in under an hour.

William greeted me warmly. The harvest was not due for another couple of weeks but preparations had already begun. He had located and secured enough flooring to fill two containers. The factory, still silent, had stockpiled a lot of production and we were able to benefit from buying a large quantity of seconds. Cardboard was still a problem so we would have to conceal the pressed blocks of cannabis carefully inside each package before vacuum-sealing it on to a hardboard base. Already William and his team had secured enough tape for the job and everything was neatly laid out in the barn ready for work. How differently William went about his work to the haphazard Charlie.

I was impressed. William had paid for everything with his own money. I reimbursed him and put him in funds for deposits and other expenditure. The Cedi, the local currency, had continued to devalue since my last visit and we would benefit yet again from lower prices. William had tried to get hold of a good watertight container from the shippers but, despite promises, he had drawn a blank. Charlie had all the shipping contacts and we agreed that, if nothing arrived in a week, we would call upon him to earn his 10 per cent. I returned to Accra much happier than was so often the case with Charlie at the helm.

Paul was at the house and we embraced warmly. He had been to the squash club to find me and was scribbling a note for me as I arrived. We fixed up a game of squash for the morning and he invited me to lunch afterwards to meet his uncle at his house.

I had been thinking in the car earlier that I was somewhat exposed. With the current schedule, I would be in Accra this time for several weeks and I no longer had a realistic cover story. Ghana was still beset with curfew, power cuts and a dearth of commodities, so there was no tourist industry. Paul and his family, friends and contacts were no fools. I could justify coming back for a couple of weeks to visit friends but any longer without a reason and people would begin to ask questions.

Paul was in no hurry to leave. He had been engaged for a year and planned to marry soon. He loved to fly but had been thinking about widening his interests in Ghana. Industry had all but ground to a halt but he figured that everybody needed to eat and farming had to be the obvious choice. I had a feeling that Paul had rehearsed this conversation in his mind already. I knew that, although he was well connected, he had limited access to capital. He had been to my house in London and knew that I had money, although he had no idea that I was anything other than a legitimate businessman.

Here, too, was my opportunity for another perfect cover.

I readily expressed interest. I tried to make him understand why I was happy to leave a land of plenty on a regular basis to enjoy the simplicity of Ghana but knew that, at best, he would attribute my attraction to Accra to a strong love interest or just downright eccentricity. In any event, if I was the conduit through which he could achieve his dreams, he would be the last to question my motives.

He had done quite a lot of research and promised to show me what he had found the next day after squash. Before he left, he told me that the lovely medical student Elizabeth had been in America visiting relatives but was expected back in about a week. I had brought some reading and was happy for the time being with my own company.

Both Paul and I were intensely competitive. Neither liked to lose and I don't remember who did on that day. We were very evenly matched. After the game, we relaxed by the pool and Paul showed me plans of two areas of farmland, which were available for purchase. The plans had been drawn by a skilled hand and showed a great deal of detail. Surveyors in Ghana had to work hard to earn their living and had no access to instruments or modern technology. I am sure that the most junior ones were chosen to survey areas deep in the bush and I wonder just how many were consumed by wild animals while on duty.

Apparently, there was a canning plant in Accra, which had fallen into disuse. Having done a lot of research, Paul was sure that pineapple farming was a good bet. He thought that the cannery could be resurrected or even purchased and I was beginning to see the wisdom of his thinking. Having purchased the tops to plant, apart from the ever present need for water, pineapple farming was a relatively low-maintenance activity.

One of the farms, about 1,500 acres, was near the Wega Dam project and not too far from Henry. I said that, if it all stacked up, I would be willing to fund the project in exchange for a 'large slice of the pineapple'. Paul offered me 51 per cent and I accepted.

There were no flies on Paul's uncle, a lifelong politician and respected Ghanaian elder statesman. We sat on the veranda of his modestly grand, colonial-style bungalow and drank a beer. Uncle, forever inquisitive, plied me with questions. I would have been foolish to stick to the story of a Ghana Airways feasibility study as a reason for my lengthy first trip and gambled on revealing a thirst for adventure. I portrayed myself as an independently wealthy man enjoying the benefits of a healthy life, a beneficial black-market rate of exchange and an insatiable curiosity. I even related the adventure in Togo and, after evident early suspicion, Uncle was visibly warming to me.

We were called to lunch and joined at the table by the ladies of the house. A feast had been prepared. There was an array of different meats and dishes, some recognisable and others more obscure. The trade-off was a generous quantity of inert glutinous *fufu*. I tried some very tasty, gamey meat with a flaky texture. On passing my plate for a second helping, my question was answered that it was from a rodent found in the bush much like a guinea pig. I asked no more questions as a selection of bush meat was passed around.

I love spicy food. There is a special preparation of chilli paste peculiar to Ghana hotter than anything I have tried anywhere else in the world. I had become quite adept at eating with my right hand but was nonetheless grateful that my houseboy provided a fast and efficient laundry service.

We returned to drinking beer on the veranda again, just us four men, for most of the afternoon. None of us was sober when the time came to leave. In the car, Paul said that he had rarely seen his uncle so animated. We had all had a good day.

The next day, Paul and I met early. The land we were to see belonged to the village on which it stood and, before we could take the first step, we had to meet the chief who lived and worked in Accra.

I was surprised to see where the chief lived. Beyond metalled roads and approached along a dusty track with an open-ditch sewer alongside, we came to an entrance and drove in. Inside was a square on three sides of which were rows of single-storey concrete buildings, each with doors interspersed at uniform distances not more than 10 feet apart. A few children, bare-footed and nappy-headed (a Caribbean term for unkempt and untrimmed afro hair) looked on curiously as we got out of the car.

A young man, not more than 30, emerged from the end of one of the buildings and approached us smiling. Obviously anticipating our visit, he was dressed in the robes of a chief and wore sandals, the soles of which appeared to have been crafted from lorry tyres.

Paul handed the chief two bottles of clear liquid and I gave him a sleeve of cigarettes. We were invited into his quarters. The open door revealed a space no larger than a prison cell. There was a crudely made wooden bed and three chairs. On the walls were some old photographs of men in tribal garb whom I took to be ancestors.

The chief took one of the bottles of home-distilled gin and, standing at the door, chanted a prayer in his African dialect while spilling some of the liquid in small spurts on to the threshold. He was joined by Paul in a loudly exclaimed 'Yow!' which I took to be the equivalent of 'amen'. At the end of the chant, we were invited to take a chair and were handed a glass each filled by the chief from the now half-empty bottle. Downed in Russian style, the foul pungent liquid, with an aftertaste of old socks, burned its way down my gullet.

The chief spoke halting English. It took a while to establish that, subject to the approval of the village elders, whom we would meet the following day, the land was available. It would be sold at a price to be assessed by the same surveyors who had prepared the plan commissioned and paid for by Paul. The chief studied the plan at length and nodded approvingly as he pointed to each feature that he recognised. We left after agreeing to collect him at 8.00am the following morning and drove to the house where the boys had prepared lunch for us.

Paul explained that the chief had a menial job in Accra and spent the weekends at the village. Most of the children and several of the women we had seen that morning were the chief's family. He had inherited his status at a very early age and was much loved by his people as a gentle and noble man.

Paul took my car home and returned the next morning with the chief alongside in the passenger seat. The journey seemed to take a long time but not much more than an hour later we pulled off the road into what I can only describe as a typical African village.

A small gathering of curious children surrounded us at a respectful distance and they all giggled when I looked at them and smiled. The chief would affectionately touch the heads of some of the little ones falling into step alongside us as the party made its way towards the only building in the village with a shaded veranda. There, as we drew close, stood a half-dozen or so older men – the elders of the village.

Having been introduced to each in turn, I was given a low stool and invited to sit down. Paul gave one of the men a handful of small-denomination notes. He returned minutes later with several bottles of old-sock gin. After several vigorously chanted prayers accompanied with much sprinkling, I began to join in with the 'Yows', much to the amusement of the assembled company.

We continued to down shots of old sock while making small talk in the searing heat of the midday sun. The plan, spread out on the dry mud floor, was the centre of attraction and animated chatter as I slid gradually into a confused oblivion in a cacophony of local dialect.

Perched gnome-like on my low stool, I was saved from collapse in the nick of time at the suggestion of a guided tour of the village. Paul was in no better state than me from the alcohol and he swayed off towards the car to find our last two bottles of fresh water. The village had no well and water was brought from the nearby river which rushed by carrying with it a high percentage of dark-brown mud. Collected in tin vessels of varying sizes, the water was left to stand for some time while the mud settled to the bottom leaving a less-than-clear proportion on the top to be scooped out for drinking.

Rather unsteadily, we joined the party of elders who were mostly dressed in a selection of clean but stained and faded long shorts – or short longs – and ragged T-shirts. All carried a long stick as a badge of office. One, crippled from a badly set broken leg from long before, needed his stick to aid his progress but led with an agility which belied his obvious disability.

We headed between the huts on the baked searing earth and joined a path going downhill towards the chocolate-brown river. There, a dozen or so happy naked children played and swam in the fast-moving current, while their mothers did their laundry and chatted. The banks were thick with verdant undergrowth from which sprang a quantity of trees of varying height.

I knew from the plan that the river bisected the land on offer to us and it would be an easy job to irrigate and water the crops. We followed the path alongside the riverbank and, a few hundred yards later, came upon a clearing sloping steeply downwards and with a rickety wooden goal at each end; here, the village football team played local villages with the ferocity of previously fought bloody battles. Beyond this, surrounded by tall reeds, was a large pond of at least four acres. It was clear from the noise that among the wildlife was a large population of frogs. As we came closer, several healthy fat specimens were visible jumping about in the reeds.

We came full circle and rejoined the village of about 50 huts from behind the gin palace. There was an all-pervasive atmosphere of harmony in this poor but happy place. Never once did I see anger or frustration.

We had pleased the elders and they agreed to sell to us. We were to instruct the valuation as soon as possible and return a week later. It being the end of the week, we bade farewell to the chief and drove back to Accra somewhat the worse for drink.

During the next seven days, I played a lot of squash, went to a couple of raucous late parties at the officers' mess and tried to avoid too much alcohol.

William reported that the ganja harvest was in full swing. We calculated that the savings we made on the black market left enough in the pot to buy an extra tonne of grass. We agreed to stockpile it ready pressed for another shipment in two or three months' time.

Paul had the report from the surveyors and they valued the land at $10,000. Having decided to buy the extra cannabis, I was left with about £2,000 so we would have to buy the land in instalments, a normal procedure according to Paul. He had been called to work that weekend but had arranged for his brother's driver to take me to the village in one of the military Land Rovers.

He arrived to pick me up at about 8.00am that Friday morning. I was reluctant to kiss goodbye to Elizabeth who had returned from America the day before. Jet-lagged, she had kept me up most of the night and I left her to sleep as I joined the party in the back of the Land Rover behind the chief. Thankful for a vehicle in which the road noise made conversation difficult, I snoozed on the wide, flat back seat.

One of the elders spoke clear English. Ceremonies over, we established that the village was happy to accept the valuation. We agreed a $3,000 down-payment and the balance to be paid within a year. This left me some working capital to leave with Paul. The village provided a willing labour pool and land preparation could begin as soon as we liked. We agreed to use one lawyer and to deposit the money with him at the beginning of the following week.

My driver, in military fatigues, had caused quite a stir. It was not long before he went off into the bush, along with some of the village men, carrying his army-issue rifle. I managed to slow down the pace of the gin swilling but was running short of conversation.

They led me to a nearby hut a little larger than the others. The inside was so much cooler than outside and the compacted mud floor had been swept spotlessly clean. I was told that these were to be my own chief's quarters.

It had begun to dawn on me that the deal for the land was a little strange. The village was plum centre in the middle of our farm. It was soon explained to me that I was indeed to become a chief. I had my house and could take as many wives as I wanted. It transpired that in the village history there had already been two Chief Pauls before me. The Ghanaians have trouble pronouncing aitches and I was to be known as 'Chief Paul the Turd'. The ceremonies would take place the following weekend. The robes would be made in Accra by the chief's tailor and my lorry-tyre flip-flops were to be crafted in the village.

That night, a feast was being prepared in my honour and I agreed to go with the elders in the morning to a neighbouring village on a courtesy call. My driver, who had returned an hour earlier with a beaming entourage, was, I was told, happy to stay. He was very popular. He had shot a good deal of bush meat and was the darling of the girls of the village.

There was no electricity; the evening descended black and early. Open fires, oil torches and candles served as the only illumination. I had commandeered the powerful electric torch from the Land Rover and put it in my hut. The radio, still containing a lot of cash, much to the amusement of the village children, played loud West African music.

We feasted on monkey, quite gamey but lean and tasty, some sort of antelope and snake. Cut into steaks and straight off the fire, snake tastes like barbecued chicken. It was not late when the party came to an end. The battery in my radio had died and I was tired. When I turned off the torch in my new hut, there was nothing whatever around me to lighten the dark of the night. I fell asleep straight away.

I woke with a start to the sound of galloping above me. Groping for the torch, I shone the beam up into the rafters. Two large rats, momentarily stilled by the light, looked downwards with their illuminated, evil red eyes. Their magnified silhouettes doubled the size of their images on the straw roof above. I was up and out in a flash, grabbing my shoes as I made for the door. With the help of the torch, I hurried to the locked Land Rover. The driver was doubtless in the arms of one of his fan club and there was nobody around. It was not hard to force one of the sliding windows and, having gained entry, I slept on the back seat.

The next morning, feeling surprisingly rested after my interrupted night, I decided to take a walk before the elders whisked me away on village duties. I headed for the river to find the launderette already in full swing. The water looked altogether too inviting. I stripped naked and dived into the muddy water. The kids, also naked, jumped out of the water and watched laughing as I swam across the fast-running current. I had caused quite a commotion but it was well worth it. Still wet, I dressed and returned to the village. It did not take long to dry out in the fierce sunshine.

My driver was by the car. The elders, already gathered, were waiting for me. It was time to go visiting. We crammed as many into the Land Rover as we could and drove slowly the two miles or so to what appeared to be a slightly smaller village. We were welcomed and led to a hut larger than any of the others with a small portable generator chattering away outside.

Inside the hut was a sight that took my breath away. A large sofa, on which sat a huge man and two big women, faced an enormous television. On both sides of the sofa two large armchairs, seating two more large ladies, also faced the entertainment. A video of very explicit American porn played away as we briefly shook hands with the chief who was obviously reluctant to be distracted. He waved his hand, indicating that we should sit and join the party and, judging from the stack of videos, they had a lot to get through. We joined their elders outside, downed a glass of gin and said our goodbyes. By midday, the driver and I were on the road back to Accra.

Elizabeth had stayed at the house and took advantage of the peace to do some studying. My eyes were itching, and when I woke on the Sunday morning my eyelids were so swollen I could not see. Elizabeth did not drive so she sent the boy for a taxi to take me to her father's clinic. He berated me for swimming in the river and gave me a large shot of antibiotics with instructions to return for another the next day. I had contracted river blindness. By the second injection, I was able to see again but my eyes remained very sensitive for weeks.

I was happy that Paul had a heavy schedule with flying duties the following week. William had started to press the fresh crop. It was so refreshing not to need to chase him. I made several courtesy calls to give encouragement but my presence was not needed on a daily basis. Charlie had done the business with his shipper; the container was ready to be loaded.

Paul and I returned to the village for the celebrations to mark the purchase of the land. Determined to avoid a night in the village, we once again accepted the services of the military driver who would be able to return us to Accra after curfew.

During the week, I bought a big aluminium frying pan and a gallon can of cooking oil. I had a plan. The week before, walking past the pond at the village, I noticed a strong smell of wild garlic. On closer inspection, I found loads of it and determined to prepare a delicacy.

We arrived to be met with our new robes and shoes and changed for the ceremonies, which, thankfully, were conducted without the need to consume too much gin. The driver once again set off with his hunting party in tow.

I presented the village with my purchase and, when asked what it was for, explained that I had noticed that the frogs were flourishing in the village pond and was curious why they were not captured for their large and delicious legs. They looked at me in horror. I had told Paul about my plan in the car and he, too, was shocked at my barbarous suggestion. I tried to explain that, in Europe, the prospect of eating monkey was not exactly encouraged, but they were unmoved by my arguments.

Our driver had bagged a selection of animals for the pot, proudly carried by his happy followers. He and I moved on to the pond and, watched in silent horror by an ever-larger gathering, we dispatched and dismembered a quantity of amphibians in short time. We quickly gathered some garlic and returned to the village where a fire was already burning beside our gin palace.

The smell of my cooking was irresistible and soon I had a plate of fat, succulent local delicacies ready to eat. Everyone I approached with the plate, including Paul, backed away from me. I stopped and, as publicly as possible, ate a couple of the delicious legs. Eventually, Paul, shamed by me, took one and, with closed eyes, tentatively took a bite. Surprised to have survived, he soon took another, declaring it to be irresistible. Finally, our young chief joined in and, within a short time, I was back at the fire cooking more. With the village now turned on to this delicacy, I am sure that the descendants of the frogs we ate that day are not quite as easy to catch.

I supervised the vacuum-sealing of the wood flooring and we loaded the container with some of the best-quality grass I had seen. The boys pressed the load for the next container, which we stacked unsealed for fear of it becoming mouldy.

Paul and I continued to research our farm and preparations were made to irrigate and plant as soon as possible.

Charlie took another ten days to get the paperwork but, eventually, I was on my way back to London.

14

SUCCESS 1983

For some strange reason, the ship carrying our container seemed to be making a world tour. At first, the information from our shipping agent led us to suspect that all was not well. We had plenty of lengthy discussions and, with the help of a large degree of paranoia, became convinced that our 'bit of work' was 'on top'. Apparently, after one week at sea, the ship stopped again around the African coast to pick up more cargo and a further three weeks later was now in Rotterdam unloading.

Convinced that everything had been done discreetly and correctly in Ghana, I decided to make some enquiries. If our container was suspect on departure, it could only be because we had been 'grassed up'. William and Charlie were the only ones to have any details about the shipping and both of them relied upon the successful arrival of the consignment for their money.

I made a call posing as a freight agent and found a friendly voice at the shipping company. It transpired that our information was indeed correct. This particular shipping line often worked in this way, which was why they could offer such a cheap service. Charlie had booked and paid for the cheaper service and pocketed the few hundred pounds difference.

Although William had been so much easier to work with than Charlie, I deeply regretted the need to give him my home telephone number. Despite several warnings, he called me on many occasions while we waited for that boat and was by no means discreet with his questions.

Six weeks after dispatch, our container arrived safely. We had a little over a tonne on board but some of the grass had deteriorated with mould during the long journey. Once again, we had the advantage of a shortage in the market and sales were fast and furious. I was delighted. Roy handled the distribution. He recruited his son-in-law, Peter, whom I knew and liked, but I remained distanced from the rest of the sales network.

The money rolled in. I distinctly remember getting fed up with counting the bundles of notes. It doesn't take long to become spoiled. The racing season was upon us and the money stuffed behind the panels of my bath would soon be put to work.

I decided to support Johnny Herbert. I gave him another test day at Brands Hatch in a more forgiving car. He was able to relax, enjoy the day and put in some respectable lap times. I duly came to a deal with Johnny to run a car in the Formula Ford Junior Championship, which that year included a young man called Damon Hill.

It was going to cost me a lot of money. I asked my solicitor to draw up a contract, which stated that, if Johnny made it to Formula One, I would receive a percentage of his earnings. Johnny and his father happily signed, knowing this to be the opportunity of a lifetime. When Johnny won the Formula Ford Festival in 1984, Bob, his father, made a point of telling me that Johnny would never have made it without me.

In due course, we saw less and less of Johnny. Eventually, he began to avoid eye contact rather than speak to me and, at that point, I knew that he had signed away his future elsewhere.

After winning the Formula Ford Festival, Johnny's career took off. He rose through the ranks, notching up success after success. Shortly after my arrest, he had a massive accident in a Formula 3000 race at Brands Hatch and it was touch and go whether he would lose his legs. It transpired that he had just signed with the Benetton Formula One team. Flavio Briatore, the team boss, made sure that the best medical facilities in the world ensured Johnny's recovery and, within months, he was behind the wheel of a Formula One car.

After years at the top in that rarefied atmosphere of Grand Prix racing, the spoils of which resulted in Monte Carlo tax-haven status, Johnny moved on to become a top Le Mans driver with Audi.

After my release from prison, at a point when I was struggling to survive, I sent emails to Johnny via his fan club, run by his mother Jane. In them, I reminded him that he owed his opportunity to make the big time to me and that, despite there being a contract between us, I had never asked him for anything in return. I asked him then for help, but never received a reply.

Oscar began to race as soon as he reached 11. His aggression often got the better of him and he cost me a lot of money in spares and repairs. I tried to get it across to him that, 'In order to finish first, first you have to finish.' Throughout his racing career, that maxim never totally got through. He was spectacular to watch and the older drivers loved to observe his skill at overtaking, especially in wet weather.

Emily, in direct contrast to Oscar, was a calculating driver, always fast against the clock and smooth. She was able to see the bigger picture and could calculate the value of taking a risk. As a result, she had far fewer accidents and would always be 'in the points'. She had a feel for machinery and was able to give valuable feedback in the pits, often surprising her mechanics with her technical understanding.

There were very few female competitors in karting. At first, Emily had big trouble with the boys, most of whom were more than somewhat chauvinistic. In the early days, she was knocked about on the track more than most but quickly earned respect. Always pretty and slim, she was very fit and stronger than she looked.

One day, after a very tough race against an old rival in which there had been a lot of contact on the track, she was grabbed angrily by the boy's swearing father. Before I could get there to intervene, Emily had floored the man with a single knock-out blow. He was too embarrassed to protest and the officials were 'busy looking the other way'. I was so proud of my protégée.

I had a fine new transporter which had been made to measure to accommodate all our karting requirements. The front section had enough seating for eight people and could be made up to sleep four. It had a fridge, a cooker, a TV and video. The rear section had enough room to take chassis, engines, wheels and tools. With an awning on the side, even the wet meetings became tolerable.

Emily graduated to National level and that year we travelled to the British Championship Super One rounds. These meetings were spread over two days of racing with the tracks open for practice two days before. They took place all around the UK and attracted the best drivers. It was a fast learning curve and Emily soon became a front runner.

I had met with increasing success with my tyre-import exploits, which brought me into direct contact with Antonio Ducati on a regular basis. Antonio, a stylish man, loved good food and his comforts. Wherever I met him in the world, he knew the best places to eat, the classiest bars and the most comfortable hotels. His instincts only came a cropper when he came to some of the English race meetings. They were usually held on tracks in the middle of nowhere, where a slice of cheese on a greasy burger was the most sophisticated culinary experience one could hope for. He had the look on his face of a man facing the firing squad the first time he encountered mushy peas in a pub in Barnsley. Antonio invited Emily to compete in a race in Parma later in the year. His tyre company would act as her sponsor.

The Junior World Championships were held at Laval in France that year. On the longest straight I had ever seen, a radar gun timed these kids at over 100mph as they raced in tight formation, 36 of them on the track at a time. Dave Evans and Gary, the duo who looked after Tony Negal that day at Tilbury, came along to mechanic. Over 100 of the best young drivers in the world competed for the top 36 places for the final day's racing. Emily just failed to make the cut but we had all learned a lot from the experience. We used special grippy tyres for international racing. These required a different design of chassis which were only manufactured abroad.

True to his word, Antonio arranged everything for the race in Parma. We had the luxury of flying in and renting a car with which to commute from track to hotel. A friend of Antonio who ran a team was at the track to meet us and provided everything we needed for the race. Our Sicilian mechanic proudly did everything for Emily and all I needed was a stopwatch. The engines were prepared by a highly respected tuner called Merlin. He strictly controlled how and when they were to be used.

Merlin took to Emily and I stepped back to allow them to establish a rapport. He immediately recognised that she was able to give him the feedback he wanted. He allocated her one of his best engines for qualifying and she surprised us all with a fantastic sixth place on the grid.

Emily finished eighth overall after some furious racing. Merlin was delighted and the Italian team manager invited Emily to join them for the following season. Antonio Ducati provided her with residency. A competition licence would be a formality.

I had been introduced to a charter company specialising in Italian destinations called Pilgrim Air. They were based in London and their boss, Flaviano, readily agreed to help with sponsorship. Emily spoke not a word of Italian. One of Flavi's employees came from Cervinia and her father owned the local ski shop. In no time, Emily was packed off to Italy for six weeks' skiing and to learn the language. She was to return, happy and fit, but with no more command of Italian than her Jack Russell, as all the boys wanted to impress *l'Inghlesina* with their knowledge of English. The 1983 season was coming to a close.

I had been in touch with William and he spent a few days shopping in London. I let him convince me that all the work had been done for the next delivery and that my presence in Ghana was not required.

As soon as the ship was dispatched, William personally delivered the documents. The agent was alerted and the duty paid. I sent William back to Ghana with strong warnings about the use of the telephone. But I had my doubts.

15

FAILURE 1983

The ship arrived about three weeks later. The agent told our manager that there was a delay in off-loading the containers but delivery should be possible within a few days.

Roy called me and asked me to come to his house to meet a 'friend' of his later that day. I arrived a little early to be told that our container had been spotted at the docks with Customs men 'swarming all over it'. His friend arrived. He did not say where his information had come from but was adamant that his source was impeccable. 'I'm telling you as a friend and you're stone fucking lucky that you know about it before you're all fucking nicked...' were his words. He declined a drink and left as hurriedly as he had arrived.

'What do you think?' asked Roy.

'It looks like we've lost it,' I replied. 'And I think we should be grateful to your mate for sticking his neck out for us.'

'Yeah, but maybe they've got friends at the docks and they're trying to nick our container from under our noses.'

'How would they know which one is our container?' I replied.

I never got a sensible answer.

'I think it's on top,' I said and left without convincing Roy that his friend had given us accurate information.

I was not surprised to find Roy at my house early the next morning. His suspicious mind had allowed him to dismiss all logic during the night. His conspiracy theory was paramount in his mind. We spent a long time discussing it but we failed to agree. Despite this, I allowed him to convince me to speak to our manager and offer him double money to accept the container.

In theory, those who worked at the delivery address were not connected in any way and were simply being paid to accept delivery and store our goods. In this case, our manager also owned the workshop where the goods were to be delivered.

Roy's friend was right. The lorry delivering our container was driven by Customs men. The delay was for the time it took to substitute the grass for sawdust and reload the container. Our manager got a message to us before he was arrested. Roy disappeared abroad for a few weeks.

Unfortunately, the manager had been seen at the timber-import office and there was forensic evidence to corroborate the eyewitnesses who worked there. After a two-week fight in court, he was found guilty and jailed for eight years. I still regret allowing myself to be persuaded by Roy to accept that delivery. Had I stood my ground, the manager would never have been caught.

I never found out why the last container from Ghana was singled out for attention. It may have been a random selection; it certainly could not have been anything sinister. The only ones who could have grassed us up would have put me in the frame, too, and there was no suspicion attached to me at all.

As expected, William never stopped telephoning. One day, he arrived in London unexpectedly. Had I been under suspicion, the calls and visit would have compromised me and I never forgave William for his dangerous lack of trust.

Shortly after Roy returned from his trip abroad, he came to see me. Our biggest dealer in north London, Harry Appiah, himself a Ghanaian, wanted to speak to me. I was worried that our 'need to know' policy would be breached but Roy vouched for Appiah and I agreed.

Later that evening, we drove to his house, which was somewhere near Hendon. He lived in a comfortable semi in suburbia, overflown, every two minutes, by huge low jets on their way to Heathrow. We were welcomed by Harry, a small and wiry man of about 40. From his speech, it was immediately evident that he had been anglicised from years of British residency.

He quickly came to the point. Through his contacts, he had been introduced to two high-ranking politicians from the Ivory Coast. They had come to London as part of an official delegation but were looking for somebody who could facilitate the importation of large quantities of cannabis into the UK. The men were staying in some style at the Cumberland Hotel and were due to return home in a couple of days, after nearly two weeks in London. There was a communication problem as they only spoke French.

We met the next evening. The two men, expensively dressed in shiny well-pressed silk suits, shared a suite. We sat in the ample sitting room which divided their comfortable quarters. I accepted a cold beer from the fridge.

They both spoke in a French accent with little hint of the African patois of my captors in Togo. They explained that in their position they could organise the safe export of anything from the Ivory Coast and, with their contacts, could offer anybody working with them total immunity. I asked whether there was a ready supply of cannabis and they indicated that there was no problem getting whatever quantity we wanted.

They were adamant that it would be safe to export the stuff concealed in containers of coconuts. I replied that, apart from needing additional paperwork for the importation of foodstuffs, I was unimpressed by their suggested commodity. I spent some time trying to explain that, while I was sure they could offer all the necessary cover at their end, the authorities in the UK were another matter. My reasoning fell upon deaf ears.

I agreed to go. I was curious and thought that there would have to be a less crackpot method than playing container roulette with a load of coconuts. This time, I took their telephone numbers and addresses, having resolved never to hand mine out again.

Ghana was finished for us. The UK Customs used a computer which, in the absence of any other information, would pick importations at random to be set aside for inspection. According to the likelihood of hidden contraband, each country had a separate factor. No doubt after our recent loss, the incidence of inspection of imports from Ghana would increase substantially. There being little history of trade between the UK and the Ivory Coast, I was sure that the odds would be in our favour if I could find a commodity in which to hide the grass that would not arouse suspicion. Appiah, who was leaving for Ghana a few days later, wanted me to meet another contact who was in London on a short trip from Nigeria.

At that time, the very best-quality grass was only grown in Jamaica. During the many trips I had made there, I was approached several times, especially when it became known that I had a pilot's licence. The rewards were high for pilots brave enough to take off at night from stretches of straight road illuminated only by hand-held flares flying the short trip to Florida just feet above the Caribbean beneath the surveillance of radar. The valuable loads of sensemilla commanded high prices in America and in human life. Scuba divers had a choice of many wrecks of aircraft on which to dive in the shallow waters off the island.

Kwame (not his real name), who had a farm not far from Lagos, had arrived in London with a sample of his best produce. Harry, a lifelong expert, declared it the next best thing to the very finest from the Caribbean. If we could only get some into the UK, he assured me that it would make double the price of anything else on the market.

Kwame, the picture of African sartorial elegance, wore a well-tailored, fawn-coloured suit. The white shirt accentuated the darkness of the skin of this tall elegant man. I shall never forget the shoes. Made of what was, I am sure, genuine snakeskin, they were set off by amber resin see-through Cuban heels.

I knew that direct imports from Nigeria were the 'kiss of death'. They were watched very closely by the authorities. Thousands of desperados with every conceivable means of concealment had been intercepted and locked up over the years. Once again, I took an

Top: My family some 70 years ago. From left, my grandfather and grandmother and my mother, an unidentified person and my aunt and uncle.

Bottom: A family outing at Biddenden. By coincidence, it's the village in which I was to buy a manor house some years later.

At 17 I thought I would be an actor and had a publicity shoot.

Top: At my wedding with my father Otto and my maternal grandfather.

Bottom left: With my business partner Jim outside the shooting lodge in the grouse moor of Tulchan. It was 1972 and I was 25 and rich.

Bottom right: Outside the lodge that same year with the family – my father, wife and two children.

Top: Me (far right) with Jools Holland (centre, wearing hat) and some friends at one of my dinner parties

Bottom: Jools and his girlfriend come to visit me at Norlesden House in Jools' car.

Top: Sharing a joke with friends.

Bottom: Cardinal Sin at a Chelsea Arts Club party in the early 1980s.

Above: At the kart track sometime between 1985 and 1986 with, from left, Oscar, Dario and Marino Franchitti. Emily is far right.

Right: Emily with Johnny Herbert after the accident in which she broke her ankle. My son Oscar stands behind her

Top: My son Oscar in the mid-1980s.

Bottom: The Formula Ford Festival at Brands Hatch in 1987. Third car from the left is Emily's.

address and several telephone numbers from this well-spoken man and agreed to contact him as soon as I could make a visit.

I made plans to fly to the Ivory Coast and arranged for Appiah to join me from Ghana on a prearranged day at the Intercontinental Hotel, which had been recommended by the politicians. When I first became involved, I vowed to do one importation only in order to get back in front. It did not take long for it to become my regular means of employment. The money was so easy but, in addition, I was becoming addicted to the excitement of it all.

16

THE IVORY COAST

My passport was becoming highly decorated. Some years later, my ten-year passport would assist the prosecution in securing a ten-and-a-half-year sentence.

I flew Air France to Paris. I had a couple of hours to kill before making my connection and made my way to the long-haul terminal at the wonderfully futuristic Charles de Gaulle airport. I checked in my bag at the UTA desk and was ushered to their hospitality lounge where I was plied with caviar and vintage champagne. Only three of us, the last to board, were escorted to the first-class section of the DC10. It was the first time I had flown with this airline, which remains, to this day, the best I have ever used. I drank more of the fine wine than I should have done on that trip.

I was looking forward to seeing the Ivory Coast. I had been told that it had much of the flavour of Togo and hoped that I would not receive a similar reception. Making my way through the formalities, I succeeded in keeping hold of most of my cigarettes. I picked my light bag off the carousel, managing to shrug off the attentions of a plethora of porters, and tried in vain to find a modern taxi in the oppressive heat of the early evening.

Abidjan, the Ivory Coast seaport capital, is built around a

beautiful natural lagoon. It is necessary to drive all the way around it to reach the Intercontinental, which stands on high ground directly opposite the airport.

I had no local currency but knew that the few dollar bills I had would do until I could get to change some sterling. At the airport entrance, my taxi was pulled over by a roadblock manned by some very scruffy policemen. I knew by now why Benson and Hedges were gold; very much an international currency.

A fairly long drive along dusty but wide roads brought us into the very imposing city of Abidjan with its tall modern buildings, which we skirted by on the dual carriageway lagoon road. Continuing onwards, the road began to narrow as it climbed steadily past a succession of imposing residential plots on which stood some fine, large houses. Ahead, the tall white Intercontinental loomed skywards.

The taxi was waved through by a man at a barrier. On the street outside thronged dozens of girls of all shapes and sizes dressed scantily for the night, in the hope of attracting some business from the passing guests.

I checked in. The marble lobby, like any other luxury hotel anywhere in the world, was staffed by young, uniformed efficient linguists. Two musicians, one with a long-necked stringed instrument much like a sitar and the other with a drum clasped between his knees, sat cross-legged on elaborately embroidered cushions and gently played to the passing International clientele. The only thing that made me stand out in this establishment was my preference for informal clothing. It was not my kind of hotel, but I had an appointment with Appiah two days later and would have to stay 'til then.

I changed only a little money knowing that the hotel would not offer the best rates of exchange and took the lift to my comfortable room cooled by whispering air-conditioning. There was a fine view across the whole of the now illuminated lagoon.

I called Harry's Ivory Coast politicians. The telephone was answered by a man who spoke the African French I knew from Togo. I was kept waiting for some minutes. I had begun to think that I had not been understood when a voice I recognised as that of one of the politicians answered. He sounded a little guarded and, from the tone of his voice, I was not sure that he was entirely happy to hear from me. We agreed to meet at his house the next morning at ten. There was no offer of transport.

Most of West Africa is on the same time as the UK, varying at most by an hour. The next day I woke early, drew back the curtains and spent some time watching the fishing boats in the lagoon below. Some were manned by as many as eight men and most, propelled by small outboard motors, headed slowly in random directions leaving behind them a narrow silvery wake.

There was a towelling dressing gown in my room which I donned over my swimming trunks. I slipped on some sandals and, with bath towel over my shoulder, made for the pool. Accessed a floor below the lobby, the sound of the city took over as soon as I opened the outside door. I exchanged 'good mornings' with a small party of young Americans and swam a few leisurely lengths of the pool.

Breakfast over, I had just enough time to find a taxi. The driver showed limited navigational skills and, together, we eventually found my destination. Set in beautiful grounds, the small tidy house was in an evidently exclusive area. There was no reception organised for me. The houseboy kept me just inside the door while he went in search of his boss.

The politician shook my hand and led the way into a dining room. His friend was already seated at the table. We made small talk while the houseboy went off to make coffee. I could feel some unease from the two men and asked if everything was OK. Coffee served, the door was shut behind the houseboy.

'We have important positions here and must be careful.'

I was not happy. 'You came to London to find a partner for this work and invited me to visit you. If you had any reservations about me you should have expressed them earlier,' I replied.

They spent a few minutes trying to appease me, after which we got down to business. It transpired that they had not yet found out where the marijuana would come from, how much it might cost or where it could be pressed. The only thing they were sure about was an abundance of coconuts and contacts in Customs to put the container on board ship without inspection in Abidjan. They did make it clear that they expected me to pay for the grass and all expenses and split the profits 50–50 with them.

I wanted to trash the bastard's dining room. Instead, I took a little while to compose myself and told them that I would not work with the commodity they suggested. They seemed to be relieved at the outcome. I got the impression that, when they returned to the Ivory Coast from London, they had got cold feet about the whole idea. While the houseboy went to fetch me a taxi, I silently congratulated myself on keeping my temper. Although I now found myself in a foreign country with no contacts and little chance of making anything out of the visit, I had at least not made any enemies. I needed to think.

I had the pool pretty much to myself. The pool boy set up a lounger in the shade of a tree, brought me a couple of big towels and fetched a waiter who served me a long cold drink. I had made the trip and was determined to do my best to rescue something from the ashes. Appiah was due to fly in the following morning and I determined to put him to work to try to find somebody who could arrange supplies and help set up a means of exportation.

I knew that the hotel was not the place to make the kind of local contacts I needed. It was not my kind of establishment anyway and I resolved to find something more to my taste as soon as I could. In any event, the Intercontinental had been recommended by the politicians. I didn't want to be anywhere they could watch me.

I ate a salad outside and stayed by the pool for several hours, reading, swimming and thinking. As the afternoon rolled on, some of the young Americans began filtering through to the pool. I got chatting to a couple of girls who finally told me that they were on an evangelical 'mission from God'. They had been in the Ivory Coast for a week and were due to fly out the next day. I was shocked to find that none of them spoke a word of French.

I asked if they had done any exploring in the evenings and was not very surprised to learn that the hotel lobby had been the boundary of their adventures. They were pleasant enough. One of the girls was very pretty, occasionally returning my glances in a very unevangelical way. I needed cheering up and decided to explore Abidjan.

My taxi driver was friendly enough. I had not eaten and didn't fancy the overpriced European fare on offer at the hotel. We plumped for Vietnamese and drove two or three miles around the lagoon road. As we turned off the road, the driver explained that the bamboo-walled restaurant ahead of us was a well-known local favourite. Opposite the restaurant was an open-sided, barn-sized room with a high thatched roof. Outside was a large wooden cage, which was home to a huge coiled snake. Directly ahead, past a small reception, there was a series of tribal-looking wooden huts, each on stilts above the water of the lagoon and approached by balustraded duckboard walkways. This was my kind of hotel.

I made enquiries at the reception. They had plenty of accommodation available and, for the price of one night at the Intercontinental, I could stay for four here. I planned to move in the next day.

The restaurant was very quiet. It was run by a couple who rented the property from the hotel owner. The husband cooked wonderfully and his wife ran the front of house. I was greeted by a willowy, beautiful woman of indeterminate age with slender, delicate hands and an aura of serenity. She wore a red *cheongsam* dress which accentuated her slender figure. I was captivated by her and heard little of the menu as she spoke to me as if I were the only person within miles. She told me of the hardships that they had experienced in Vietnam and their struggle to get to the Ivory Coast. I was treated to a fine meal.

I had asked the taxi to wait for me. Although it was still early, I decided to be sensible and get a good night's sleep before Appiah's arrival. I fancied a joint but would have to settle for a couple of drinks at the hotel bar.

The two evangelists from the pool were at the reception desk. I was quite pleased to hear the loud nasal 'Hi'. I mimed a drinking gesture and pointed to the bar. Five minutes later, they joined me.

They explained that their flight, due to leave very early in the morning had been delayed and they had been calling their families from the lobby with the new arrival time.

After one drink, one of the girls got up, explaining that she still had packing to do. She shook my hand and I bade her a safe journey home. The one who had intrigued me earlier in the day told her friend that she would see her later. As soon as her friend had disappeared from view, she fixed me with a challenging smile.

I ordered a couple of long G and Ts and took a bowl of nuts from the bar. We headed for the lift with our drinks. Another couple of passengers got in with us and I called my floor number. I was pressed against the back of the lift and we snogged unashamedly, while I tried not to spill my drink and the bowl of nuts.

The room had been prepared for the night but I felt a need to share what was to come with the wonderful view of the bay. I drew back the curtains.

I don't know where she had learned some of the things she did to me that night, but all I can say is, hallelujah!

17

THE FRENCH CONNECTION

The curtains still drawn back, I woke to the dawn. Not knowing Appiah's arrival time, I left a message with reception and went for a swim, which I followed with a hungry breakfast from the dining-room buffet.

I returned to my room and snoozed. The telephone rang around 11.00am, waking me from a deep sleep. I asked Appiah to join me in the room where we could talk in private.

I told him about my abortive meeting the day before but that it had made me even more determined to make something from the trip. He had a family contact in Abidjan and readily agreed to stay on longer than planned if we made any headway. He had run out of money but I had brought plenty and was prepared to underwrite his expenses.

We agreed to stay in separate hotels. I checked out and we took a taxi together. Our first stop was where I had been the night before. The room was superb. Surrounded on all sides by the lagoon full of small silver fish, the round building had a small balcony above which was a sun deck reached by ladder through a hatch. Inside was a small bathroom matched on the opposite side by a long fitted wardrobe. The ceiling rose to the full height of the pointed thatched roof from which hung a three-bladed electric fan. There was a noisy air-conditioning unit beneath the large fold-back louvered wooden window. I was very happy.

Appiah wanted to stay in something more African and anonymous. We took the taxi onwards and found just the thing down town in what appeared to have been the main street before the new redevelopment of glass and concrete. We parted company, he to go in search of his 'cousin' and me back to my new hotel at the lagoon.

Appiah returned after dark. He had found a supplier. The taxi took us well off the beaten track into a distinctly poor area of town. We stopped at a row of rendered concrete housing and made our way on foot past the stinking open drains. A young man was evidently waiting for us at the end of one of the accommodation blocks. He shook hands and indicated for us to follow him to his 'brother'.

Tundi (not his real name), a small man crippled with an atrophied right leg, was at the door. Balanced on a single crutch, he shook my hand and invited us to be seated on an expensive suite of furniture. He was Ghanaian, spoke English and had lived in Abidjan for many years. He explained that, although he had control of what was a limited market locally, there were not enough plantations in Abidjan to supply the quantities we had in mind. He obtained much of his own supplies in Ghana which were carried across the long largely unmanned border in the bush.

Prices were high. The Ivory Coast had a steady economy and local currency had an international value. There was no black market and no spiralling inflation. As a consequence, a pound of cannabis cost 20 times what we paid for it in Ghana.

Tundi had all the local connections. Appiah said that he had the contacts in Ghana to get hold of the quantities I had in mind and Tundi offered his services to help carry the stuff across the border by porter at night. We discussed money for a while and agreed a flat fee per pound weight delivered to our transport in the Ivory Coast, out of which Tundi would pay the porters.

He told me that, with the quantities we were discussing, word would soon get round. I would need the assistance of the police. He would try to fix up a meeting as soon as possible with the contact he had worked with for some years.

Tundi's 'brother', who had left the room some minutes earlier, reappeared. He had changed into a pair of expensive jeans. A big cream silk shirt contrasted with his dark skin. The wide smile said only one thing – we were going out.

Tundi accompanied us to the waiting taxi, shook hands and waved us goodbye. His brother gave directions in perfect French and we headed off on a journey to the edge of this big sprawling city; sometimes modern, other times commercial, rich, poor, imposing and ramshackle. The ever-changing districts gave way to a crazy madness of neon. There was street after street of brightly illuminated buildings outside which thronged hundreds of people. Each bar and club had minders gesticulating to every passing vehicle to pull in and sample the particular delights they had on offer.

The taxi came to a halt at a building larger and more permanent-looking than those around it. There was something of the Wild West about this place. It stood alone and had a deep balcony all along the front. The wide central entrance was flanked by two large men permanently busy welcoming those they considered had money to spend and rejecting the rest. Above them, the large neon sign flashing in time to the throbbing music from within was shamelessly shouting temptation.

Tundi's brother was obviously a regular. We were fast-tracked to the best table right beside the dance floor. We ordered food and downed a couple of local beers while we waited. Females outnumbered males on a ratio of at least ten to one and the dance floor was already busy with a varied assortment of nubile gyrating girls. We were subjected to a sea of inviting smiles from some irresistibly sexy young women. Dinner over, Appiah remained seated while we got up to dance.

Tundi's brother, tall and fit, like a proud warrior, moved well. Soon we were surrounded. The heady loud rhythm, coupled with the effects of a couple of strong joints I had smoked earlier after a few days' abstinence, fuelled the air.

After a short while, a girl came over to me. Lightly holding my arm, she moved close enough to be heard above the music. She pointed at a tall, light-skinned, slim girl in tight blue jeans dancing on the edge of the floor looking in my direction. 'My friend wants to make love with you.'

I blew her a kiss and she giggled. I was approached similarly several times during the evening. Tundi's brother explained that all the girls wanted to find out what it was like to have sex with a white man. I was in heaven.

The next morning, I sent my new friend in the tight jeans off to work in a taxi and spent a couple of hours relaxing to classical music and some strong coffee. I had arranged to meet up with Appiah for lunch. The telephone rang.

'Mr Newman?'

'Yes.'

'There is a gentleman in reception to see you.'

'I'll come over.'

I pulled on a T-shirt, slipped into my sandals and made my way across the walkway towards reception. A tall man in a suit wearing heavy-rimmed spectacles came towards me.

'Monsieur,' came the deep, slow authoritative voice. We shook hands. 'My name is Lamine, policeman.'

'Follow me,' I replied and led the way the few short steps to the balcony of my hut on the water. He asked for juice, and I ordered it to be brought to the room along with a fresh pot of coffee.

'I have come to see if I can be of service to you.'

I decided to be frank and open. I explained how I had come to be in Abidjan. There was a look of some discomfort in his eyes when I referred to the two politicians I had met in London. Lamine explained that one of them had apparently been caught with a hand very publicly in the till and had become something of a hot potato. He added that, although the politician could have been a somewhat dangerous contact, he would be too busy fending off much bigger monsters of his own to take any continuing interest in my activities in Abidjan.

When I explained the scale of the proposed operation, I began to detect a glint in his eye. He would be only too happy to assist with security transporting our '*marchandise*' from the border. He made it clear that his protection would go no further than cannabis and I assured him that I had no interest in anything more.

Thinking of Nigeria, I asked him if he could assist with safe importation by sea or air and he assured me that he could. He concluded that he was satisfied that I would be discreet and he would be happy to work alongside me.

'How will you conceal the *marchandise*, monsieur?'

I replied that I was not yet certain. I knew that there was a market in the UK for exotic timbers from the Ivory Coast but needed to do more research. He responded that he knew a Frenchman working locally who might be willing to assist and might be prepared to share his experience. I gladly accepted his offer of an introduction.

He stood up and shook my hand. 'I see you are a man who enjoys taking risks,' he said reaching into his jacket pocket. Handing me a small revolver, he continued, 'Take this for your protection, monsieur.'

As he walked away, I looked at the weapon he had given me. It was like a miniature version of a service revolver. I flicked open the chamber to see that it was loaded with 7.25 centre-fire brass and lead bullets. I took the light jacket I used for travelling from the wardrobe, zipped the gun into one of the inner pockets and, carrying it over my arm, made for the reception to get a taxi. I was late.

While I was waiting for the car, I decided to take a closer look at the snake. Since I had last seen it, somebody had introduced a live chicken into the cage. The snake, still coiled immobile at one end, seemed oblivious to the offering, while the bird was in an obvious state of high anxiety pressed against the far end of the cage.

Across the drive, I noticed an Oriental girl stepping out of the Vietnamese restaurant opposite. She took my breath away. I stared open-mouthed as her long legs straddled a Mobylette. She waved at me happily as she rode off. I had not been back to the restaurant a second time but planned to do so very soon.

Appiah was stressed. I found him at the hotel bar holding a large glass half filled with brandy. I was an hour late. I told him why I had been delayed and gave him a rundown of what had been discussed.

He was happy at my suggestion that he return to London via Accra where he could establish his contacts and set the ball rolling for a large order from the next harvest. He told me that he had a reliable courier service between London and Accra which could safely be used to send hard currency undetected. I gave him money for his ticket and, after a leisurely lunch, we agreed to meet up again in London.

Things seemed to be falling into place. I would have to do more research when I got back to London but it appeared that timber was the best method of concealment. For some time, I had been looking for a method which did not necessitate the use of containers. From what I had observed, Customs were much less interested in goods that could be identified visually. If we could conceal the cannabis in large bales of timber, I felt sure that we stood a much better chance.

That night, I ate at the Vietnamese restaurant at the hotel. The lovely proprietor confirmed my suspicions that the girl I had seen on the moped was her daughter. She was expected back at any time. I was invited to stay around to meet her.

When I had finished my meal, a man about the same age as me approached my table. His huge Gallic nose told me that this was a Frenchman. He offered his hand.

'Monsieur, my name is Jean Marc... I am a friend of Lamine.'

He had a firm handshake and made strong eye contact. I liked this man straight away. I offered him food but he had eaten. I had a bottle of good brandy in my room which I had bought at Heathrow. Jean Marc happily accepted my offer to share it with some fresh coffee on my veranda where we would be more private.

This man could drink! Within an hour, he had demolished most of my bottle of rather good brandy and I could see that he wasn't even out of first gear. He explained that he worked for Air Afrique as an aircraft engineer and would have to leave at around 10.00pm for the night shift.

At first, he was cagey and reluctant to open up. I had already told

Lamine everything he needed to know and had no reason to withhold anything from Jean Marc. I did most of the talking for the next couple of hours. By the time Jean Marc had to leave, he had loosened up a great deal but I could tell that something was troubling him. He was keen to know what was in it for him. I offered him a share in the operation and he responded by asking for a flat fee per consignment, successful or not. We agreed to try to resolve the impasse the next day, the first of his four-day break before changing over to dayshifts.

On the way to his car, I mentioned that I would have to get some transport of my own if I was to stay in Abidjan to work. I quickly accepted his offer of the loan of his motorbike. We agreed to meet again at the hotel around mid-afternoon the next day after he had slept off the night's work.

It was nearly 11.00pm; I was in good spirits and there was nothing to do the following morning. I decided to take a taxi on a tour of Treichville, the nightclub district. I asked the driver to wait while I sprinted back to secure the room and pick up my loaded jacket. Another night of debauchery was in store.

I paid off the taxi as soon as I saw a bar which looked interesting. Until the early hours, I did a tour of quite a few Abidjan '*boîtes*' and not for one moment did I feel vaguely in danger. Even at night, the temperature remains quite high and my jacket was more often than not slung over a shoulder. I felt that the gun was more of a liability than a comfort.

Jean Marc accepted my terms. I offered him an 'open books' arrangement and he agreed to trust me. He came to pick me up earlier than I expected. Both of us hungry from our respective night shifts, he took me to an open-air fish restaurant near his house.

He lived in a large apartment with an all-round balcony woven with so much bougainvillea as to impede any chance of a view. The motorbike was up for sale. All I needed was one look and a quick run up the road before I had bought my Ivorian transport, a black Honda 750. It was a few years old but in good condition, and Jean Marc had fitted a chrome four-into-one exhaust pipe, which made wonderful loud music revving through the gears. The price we agreed reflected the agreement that, when I was not in town, he would have use of the bike and, in return, keep it in good condition.

I let him open up to me in his own time. He had made several trips to France over the years with cannabis in his suitcase and never been caught. More recently, he had established contact with an 'opposite number' working in Paris and together they had been successful with larger quantities concealed in parts of the aircraft they maintained. The partner had been arrested with the last consignment as he left the airport, having successfully removed it from the aeroplane and passed through security. He had been sentenced to five years in prison.

Lamine joined us in the early evening. After some small talk, he told Jean Marc that, if we were to go to work together, he should come to an arrangement with Albert. This was the first time I had heard the name. Albert, a Ghanaian who had lived in the Ivory Coast most of his life, had supplied Jean Marc with his cannabis. They were equal partners with the Parisian.

It soon became evident that Jean Marc hated Albert. He strongly suspected him of having something to do with the arrest of their partner but could not prove it. Albert had connections and Lamine made it clear that Jean Marc would not be able to keep his new business a secret for long.

Lamine departed, leaving Jean Marc and I to spend most of the night bonding. We did a tour of Jean Marc's favourite bars until late. It was clear that he knew most of the girls along the way rather well, making a point from time to time of quite openly showing me the various bits that he found particularly attractive. The girls seemed to be willing participants and his behaviour became more outrageous the more he drank. He told me that he estimated that he had sex with about 500 girls a year and never used a condom. Jean Marc eventually died of AIDS not long after I was arrested in 1988.

At one of the bars, I told him that Lamine had given me a revolver. He asked me where it was and I passed him the jacket. He took the revolver out and started waving it around. I grabbed it from him just as he thought it would be a good idea to fire a few shots into the air. Having spooked the girls and clientele, we moved on to another establishment. I left a generous tip.

At the next bar, Jean Marc apologised. He was by no means sober but I knew that he was trying to impress me. He said that it would be a great idea if I shot Albert. He didn't know me and there would be no reason for me to be suspected. It would guarantee our security. I stopped drinking a few bars earlier and made it clear that it was up to him to make sure that Albert was not a threat. He would have to come to some arrangement of his own to keep Albert quiet and I offered to meet Albert to help him make his point. I made it clear that it was not my problem and the only shooting I planned to do was back in England after the pheasant season opened in October.

I was happy to let him make light of his suggestion but I knew that, for a while at least, he had been serious. The following day, I returned the gun to Lamine. I was pleased to see the back of it.

We went to see Albert. I could tell that there was bad blood between them. Jean Marc made Albert an offer in exchange for any assistance he may need, which was readily accepted. Albert was to die of liver failure in 1986.

Jean Marc had a friend in the timber business. He established that the Ivory Coast did supply the UK with an indigenous hardwood called iroko. It was exported mostly in rough-sawn bales about 15 feet long and 4 feet square. Each bale weighed about two tonnes.

Over the next few days, we made a great deal of progress. We had a good look at a bale of timber. The planks were not sawn on the sides; they still had the bark intact, following the contours of the tree. We established that, with care, the planks could be cut in a way to provide a big open space in the centre and, if nailed back together in a carefully selected order, we could conceal several hundred kilos of cannabis in each bale. Shipped as 'deck cargo', they would be exposed to the elements so we would need to construct a waterproof lining to protect our '*marchandise*'.

We registered a timber-export company, obtained a licence to trade in foreign exchange and opened a bank account with a small deposit. Lamine found some premises in an industrial area surrounded by a high wall which we could rent on a month-to-month basis for cash.

We decided to do a dummy run. Not knowing what pitfalls we might find with this new method, we considered it a good investment to buy half-a-dozen bales of iroko and send them to the UK. I would have to organise a new import company and find premises as soon as I got back to receive the wood and would try to find a market for the stuff in England.

Jean Marc was due to return to France in a month's time for his annual four weeks' leave. We decided to try to send a few bales before he left.

I would need a cover to justify what would become regular journeys to the Ivory Coast. In little time, I discovered some land for sale beside the lagoon and instructed a local architect with a view to building a resort complex. I would need to register my interest at the Chamber of Commerce.

It turned out to be a simple procedure. As a potential investor, I was cordially invited to a reception the following week. I made my excuses, explaining that I would be returning to London to report my findings to the Board. I would not be able to avoid these affairs on future visits.

One afternoon, while Jean Marc was doing his bit at his friend's timber yard, I was taking a rest after a spell at the deserted hotel swimming pool. I had a shower and was lying on the bed with a towel wrapped around my waist. There was a light knock on the door. My fantasy girl on the moped had come to introduce herself. We climbed up on to the sun deck and chatted easily for some time. She asked me if she could take a bath. After a couple of minutes, she called me to wash her back. She made love to me gently and unhurriedly, dressed, kissed me and left.

My new motorbike already knew its way to the fleshpots of Abidjan and we made a few trips together before I returned it to Jean Marc, whom I arranged to see next in Calais. I then called Kwame and bought a ticket to Lagos.

18

NIGERIA

It was a short flight from Abidjan. As soon as I arrived at Lagos airport, I could feel the difference. The whole atmosphere was tense – pushing, shoving and arguing, there was not a happy face to be seen. Kwame was waiting for me beyond Customs, by which time I had already encountered more than one possible confrontational situation. I was happy that I had booked my return flight the next afternoon.

Kwame had brought his driver, who took my bag and led the way to the car which was parked arrogantly on the pavement directly outside the terminal building. The shiny black Mercedes drew a fair amount of attention and set my man apart as one of the 'haves'.

The car cooled quickly and I sat back in comfort beside my well-dressed host. The traffic was horrendous. It seemed as if every vehicle was fighting for the same small piece of road – hooters blaring, tempers flared, road rage all around. It took a good half-hour before we arrived at my hotel, which was clearly visible from the airport. Kwame had done me proud. This was the best in Lagos. All I had to do was show my passport, the bill was already paid.

The farm was a distance from the city and we decided to make our way there directly. After a while, the traffic began to thin. We made reasonable progress and, a few miles later, the wide highway narrowed as the roads became increasingly potholed. It was many miles before the sporadic industrial areas finally gave way to bush and village.

The back seat of Kwame's chilled Mercedes was as good a place as any to discuss our business. The driver was an old retainer and Kwame guaranteed his discretion. By the time we reached our destination, I had confirmed our ability to tranship safely to the Ivory Coast with the assistance of Lamine's Customs contact. We discussed prices and arrived at a mutually acceptable deal, subject to quality. Kwame would pay for shipping. We agreed that he would initially send one tonne concealed in cartons of canned orange juice and exported in a 20-foot container.

The farm was impressive. The large white single-storey house stood surrounded by fresh green manicured lawns watered continually by several mechanical sprinklers. I followed Kwame through the heavy, double front door into the cool of the large parquet-floored hall. By the time we reached the sitting room, a houseboy had arrived with a tray of assorted drinks.

When we were alone, Kwame crossed the room to a large bureau. He unlocked the flap and brought me a large silver cigarette box. The small pressed block of bright-green cannabis inside smelled divine. My memories of Jamaica rekindled, Kwame invited me to try it. It was indeed just as Appiah had described and, after a couple of draws, I knew that I would be spangled if I finished the joint.

Kwame explained that he had a quantity of blocks from the recently gathered last crop. We took a walk to a nearby outbuilding and I opened a couple of the tightly pressed packages at random to reveal a quality equal to the sample. I explained that it could be some time before we were ready to accept delivery in Abidjan and we agreed to reserve a tonne from the next harvest due about six months later.

Kwame invited me to lunch. The table had already been prepared. We were joined by the lady of the house. She was large, elegantly dressed in traditional costume and festooned with expensive gold jewellery. She was an experienced hostess, educated and well read.

We took some time eating and, as soon as it was over, Mrs Kwame withdrew. I never knew her name.

After lunch, Kwame explained that he had been growing cannabis for several years. He had been exclusively supplying a Dutch customer who was an expert in cannabis horticulture. Together, they had developed Kwame's product and the Dutchman came to stay once a year. The last consignment had been discovered by Customs in Rotterdam and, although Kwame's contact was not implicated, they had decided to take a short sabbatical.

I asked why he had come to London to find a market. He replied with disarming honesty that it was only because he knew the prices there were higher. I urged him to be discreet and he assured me that he would give our business his personal supervision. I lived in hope but knew that this man had never done a stroke of work in his life.

We established lines of communication but, as with others before, I had no alternative but to give Kwame my telephone number. He insisted on accompanying me back to Lagos for the long drive back and it took me some time to persuade him that I would take a taxi from the hotel to the airport. Kwame was a stylish host. He was due to come to London again on business and I promised to take him for a good dinner. We shook hands cordially and parted company in the hotel lobby.

My room was of top international standard. By the time I had showered, it was quite late. I smoked the rest of the joint I had extinguished earlier and cruised down to the bar. It was full of Europeans, some of whom had accepted the company of a selection of very well-dressed girls hanging around in the lobby. I ordered a drink. While I was waiting for the barman to add the lime and ice, a tall slim girl in a tight short cocktail dress edged up beside me. Before I knew it, she had her hand between my legs and was squeezing my balls. I sent her away and, from her reaction, she could have spat at me as she strode away on her high heels.

Some Englishmen at a nearby table were laughing at what they had seen and I joined them with my G and T. It turned out that they were employed by an oil-exploration company and had been resident in the hotel for several months.

They were very well paid for their work but all of them hated Nigeria. It was not safe to go out at night and each of them had a mugging story to relate. One of their friends had been hijacked in a taxi one night. His body, just in a pair of underpants, was found the next day in a ditch. He had been shot in the head. Most of the assembled company had received treatment for venereal disease caught from the elegant hostesses at the hotel and two of the men had the added indignity of losing their wallets at the same time. We drank well into the night; the men appreciated new contact with another Englishman.

I swam in the hotel pool the next morning and, when I went to reception to pay my bar bill from the night before, I found that Kwame had left strict instructions that I was to pay for nothing. There was a courtesy bus to take me to the airport and I was able to check in at a travel desk in the hotel lobby.

In true Papal style, I could have kissed the ground back at Abidjan airport. It was good to be back in the Ivory Coast.

19

BACK TO LONDON

I gave Jean Marc enough money to cover the expenses of the first shipment of timber. We spent another night on the town and, the following day, a little worse for wear, I took the UTA flight to Paris, before making the connection to London with only a few minutes to spare.

I needed to move fast. If we were to be in a position to take delivery of the timber before Jean Marc left for France, everything would have to be put in place within two weeks.

I reported my progress the next morning. I had already discussed the possibility of work with our racing mechanic Dave Evans and found him more than happy to join the gang. I spent the best part of the day with him explaining in detail what he had to do. We needed an import company, a bank account and premises. This time, we decided to register for VAT and run the company books as legitimately as possible.

We added a further sophistication – we would need help to man the warehouse. Dave needed time out to keep up his engine-tuning business and go motor racing as soon as we started to make some money. We had recently met a young chap who started kart racing a few months earlier. Steve was keen to progress but was limited by a shortage of funds. He jumped at the chance to 'go to work' with us.

Once the company was set up, Dave would place an ad in the *Evening Standard* for a warehouseman, inviting applicants to write in. Steve would respond and be invited by letter to attend an interview. In the event of an import going wrong, Steve would have evidence that he was a bona fide employee. Unless he had been 'under surveillance', there would be little chance of a successful prosecution.

Dave, a conscientious man, got to work and we all kept our eyes peeled for suitable premises. Within a week, he had set up the company and opened a bank account. I decided to take the risk of starting the ball rolling before we had found a warehouse and told Dave to begin some fax traffic with Jean Marc's export company in Abidjan. He sent a request for prices. After he got a quotation, he responded with a firm order for the first delivery to be sent as soon as possible on the first ship travelling to Tilbury Docks.

Within a few days, Dave received a pro forma invoice for the timber which included the cost of shipping from the Ivory Coast. Dave gave the bank instructions to pay the invoice by telegraphic transfer and, a few days later, a fax arrived from Abidjan with details of the shipping.

Steve happened upon a suitable warehouse. Dave negotiated a deal and, within a few days, he was given the keys. The advertisement for the warehouseman went in the paper and I think there were ten or so replies. Steve, the best qualified for what we had in mind, got the job.

Jean Marc got the shipping papers a short while before he left for France on leave. He had a sister who lived in Calais. The short journey from Lille took less than an hour on the new Kawasaki he had bought with his holiday money.

There was a seafood restaurant not far from the ferry terminal and we met there for a long and boozy lunch. I returned later in the day with the bills of lading, which Dave delivered to a shipping agent with a cheque for duty and VAT.

Another firm on the industrial estate had a forklift truck. They were happy to lend it to us to unload the first delivery. Neither Steve nor Dave had driven one before. In a stroke of genius, Steve confided in the regular driver that he had lied on his job application. He got a couple of secret lessons and mastered the controls in a short time. I knew Tilbury reasonably well. The docks are about a mile away from the kart track. A couple of days before the ship was due to dock, I decided to take a look. I was surprised to see that there was no security to speak of in the area where non-container goods were being unloaded. I was able to watch as long as I liked as the tall cranes straddling the wide rails on which they stood went about their laborious work. Ships of all sizes sporting flags of obscure nationalities lined the docks as they were steadily disembowelled of their ever-varied cargo. Great stacks of timber patiently waited for collection on one of the quays. In direct contrast, the container terminal further round the dock was seemingly impregnable behind high walls and permanently manned secure metal gates.

I went back to the docks two days later. Our boat had arrived during the night and, by mid-morning, unloading had already begun. Streaks of rust stains ran down the hull of this white-painted workhorse of a ship. I could see that the crew working on deck were mostly Asian. I wondered where, in a God-forsaken place like Tilbury, whatever they might be in need of after a long voyage could be found.

The following afternoon, our timber was delivered to the warehouse. The bales were so heavy that the neighbour's forklift made hard work of the job. We would have to buy one of our own capable of lifting heavier weights.

Dave sold most of the wood to a timber merchant who was curious to know how he was able to buy this rare and precious commodity so cheaply. He made out a couple of fictitious cash sale receipts to show a profit on the importation and, in due course, filled in his first VAT return. Claiming back the VAT paid on arrival and for other expenditure, the return quite correctly showed that Customs and Excise were in debt to the company. A week later, an official came to inspect the books. Satisfied with what he saw, he congratulated Dave and wished him well with his new venture. Our

VAT inspector was not available as a character witness at the subsequent trial.

I flew to Paris to celebrate with Jean Marc. We shared a suite at the George V Hotel and consumed a massive plate of *fruits de mer* washed down with several bottles of fine wine. It was no surprise when he took me to a club called Le Baron; that Gallic nose never let us down.

My daughter Emily had her first race the following week with the Italian karting team. The track was situated at Jesolo, a seaside resort on the Adriatic and a short drive from Venice. I invited Jean Marc to join us there, and he readily agreed.

20

RACING 1984

Flaviano Preston, the MD of Pilgrim Air, had been very generous. He provided the whole family with free flights, car hire and accommodation for Emily's first international race. I had a warm feeling of pride as I felt my own ambitions of a motor-racing career transferring to my daughter.

Merlin had prepared some racing engines for Emily and they all had to be run in with precision. Much testing had to be done and our presence was required at the track the Wednesday before racing began on Saturday morning.

There was a flight into Marco Polo airport on Tuesday evening where a very smart hire car was waiting at our disposal. We had a dinner engagement with the team manager that night and there was little time to get ready. I found the hotel easily enough. The manager welcomed us at the busy clubhouse which incorporated a restaurant large enough to cater for the whole team and their support crews during the compulsory two-hour daily lunch breaks.

A table had been laid for us in the corner of the room with a clean white tablecloth. Throughout the meal, which included copious pourings of wine, there were interruptions by other team members paying their respects to our host and taking a closer look at their pretty team-mate. Eventually, one found the courage in halting English to invite Emily to join him. They went off together to the track, which opened every night for holidaymakers to race rented fun karts under floodlights.

We emerged to find a gladiatorial contest taking place. Many of the team members had rented the leisure karts. They were wreaking havoc, punting each other off the track into the straw bales. All of them were driving as fast as they could with one hand on the wheel while making rude gestures with the other. The concession owner, far from being upset about the abuse of his machinery, let the kids carry on with an indulgent smile.

Starting early the next morning, we arrived to find that the circus had already hit town. Expensive transporters and brightly coloured awnings filled the pits. Mechanics were busy building up new chassis, putting race tyres on rims and arranging the equipment in a way that always showed it off as if on display. Here and there, team owners and managers could be seen in small groups deep in conversation. This was the politics of the sport and the Italians were past masters.

It was hard but happy work. Everything was well organised; there was a permanent sense of preparedness and mounting excitement as the competition drew nearer. The lunch breaks with communal eating drew everybody close. One of the mechanics in our team had trained as an operatic baritone, half a bottle of *vino rosso* being all the fuel necessary for an aria or Neapolitan song.

Emily became friendly with a young driver called Giovanni Bonanno, a redhead with a volatile temper. The first time I saw his father Angelo, he drove into the pits in a bullet-proof Mercedes. Sitting alone in a corner of the grandstand, his vigilant chauffeur was never far away.

One day, curious, I went to introduce myself and we sat together for a couple of hours watching the preparations for the next day's racing. Armed with stopwatches, we timed Giovanni and Emily's laps and discussed their prospects in the sport and plans for the season. He was pleased to have company and invited the whole family to join him later for dinner.

Jean Marc flew in later in the day and joined us as we followed the bullet-proof Mercedes several miles into the Italian countryside. We arrived half-an-hour later at an imposing country house, stylishly converted into a fine restaurant. Angelo would not allow us to make a contribution and paid the bill with a handful of large notes. It was to be the first meal of many we would enjoy together. Whenever our respective offspring were racing, Angelo and I would spend time in each other's company.

Jean Marc would begin drinking from the crack of dawn. We used to start practice early in the day and the café was always open. Several coffees with generous double shots of brandy would give way to a few beers before lunch followed by bottles of wine. Onwards through the day, he never stopped. I did see him drunk on a few occasions but never legless. He also had the unnerving habit of giving vent to his temper when under the influence. The Ivory Coast was used by the French Army and the Foreign Legion for military training. The young soldiers flocked to the bars and fleshpots of Abidjan when on leave. For some reason, Jean Marc hated these soldiers and berated them with abuse whenever he was drunk. I never found out why.

The racing was fast and furious. The standard of professionalism, so much higher than back in England, ensured a very high level of competition. Every tenth of a second was crucial and small changes to settings could make the difference of ten places. Emily finished inside the top ten, a result which pleased everybody in the team.

Italians love to put on a good show. Always theatrical and stylish, the race meeting at Jesolo had a sense of Grand Opera about it. Marching bands and singers put on a display to the large crowd before the drivers were paraded on foot, waving to the main grandstand. Each official, identified by a proudly worn uniform, was further adorned according to rank. The medical crews were no exception. At strategic points around the track, teams of medics, appropriately dressed and each with stretcher, oxygen and equipment, stood by.

At one point in the racing, two karts came together. One of the drivers was thrown out of his somersaulting machine at high speed.

He landed inert at the side of the track directly in between two of the medical stations. Each one, desperate to claim the patient, picked up their stretchers and ran as fast as they could to the scene.

Both arrived together. There followed a violent argument between the crews as to whose patient it was. The unfortunate driver, now forgotten, was left lying on the ground while the medics, encouraged by the spectators, steamed into each other with fists flying. The driver recovered without injury but two of the medics were taken to hospital for treatment.

The season proved to be very successful. We travelled and raced all over Europe, made a trip to Perth to compete in the Australian Championships and spent a great deal of money.

Emily won the Junior British Championship, the first female to do so. She followed it up with an excellent fourth place in the International Championship. Oscar, too, was achieving success in England. He had a mechanic from Birmingham with a great dry sense of humour. Oscar had grown and, because he was about 10 kilos above the permitted minimum for driver and machine in his class, his driving skills were insufficient to make up a deficit of about half-a-second a lap. After scratching our heads in an effort to find where we could shed some weight, his mechanic piped up in his broad Brummy accent, 'I know... we'll circumcise him.'

Oscar took second place in his class in the Junior British Championship.

We drove to a race in Parma in my transporter. Tim, Jason Plato's father, the British Touring Car Champion, came as Emily's mechanic. We were accommodated in a hotel near the centre of town. A couple of very shady-looking men were staying in one of the rooms on our floor next to Tim. After the racing, Tim drove off back to England in the transporter, leaving Emily and me to fly back the next day.

The two men appeared in the lobby in a state of panic. They told me that they had been minding a stash of emeralds, which had gone missing from their room. This was very obviously not a matter for the police. Suspecting Tim, they set off in pursuit of the transporter now two or three hours out of town.

They stopped Tim on the highway at gunpoint and proceeded to pull the camper apart in the search for their emeralds. Some time later, the camper continued on its journey and the men drove off, to continue their search.

That year, Johnny Herbert won the coveted Formula Ford Festival at Brands Hatch in fine style. He was on his way to the top.

21

FELIX

Appiah took his time returning from Ghana; I had been back in London a full two weeks before I heard from him. He reported that everything had gone well and some good-quality cannabis would be on stream within a short time.

There were no flaws in our set-up in London. The system had been tested and we were ready to go. The expenses of running the warehouse were mounting and the new recruits were keen to see some rewards.

Appiah was sent back to supervise the purchase of two tonnes of grass. This time, the size of the pressed blocks was not so critical. It would not be difficult to arrange them inside the large voids of each of the bales of timber. This would reduce the timescale by quite a margin. There was a limit to how much money we would be happy entrusting to Appiah. We gave him about half the necessary funds needed to do his work. The rest of the money was to be handled by Jean Marc and would be handed over upon delivery of the goods in Abidjan.

Jean Marc returned to the Ivory Coast. He had to order in some more timber to be prepared for the delivery. We estimated that we could get about 500–600 kilos of grass inside each bale of wood and decided to order eight for the next shipment. Four would remain untouched and double our chances in case of a random inspection by Customs at Tilbury.

Tools had to be purchased. We would need a powerful saw to cope with the very dense hardwood and plenty of spare blades. Nails, banding machine, hammers and crowbars would all be needed. Fibreglass sheets, resin and plywood for the weatherproofing had to be in place, too. For good measure, we decided to buy a vacuum-sealer to double wrap our little babies before consigning them to the elements.

Lamine, our colleague and Ivory Coast Police Chief, would be alerted to set up his counterpart in Customs for the arrival of the container from Nigeria. I had a feeling that Tundi, our crippled supplier, would do his work efficiently.

I agreed to meet up with Jean Marc in the Ivory Coast after he confirmed the need for me to be there. It was not long before I got his call. We had an arrangement for communication. Jean Marc would call me as my architect. We would make reference to the site in Abidjan and, if the conversation could be engineered to refer to our exports while sounding resort-development orientated, we would say what we could. On this occasion, it was quite appropriate.

'The men are on site and they have the machinery they need.'

'Good,' I replied.

'However, they need more expertise and the ground is very hard. I think you should come over.'

'OK... I'll let you know my plans.'

In accordance with our arrangement, I telephoned Jean Marc six hours later from a call box. He explained that the physical work had turned out to be much harder than we thought. Jean Marc had enlisted a couple more pairs of hands but, with his Air Afrique schedule, too, they were unable to keep up.

Three days later, I was back in Abidjan. Much as I loved the hotel on the lagoon, we agreed that I should move on. The problem at the lagoon hotel was simply that, in order to access any of the rooms, everybody had to pass reception, so it was not nearly discreet enough.

Jean Marc took me to another hotel a couple of miles around the lagoon. It was a complex of bungalows, each very pleasant but not on the water. There was a good pool which was always busy. There was a great deal more footfall here and I would be less conspicuous.

We drove together to the warehouse. Only one bale of timber had been prepared. Jean Marc began to explain the difficulties but we arranged to meet at midnight after his shift and work together at solving the problem.

I collected the motorbike from Jean Marc's house which was quite close to the warehouse. Foolishly, I never wore a crash helmet or gloves; the only protection was a pair of dark glasses to shield my eyes from the dust and sand. There was one piece of highway in town at the end of which was a large roundabout. A left turn led to the airport and right to a lesser potholed piece of dusty road which followed the edge of the lagoon. I used to wind the bike up, red-lining the wonderful-sounding engine in every gear and braking hard for the roundabout. Too much exuberance on the dusty route to the hotel was not advisable.

Greeted by a large gathering of girls looking for business, I parked the bike and made my way through endless propositions to get my key from reception. A couple of the bolder girls knocked on my door but I made it clear that I was not buying.

Waking slowly and luxuriously to the realisation that this was a strange bed in a hot foreign country, I had a little time before I needed to go to work. I leaned over to the bedside table for the remote for the television. I watched the local news for a short while and flicked over to find a porno movie playing on the next channel. The hotel, I found out later, played them late every night from a very large library of videos kept in reception.

I had brought a lot of money with me, stuffed into the inside pockets of my jacket. Before leaving, I decided to leave half of the money in a safe at the hotel and give the rest to Jean Marc. At night, although by no means cold, a light jacket was advisable on a motorbike at speed. Again, I ran the gauntlet of the girls of the night, now pretty much resigned to drawing a blank, and headed to the warehouse.

The men were already hard at work. One man was beating a 6-inch nail into the unyielding hardwood with a very heavy hammer. Around him on the concrete floor lay several previous efforts, bent, deformed and spent.

Jean Marc hit the red button on the screaming circular saw, called a ten-minute break and distributed bottles of beer from a very battered old fridge leaking water from the cooling pipes behind. A stack of crates beside it waited their turn for a spell in the cooler. The atmosphere was one of despondence.

We worked through the night. The problem was that the wood was so dense and hard that it was almost impossible to work with. A solution was found for nailing the boards together. By first drilling a pilot hole less than half the diameter of the nail, it was possible to drive it through the thickness of three boards with less effort.

Once the stack of timber was cut to make the large central opening, it lost all its strength. Apart from the undisturbed bottom layer of planks and two layers placed back over the void, the whole of the rest of the bale had been cut. Many of the big nails had to be used to bind the bale back together. It was a complicated job because the nails had to be concealed.

By the end of the night, we had deconstructed and cut a second box ready to be nailed together the next night. We lined the first box with half-inch plywood and painted the inner surfaces with resin, covering the gaps with sheets of fibreglass. The fumes from the resin knocked us out and we had to take turns, just a few minutes at a time, before practically passing out. The horrible stuff got everywhere and left dirty sticky stains on our fingers.

We were knackered. Encouraged by some measurable progress from our combined efforts, along with finding a solution to some of the problems, we decided to split up and meet again later in the day.

I woke early in the afternoon. Before taking a look at the swimming pool, I had to call the Ivory Coast architect I had appointed as part of my cover. He had been busy on my behalf and asked me to meet him the next day at the Chamber of Commerce. We expected some good news about the zoning of the land.

The poolside was something of a revelation. Certainly, this hotel, although very comfortable, was not the best available in Abidjan. However, beneath the shade of the large parasols was a selection of privileged European ladies lounging, chatting and preening. Some would occasionally smile or wave at their small children being dunked by their uniformed nannies. Evidently not holidaymakers, this truly colonial display was a collection of spoiled diplomatic wives with little or nothing to do in their overstaffed households.

Noticing that some were eating what appeared to be well-prepared poolside snacks, I ordered some food. I sat on a high stool at the outside bar beneath the shade of a thatched roof observing some of the very elegant and bronzed young ladies. My glances were often returned with ready smiles.

After lunch, on my wooden sun chair, it was not long before I was engaged in conversation with three women. All of them were married; two in particular had lived in Abidjan for some years. One of the women used the hotel pool several times a week with her two young children. Both had been born in Africa but were not yet old enough to be sent to boarding school in France.

My newfound friends were keen to find out what I was up to in the Ivory Coast. I explained my interest in resort development and told them about the piece of land by the lagoon. The older lady in the group said that, during the years she had been resident, the tourist industry had been in decline. I bluffed that I was aware of the situation but considered that it would not be many years before holidaymakers would begin to tire of the usual destinations. I explained that I was sure that in the long term the demand for more exotic locations would increase.

I accepted an invitation to a small reception at the French Embassy the following week. A little nervous at the prospect of continuing the charade, I was nonetheless excited to have landed a new part in another soap.

Jean Marc came to see me on his way to work. Lamine had contacted him to say that we would be receiving our first delivery of cannabis within 24 hours. The porters had been hard at work at the border for a few days. As soon as the stockpile was sufficient to fill a lorry, it would be brought directly to the warehouse.

Not long back from annual leave, Jean Marc could not take time off. Already short-staffed, Air Afrique needed his services. I was there to work but could see that another pair of hands would help a great deal.

On my way to the warehouse, I stopped at a small hotel and called London from the lobby. We had a prearranged method of communication. Fifteen minutes later, I was speaking to Roy in a phone box near to his house, the number of which I had written on a piece of paper in my wallet.

'I need another man on site.'

'How soon?' he replied.

'Yesterday... send Steve out here.'

We had already arranged that I would receive Steve's flight details by telephone from Paris should he be needed.

The fibreglassing had set well. There were a couple of gaps which we filled in, but, otherwise, box number one was ready to be filled with contraband. The next five or six hours were spent nailing the planks of number two together; it was back-breaking work. By the time Jean Marc arrived, the second bale had taken shape and bale number three had been taken apart, measured and marked with pencil ready for the circular saw.

Jean Marc was weary. He was happy to learn that Steve would be coming to help. I was feeling good about what had been achieved with the two employees. They were willing and strong but had no initiative. They could not be left with instructions to do anything other than menial work. There was an audible sigh of relief when I suggested calling it a day. The men were left to clean up the warehouse and return all the tools to their rightful places. Jean Marc declined my invitation to go clubbing. I knew from his smile that he had a small *divertissement* to make on his way home.

There was a shower at the warehouse; there was no heater but the water was never cold. I changed back into the clothes I arrived in and hit the road to Treichville. It was already about 1.30am and the place was in full swing. The last time I had been there, I had passed by a small club playing more mellow music than many of the others. My bike caused a stir and I kept moving slowly from street to street until I recognised the tidy little neon-lit bar. As soon as I parked the bike, I was surrounded by happy admirers. I was warned many times about the dangers of the area but never once did I feel threatened.

The doorman was already at the bike, officiously trying to move everybody away. At the sound of the commotion, three girls came to the entrance. I smiled up at them and calmed the doorman, assuring him that everything was OK. In Ivorian fashion, I was welcomed by all three girls with a kiss. The place was empty. The tallest invited me to sit at a table and gave instructions to the other two to bring us both a drink. It turned out that she owned the bar.

Ami was gorgeous, tall and slim with long braided hair. I was entranced by her. I could see from the hang of her large T-shirt that she had enormous firm breasts. I don't know how long we sat together before she moved closer to me and began to caress the back of my neck. She locked the bar at about three and teased me with her fingers from the pillion seat all the way back to the hotel.

She devoured me. Despite her total lack of inhibition, it was some time before she uncovered her breasts. The T-shirt came off eventually as we shared some post-coital relaxation. She was always self-conscious about those magnificent tits which could have earned her a fortune in the British tabloids. We discussed fantasies and she told me that she liked sex with girls just as much as men. She left me exhausted as the dawn was breaking to return to her French husband.

Infidelity and adultery seemed to be a national sport here; maybe that's why I felt so at home. A few years after my release, I travelled to Iran to design and make a new collection of glass vases and drinking glasses. While I was there, a man and woman were publicly executed in Tehran's football stadium for adultery. It was not something I wanted to watch on television.

Steve called the next day from Paris; he told me that the next flight to Abidjan was the following day. I agreed to meet him at the airport.

I decided to take a taxi to the afternoon meeting at the Chamber of Commerce thinking that I might appear somewhat strange arriving on a motorbike. The architect was waiting outside and greeted me excitedly. He proudly told me that he had negotiated an agreement to grant planning permission to construct a resort complex in exchange for a few small personal 'fees'.

The planning officials welcomed us with coffee and a bottle of brandy, which we worked our way through during the long meeting. Unrolling the plans, which contained a great deal of detail drawn in freehand, the architect took the floor to outline our adventurous new scheme. We were all impressed at his ideas and attention to detail and I was left in no doubt that the planners were very much in favour. I was invited to attend an overseas investors reception the following evening. I would have just enough time to collect Steve from the airport, but considered it unwise to bring him.

I spent a little more time with the architect after our meeting and paid his modest fees with some cash that I had on me. The total palm-greasing exercise would only add another £150.

I got to the warehouse early at about 8.00pm. A very old ramshackle, curtain-sided lorry was waiting outside. Tundi's brother, in a cap and dark glasses, waved at me from the passenger seat. The first delivery of cannabis had arrived. The young guard who worked with us looked anxious. He explained that he had strict instructions to keep the gate locked and only open it upon the direct orders of Jean Marc. I told him that the truck was expected and asked him to open the gate. The lorry had been kept outside for over two hours. As the guard was opening the gate, Lamine arrived in his Mercedes. Alerted by the young policeman he had instructed to accompany the truck, he had gone in a vain search for Jean Marc.

The blocks of newly pressed cannabis were on open view in the back of the truck with nothing loaded around them.

Lamine shrugged his shoulders. 'The lorry has my protection,' he said. 'It would not be stopped.'

'What if it stopped of its own accord?' I responded.

'No problem,' he replied nonchalantly.

The truck was unloaded within minutes and left immediately.

Tundi's brother stayed while we weighed the cargo and we inspected a few packages together at random. We had about 600 kilos, more than enough for the single bale of timber we had ready prepared.

In amongst the varying-sized packages were some which felt lighter than they should. Upon inspection, it was immediately obvious that the dry crumbly contents were from an earlier crop. I needed to get a message to Appiah and asked Tundi's brother to pass the word on that I was not happy. So far, about 10 per cent of the packages were under weight.

The atmosphere was a little stressed that night. We eventually finished fibreglassing number two and had made a fair bit of headway with the third. During the night, both the circular saw and the vacuum-sealer gave up the ghost, the saw from straightforward exhaustion. It could be replaced the next day. The sealer was another matter. It seemed to be beyond repair, having begun smoking shortly after it was plugged in. Jean Marc was sure that there were none to be had in Abidjan. The big pile of cannabis smelled. No doubt, in the open air, it would not be quite so strong but I figured that, if the smell could get out, the elements could get in.

We would have to re-tape all the packages by hand and that would take an age. Furthermore, until we had the tape, we would be unable to load any of the bales. We packed up around 4.00am.

A visit from Ami was not what I had in mind. But there she was with one of the girls from the bar, sitting smiling on my veranda. Looking at those two naughty girls, it did not take me long to conclude that it would have been churlish to send them away. They had started without me while I took a shower and I was wide awake by the time they left me later in the morning.

Steve's flight arrived a little late the next afternoon. Fortunately, Lamine was with me at the airport. He gave Steve a lift to the hotel while I made my excuses, promising to get back from the investors reception at the Chamber of Commerce as soon as I could. I had already arranged a room for Steve at the hotel and I told him to get some rest. We had a long night ahead.

The drinks party was a doddle. I was a little late and was the only

English-speaker there. As soon as I entered the room, I could see that at least half the young guests at the reception were fellow adventurers up to no good.

I left Steve to sleep, before finally waking him in time to go to dinner at my favourite Thai restaurant near the warehouse. He had needed the sleep. Two of the others who worked on the distribution side had decided to give Steve a lift to Paris. They decided to make a pilgrimage to the Baron Club where I had been taken by Jean Marc. It had apparently been a long and heavy night.

Steve was easy company. He was happy to have the opportunity of an adventure in a strange country. We ate well, had a few drinks and continued on to the warehouse.

Another lorryload of grass had arrived. Jean Marc was halfway through weighing the packages with Tundi's brother; it was the same as the day before, about 10 per cent old and dry. I was not happy but knew that the chances of reversing the situation at this stage were slim. I did not expect to see Appiah until the last of the consignment had arrived, by which time I estimated that we would have about 20 kilos of the last year's crop. I sent a message to Tundi to see if he would take the older stuff off our hands but expected that the idea would not appeal to him. The only other alternative was to send it to London in the hope that Appiah would find a market for the stuff.

We made good progress, deciding to graft through the night in the hope that we could break off early the following night to show Steve the sights. For some reason, we found that the fibreglass resin was inconsistent. Sometimes the stuff would set rock-hard before you had finished working with it, and other times it would remain fluid for hours. The warehouse stank with it that night and we were all red-eyed by the time it had come to lock up.

Steve and I met at lunchtime the next day. Many of the diplomatic wives spoke good English and we spent a leisurely afternoon in the sun. I introduced Steve as my construction manager, a role that he played very well. He got very pally with a pretty new member of the group and they spent a lot of time basting each other with French sun oil.

That night, we caught up with the workload. Jean Marc was on a mission and must have drunk two crates of beer. He always enjoyed manning the circular saw but that night I was unable to watch, fearing lurid scenes of amputation. He was very unsteady on his feet by the time we called it a night. Steve and I drove off to enjoy a night of revelry.

We overcame most of the difficulties as they arose. Only the vacuum-sealer refused to rise from the dead after exhaustive efforts of intensive care. The resealing of the packages was very time-consuming but, in comparison with the rest of the work, it was a light option. We adopted a system of job rotation according to effort, which proved to be a success. This time, we packed just over two tonnes, of which about 190 kilos was of inferior quality.

Appiah tried to reassure me that he would have no trouble selling the older stuff but I had my doubts. He had little excuse for sending it and I made it clear that it was his responsibility. I decided not to press the point and was happy that the job had been a logistical success.

Steve was reluctant to leave. We had worked hard and played hard; he was good at both. I enjoyed his company and we all welcomed his input. As the Cockneys say, he was 'as game as a bagel'.

I attended the reception at the French Embassy and had a good time. The next day, Jean Marc presented me with the shipping documents and a day later I was on my way back to London.

I returned to find that Steve had begun to feel unwell on the flight home. Unable to make a diagnosis, his GP sent him to the Hospital for Tropical Diseases. He was admitted straight away. For more than a week, his condition worsened as the specialists failed to find what it was that he had contracted. Eventually, one of the tests indicated that Steve had a virus which only affected cats. The 'chicken' used to make the curry that Steve had come to love at our favourite Thai restaurant must originally have had whiskers.

To add insult to injury, while Steve was recovering in hospital, his mates had put a new registration number on his car – FEL 1X.

22

INSURANCE PAYOUT

Despite nearly going to pussycat heaven, Steve was so enthusiastic about his time in the Ivory Coast that his co-workers formed a queue for the next call for a volunteer.

I went to Tilbury one sunny morning in 1985 to watch our cargo being unloaded. Having every confidence that everything was in order, it was curiosity and a sense of triumph that took me to the docks.

The crane was attached to slings around each bale of timber; I recognised each and every one as it was hoisted on to the dock. About halfway through the operation, hovering about 10 feet above the ground, the crane jerked to a stop. The bale began to sway jerkily and one of the slings slipped towards the middle. Almost in slow motion, with the weight of the wood now uneven, one end of the bale swung down vertically. At this point, unable to hold on, the other sling released its grip and the timber crashed end first on to the concrete below. Two of the three steel bands burst open and the planks spread apart like an open fan with one end still secured.

Somebody was smiling down on us that day. It was one of the extra 2:1 odds insurance I had insisted upon. Dockers scurried around with all the tools needed to push the planks back together into the semblance of a bale and cleared the dock quickly to avoid impeding the work of the cranes any longer than necessary.

Dave received an apology via the shipping agent. We never pursued a claim. The consignment was delivered to our warehouse the following day and unloaded by Steve with our new heavy-duty forklift.

The fibreglassing was a success. Exposed to the elements and enormous swings of temperature and humidity, it was a racing certainty that our cargo would deteriorate in transit. This time, it was not as bad as I had feared.

We chose to select the best of the cannabis first to get as much money in as possible at the best prices. Roy was responsible for distribution and he had a network of customers. Some would take large quantities at a time and distribute to their local area and others were more small-time. Most were allowed credit, paying for each delivery when they received the next.

I had come to know the father of one of the boys racing against Emily who was called Jim Kavanagh, a South African bull of a man with a heavyweight-boxing pedigree. He and I had become friendly and, after a while, he let it be known to me that he was in the business of wholesaling cannabis.

Initial sales were astronomic. Word got back to us that we had flooded the market so effectively that the police were hotting up with enquiries in the hope of nicking a major gang. The money rolled in. Carrier bags of the stuff arrived daily on my kitchen table at Norlesden House. Everybody was paid and Steve and Dave were able to get rolling with their respective motor-racing plans.

Just as our best-quality grass was running low, another firm had begun to make themselves busy supplying London. Word was that this firm was based up north and the stuff they had on offer was at least as good as ours.

Appiah could no more move the old crop than anybody else. We still had more than half the delivery to sell. I approached Kavanagh who was happy to work with us. He began with a reasonable quantity, calling for double the next day and so on. Within a couple of weeks, he had built up his credit to 100lb weight at a time until, one day, he went missing.

His telephone number was unobtainable, there was nobody at his house and his son was no longer to be seen kart racing. He had disappeared. Roy put out feelers and we began a major search. He was nowhere to be found. I never saw him again but, about a month later at a local race meeting, somebody told me that he heard that Kavanagh had been nicked with a large quantity of drugs. I reported back. We called off the search and wrote off our losses.

We still did well. In time, all but 100 kilos was sold at ever-diminishing prices. One night, the boys took the remaining unsaleable packets to a slipway on the Thames near Greenwich and launched it down-river. Roy reported that it looked like an oil slick slowly floating away on the ebb tide in the moonlight.

23

TORTOLA

Life was good. The importations continued, and I was happy that the personnel we had selected were more than able. The quality, though, was never as good as promised. The quantities seldom matched the estimates and delivery times were usually fictional. Kwame, my Nigerian supplier, scared me shitless with his indiscreet telephone calls. He had an uncanny knack of arriving at Heathrow just when I least wanted any kind of African contact. He would call me daily from wherever I took him to stay, and the more I remonstrated, the more he called.

I was in no position to complain. The money was rolling in like there was no tomorrow. I remember at one time having three-quarters of a million pounds behind the panels of my bath. Packaged in bundles of notes of £1,000 each in mixed denominations, it filled enough carrier bags to stack round the whole of the bath.

Roy caused me concern. In the space of no time, he had moved from struggling to pay the rent of his council flat to buying a very big house in Surrey. Along with a partner with whom he held the leases of several pubs, he bought a club near Streatham. Here, he employed Bob Westbury as his manager. I didn't know him well but this strange man –who, within one sentence of first meeting, announced himself to be ex-SAS – had a collection of firearms that

Rambo would have been proud of. Always in need of help to distribute the cannabis, Roy recruited him. Westbury, the loyal employee, the brave soldier, the hero of Goose Green, buried us all when he did a deal with Customs and turned Queen's Evidence just before the trial. Tattooed as he was with proud army motifs, I would have added one with the words 'Dishonour Before Death'.

The 'need-to-know' principles, which are essential in a large conspiracy involving many people, went out of the window. I should have nipped it in the bud but life was good and I didn't want confrontation. Everybody knew everybody else and, in those circumstances, it only took one grass to nail us all. We ended up with two grasses and no small measure of dirty dealing to throw into the mix.

The racing took up a great deal of my time. We travelled the world to all the most important karting events. Emily was winning regularly and beginning to be tipped for success as a future racing driver.

We competed in a big race meeting in Perth, Western Australia, and arrived at the airport to be met by my friend Angelo. Our equipment had been shipped ahead of us and a local workshop was put at our disposal. The two-day race meeting was restricted to the use of only one set of tyres per day per driver, each set being marked with a special branding tool by the scrutiniser.

There was a monumental punch-up at the prize-giving dinner. After the race, I sold every last piece of equipment to the locals and we left for England with nothing apart from our trophies. One day, Roy came to see me. He loved boats and had found an advertisement for a marina in a magazine. The photo of the place looked idyllic – it was on Tortola in the British Virgin Islands. He asked me if I wanted to go into it with him. I agreed to make some enquiries. The agent, in smart offices near the Houses of Parliament, confirmed that it was indeed a whole marina and his clients were looking for a speedy sale at around $1 million to include quite a substantial inventory which included, amongst other things, a rather fine sailing yacht. The price was too good to be true and, when I learned that the vendors were a very large brewery, I was intrigued. We made travel plans.

The flight took us to Costa Rica. There, we changed aircraft. I was thrilled, as the onward flight was to be in a very old Dakota DC3. Climbing in at the tail, we had to walk uphill to our seats. The flight did not take long and this elderly twin-engine hero of the Berlin Airlift carried us noisily but sedately to our destination.

The little island was a revelation. It boasted a militant Prime Minister who would only issue a work permit if there was nobody else on the island who could do the job. After I found his telephone number in the phone book, he gladly came to meet us to lay down the law. I admired him. The island was still a British protectorate and the Governor drove about in a London taxi. There was a Yacht Club, the last bastion of the British Raj and a very snooty elderly English couple who sent their old and infirm Rolls with a hand-written invitation to tea.

The almighty contrast to this quaint little island with its smart restaurants playing classical music was the enormous selection of huge banks. This was the 'laundromat' of the world. Vast private fortunes hiding from authorities of every kind lurked in the vaults of these disproportionately large establishments.

We arrived at the marina to learn that the yacht on the inventory had slipped away under cover of darkness with a director of the said large brewery at the helm. It was no longer included in the sale. The site was beautiful. Evidence of heavy expenditure on the best of everything was all around. The construction of a small hotel on the site had been abandoned at ground-floor level.

I was taken on by an American girl whom I met at an outdoor disco and shown the island. By the end of a week, I had seen enough. This was not the Caribbean that I knew and had come to love. It was very evident that, after years of heavy losses, serious changes would have to be made. I formed the opinion that, even if one took up residence, the labour laws would conspire to defeat the objective. It was impossible to lay off or sack staff, no matter what they did.

I took a trip to Virgin Gorda; I did a night dive on a wreck; I went marlin fishing and enjoyed intimate Anglo-American relations, but the highlight of that trip was the return to Costa Rica in that wonderful Dakota.

By the time my two older daughters reached 13 and 14, they issued me an ultimatum. Already expelled from a small selection of local educational establishments, both of them were now in militant mood. They approached me together. 'We're leaving school,' they told me, 'and there's nothing you can do about it.'

They were right. Furthermore, fed up myself with a daily reveille that usually ended in tears, anger or both, I would quite welcome some peace.

The house was big enough. I set aside a room in the attic for schooling and fitted it out with everything needed for a home education. I received a visit from the local education officer whom, I suspect, was quite happy to be relieved of two more delinquents from his books. I placed advertisements in the local paper and was surprised at how many teachers were attracted by the challenge. Given the choice, I think I would rather have followed Kitchener's call to the First World War trenches than take on these two. In due course, I was to encounter many a hardened criminal and suffer privations of massive proportions. The combination of my public-school education and confrontations with my daughters were a perfect apprenticeship for a lengthy spell of incarceration.

They systematically drove one applicant to drink, another to attempted suicide and a third into psychiatric care in the space of six months. We finally ended up with a token teacher who satisfied the education department but taught the girls nothing. On the contrary, it was they who taught him. By the time he left my employ, he had learned how to roll a party-sized joint, hot-wire a car and swear like a trooper.

I was spending a fortune on motor sport. By the time it all came on top, there was nothing left. Nobody believed me and, looking back, I find it hard to believe myself.

Shortly after my arrest, Westbury, a long time before he went wobbly, told me that Roy, who was in charge of distribution, had been systematically cooking the books heavily in favour of himself.

It was a period in my life of rich pleasure. When I look back, I have happy memories and no regrets.

24

TARZAN

Jean Marc and I met regularly during the summer of 1986. Our favourite venue was the seafood restaurant in Calais and, true to form, we would consume a fair quantity of wine and cognac. The trip from his house in Lille and mine in London took about the same time. I always brought money, never less than £20,000 and more often £50,000 at a time. We had decided to do a big one – three to four tonnes of cannabis, along with all the other associated expenses, cost a lot.

Jean Marc still worked for Air Afrique and had to return to Abidjan where, on Lamine's advice, we had rented a much larger warehouse closer to the timber merchants and, more importantly, in a location not overlooked by anybody who might be looking for a pension.

I received a call about a month later to say that I was needed and, as usual, took a flight to Paris and connected by UTA to Abidjan. I had bought a poacher's jacket at Holland & Holland with several concealed pockets. In these, I carried another £75,000 in cash.

I had to clear Customs where a few packets of cigarettes ensured smiles and fast-track service to the public area. I was surprised to find that Jean Marc was not around to greet me as arranged.

I always travelled light and, taking my bag and jacket, hailed an old Peugeot 504 taxi, which rattled me to my usual beachfront hotel. Along the way, we were stopped at a couple of police roadblocks looking for a little money to enable them to eat.

The last time I was there, Lamine had told me that the French drug squad had sent the Abidjan police four highly trained sniffer dogs earlier in the year. Apparently, they lasted about three days before being sacrificed and barbecued at a roadblock near the airport where they were consumed with great relish. Lamine had been asked to say that the dogs had been sent up country and to request further supplies.

I arrived at the hotel with its down-at-heel bungalows and the usual army of prostitutes looking for business by the gates to find that Jean Marc had already checked me in. He had left a note at reception and my Honda 750 was parked waiting for me. I found the keys inside the envelope and a letter explaining that he had to work a night shift at the airport.

It had been six months since I was last in Abidjan and I had no intentions of sleeping before my breakfast meeting. I am ashamed to admit that I never wore a crash helmet. Despite being regularly stoned, drunk and reckless, I never crashed or fell off. I checked the fuel and stopped to hand out a few Bennies to the prostitutes who were always friendly and cheerful. Despite knowing by then that I wasn't going to give them any business, they never stopped trying.

It must have been about 1.00am. I zipped up my jacket and took a left along the industrial coast road to Treichville, the centre of shanty-town nightclub heaven. I felt exhilarated to be riding the bike again. I passed the succession of shacks, houses, stalls and roadside food, which served to feed staff employed in a wide variety of light and heavy industry. Flaming refineries dwarfed tiny shacks. In these, workers re-treaded by hand massive lorry tyres which had long since lost their grip, alongside many other labour-intensive activities.

As I neared town, I remembered to be careful at two precarious railway crossings. The tracks made huge indentations in the road, which at that point became cobbled, adding to the hazard. This was, for me, the point of no return as a gradual crescendo of humanity, noise and smells took me to street after street of shacks, one leaning against the other, alive with music and activity of a kind of restlessness I had not encountered anywhere else in the world. Each establishment had its own unmarked but always respected set of boundaries and minders who would look after whatever you arrived in or on. The big Honda always attracted a large crowd of admirers who also applauded my departure. The applause was always directly proportionate to the amount of noise and drama created as I took off. It was easy to make friends.

I headed for Hello Dolly, Jean Marc's favourite dive, where, after a fine welcome from the doorman, Dolly greeted me with the hug of a long-lost sister. She had come to Abidjan from Liberia some 12 years earlier. She had worked as a dancer, sending back home what she could to feed and clothe a growing son she had left in the care of a sister.

Over the years, she made enough to set up her *boîte*. As she prospered, so did her Liberian family, who moved into a large house built by Dolly and into which she planned to retire. The years had not been kind to Dolly, who cared little for her appearance but, having discovered a preference for other women, remained true all the time I knew her to a beautiful young Abyssinian girl who adored her.

She led me into her bar, which contained fewer revellers than usual, and bought me a beer. She explained that business had been bad which was why she had to double her already extortionate prices. I tried a little commercial reason and failed. I liked Dolly; she always told the truth. I often wonder what became of her and her family in a Liberia since ravaged by civil war.

I went on to see Ami, whose bar sported a much greater degree of investment, bankrolled by a French ex-pat with whom she had arranged a mutually beneficial repayment plan in kind. She closed up at about 4.00am and I took her back with me on the pillion of the Honda. Jean Marc arrived at 7.00am. Ami took a cab back home while Jean Marc and I went to check on progress.

I had not seen the new warehouse, which stood behind a pair of large steel gates and was opened by the guard who had worked for us for some time. Lamine had recruited him and, as far as I knew, he was still employed as a policeman. The salary he received from us would have paid for a whole police station in Abidjan.

The building was about 120 feet by 40 feet with brick walls and a corrugated-iron roof. There was strip lighting and a few old electric fans rotating uselessly at precarious angles suspended from the rafters. Inside were about 14 bales of timber each about 15 feet long and 5 feet square, consisting of about 12 layers of rough-sawn uneven planks of iroko and held together by steel bands, tensioned and stapled by a powerful machine.

The laborious task of preparing the bales had already begun but I calculated that, if we were to export between three to four tonnes of grass, we would need to hollow ten of the bales. This time, I would have to reduce my 2:1 safety ratio and we settled for an extra six bales to be left untouched. Our warehouse in London would be full to the brim.

Jean Marc told me that he expected the first delivery of cannabis to arrive in about a week and, between us, we had another eight bales to prepare with the help of the guard and one other employee. We had less than a month to prepare the shipment if we were to make the boat on which we had reserved space. Jean Marc was now working the early shift at the airport, which meant that we could only work from about midnight until we dropped.

We gave it a go but both knew that we were unlikely to meet the deadline with the workforce we had. Although it would have been easy to recruit as large a workforce as we needed in a matter of minutes, we did not want to risk wagging tongues. We arranged to meet at the warehouse at midnight and went our separate ways.

I slept until about midday and went for a swim in the hotel pool where one of the more attractive diplomatic wives I'd met before was pleased to see me. She left the children with their nanny while we sat at the bar and ate a light lunch together. She complained of boredom and invited me to a reception the following evening at the embassy.

I gratefully accepted and said my goodbyes. I had a meeting uptown at 4.00pm and went to get changed.

Kwame and I had arranged to meet at the Intercontinental and I arrived early to see him in the lobby dressed in a fine suit and those wonderful tan shoes with imitation amber Cuban heels – the perfect Nigerian businessman. He had flown in from Lagos and the flight had just arrived, three hours late. He checked in and we went to his room. He handed me some shipping documents and proceeded to tell me that his expenses were much higher than anticipated and that we should give him £30,000 more for his trouble. I asked him if he had managed to load the two tonnes we had agreed to pay for, which he confirmed. I could see from his eyes that he was lying.

He pressed me to pay him the balance for the consignment and I told him to wait until we had received the container and weighed the contents. As expected, he told me that he had to return the next day, but I resisted his demands.

The ship was due to dock the next day and I was assured that the two tonnes of best-quality sensemilla were in the container carefully concealed behind cases of canned fruit juice. We had prepaid Kwame for everything bar a balance for about 500 kilos.

I rode back to my hotel where Lamine, the Chief of Police, was waiting to meet me. I gave him the documents and he left to meet with his contact in Customs with a present from me of £1,000. He returned about an hour later to say that the ship had arrived that day and would be unloaded during the night. Our container had 'cleared Customs' and we could collect it in a couple of days. I slept until late, listened to some music and left for work.

We worked through the night hammering, beating, lifting and sawing and made enough noise to wake the dead. I could not believe the amount of beer Jean Marc consumed during the night. We looked like coconut-coated marshmallows from the combination of sweat and sawdust, by the time we piled into Jean Marc's Peugeot to his apartment where we showered and ate an enormous breakfast cooked by his houseboy.

Using my prearranged system of communication, I called London.

Fifteen minutes later, I was speaking to Roy in a London phone box from a hotel lobby I had stopped at on my way back.

'We need help.'

'How many do you need?'

'Send me Peter, he's strong. Get him to call me from Paris with his arrival time.'

Peter, Roy's son-in-law, worked with us in London and was good at distribution. After Steve had returned from Abidjan, Peter had wanted to make the trip. We got on well and, although he had travelled abroad on holiday many times, he had never visited Africa. He had an army training, a good sense of humour and a desire for adventure. He was discreet and careful and kept a low profile.

I got back to my bungalow to find the words 'Ami come' written in big letters in lipstick on the window. Mercifully, I slept uninterrupted and awoke refreshed, feeling a need to see someone special.

During earlier visits, I used to stay in a hotel on the lagoon where the round rooms with thatched roofs were built on poles over the water and accessed by a pathway, which passed the reception. I loved the location and to sit on the balcony watching the fishing boats silently sliding by and pelicans lazily plopping into the water, but I was concerned with privacy. Every visitor could be observed and logged coming and going, so I moved on.

At the entrance to the hotel was the Vietnamese restaurant run by the couple who rented the property from the hotel owner. I had eaten there a couple of times before I met her 19-year-old daughter; I was stricken. She seemed to come and go with no pattern of regularity and would stop to chat from time to time or wave en passant.

One afternoon, she came to visit me on my balcony. We chatted a while and she asked if she could use the bath. She took my hand and led me to the bedroom where she undressed me and made love to me. We would meet from time to time, never by arrangement, but almost with an intuitively perfect sense of timing. The clocks seemed to stand still to allow us whatever time we needed together.

She was sad and strangely distant. She told me that the restaurant was closing and that she and her family were planning to go away.

She promised to stay in touch but never did. Looking back, I never knew what she did and never asked her.

I had little time to get ready for the reception and changed into a light tropical linen suit, which always did the job on such occasions. I have always wondered how colonials and ex-pats in the tropics have been able to stand overdressing as part of an age-old tradition. Even now, with the benefit of air-conditioning, you can still melt just in the process of arrival.

On these occasions, most tended to wear suit and tie. The French, ever chic and stylish, seem to have mastered that 'just-off-the-tennis-court-and-rushed-from-the-shower' look. I mingled, deferred and conversed until Mme Diplomat, looking very lovely, took my arm and steered me to a gathering of rather serious business people. 'This is Paul Newman... he is from England and is building a hotel.'

The general conversation revolved around the decline of the Ivorian economy and the need for caution. A woman I had not seen before left the group and joined me with a card in her hand. I was surprised to hear her introduce herself in perfect English; she was attached to the British embassy with responsibilities for trade. She fired some questions at me and asked what I had that would ensure success in a tourist industry where others had failed. She knew that Air Afrique, unwilling to lose their monopoly, would oppose charters and that the lagoon was becoming ever more hopelessly polluted. She said to call if I ever needed any help but, from her look, I knew that she had dismissed me as an adventurer. I left for work.

That night, we worked well together and succeeded in preparing two whole bales. Stoned on the smell of glass-fibre resin and drunk from a crate of beer, Jean Marc took a piece of chalk and wrote in one box 'For ze queen', and in the other 'For ze princesse'.

Lamine came by as we were cleaning up and said the container from Nigeria could be picked up from the docks in the afternoon. One of us should be there to meet it because a junior Customs officer had to accompany the lorry with instructions to open the doors just to confirm that the contents were as stated on the bill of lading. I volunteered and Jean Marc left to arrange the lorry.

I returned later to find the lorry already waiting outside with the Customs officer sitting in the passenger seat. I called the guard who opened the gates and asked the driver to reverse into the yard outside the warehouse building and leave the trailer with the container on board. He replied that he had instructions to return with the empty container but said that, if we all worked together, we could discharge it in an hour. The young Customs officer nodded in agreement.

I gave the driver some money and told him that I wanted the container left undisturbed in the yard overnight and he agreed to return the following morning. We duly opened the back doors and were nearly smothered by a cascade of thousands of coconut husks, which fell to the ground revealing the packets of badly sealed and very smelly cannabis. I quickly steered the somewhat shocked Customs man to the office where, with the present of £200 – more than six months' salary – he readily agreed to sign the papers and keep *schtum*.

I gave the driver some more silence money and we agreed to return to plan 'A', kicking the remaining coconut husks off the back of the container on to the ground and forming a chain to bring the packages of grass into the building. In less than an hour, the lorry had gone.

I got the guard to fetch some scales. Before we could start weighing, Lamine arrived, obviously angry. The young Customs man had told his boss how the cargo had been loaded and he had, in turn, called Lamine. Fortunately, the young man was reliable and, after we shared a beer together, Lamine left laughing.

The grass was good quality but needed resealing. It was 600 kilos under weight. We had overpaid Kwame by £10,000; little wonder he had fucked off back to Lagos as quickly as he did.

Jean Marc had bought a new vacuum-packing machine in Paris and shipped it to Abidjan, but the instruction book had gone missing and, so far, nobody could make it work. I managed to achieve some measure of success and, at midnight, we had sealed the packages, filled up the 'queen' and the 'princesse' and stuffed another for 'Prince Charles'. By 2.30am, we had nailed the tops on the three full bales and banded them all. By way of celebration, we spent the rest of the night clubbing in Treichville.

I was woken by the telephone; it was Peter. He was staying in Paris until the following day and would be on the evening UTA flight. We agreed to take the following evening off to welcome Peter and to do as much as possible in the warehouse before his arrival. We were tired. To add to my worries, we received word that two of our porters had been arrested up country at the border. I was assured that it would be sorted out and that supplies should be on stream again within a couple of days.

I spent some leisure time by the pool until early evening when Lamine came by to take me to the airport. He wore that kind of military police dress uniform prevalent in Africa and South America which, set off by a pair of wrap-around shades, white gloves and a swagger stick, looked very sinister indeed. We left in the back of his black Mercedes and drove on to the apron as the DC10 was taxiing to a full stop.

We waited until the steps were rolled to the front section and the door opened before getting out of the car. I stood beside Lamine and prodded him the minute I saw Peter. Lamine drew smartly to attention. Peter looked incredulous when he spotted me in the reception party and, as I shook his hand, Lamine saluted.

'What the fuck's going on?' said Peter *sotto voce.*

'Don't worry and get in the car,' I said with a smile.

He climbed in the back and we sped past the opened barrier to more salutes.

Outside, the car came to a halt in front of a line of about 12 policemen standing smartly to attention. Lamine explained that Peter had to inspect the honour guard before we could continue and I translated. After some hesitation, Peter obliged and, as we got back in the car, a deep belly laugh began from Lamine. Soon, we were all crying with mirth with Peter shouting obscenities at us all.

We drove to Jean Marc's house where Lamine said his farewells and three of us continued to a restaurant for a dinner washed down with more than enough alcohol. We dropped Jean Marc back at his house and took his car to the hotel to get freshened up before Peter's first taste of Abidjan night life. He was asking so many questions.

'Peter, just imagine you've landed on Mars...' was all the advice I could give him as we headed straight for my usual haunts.

After a couple of establishments, I could see that Peter was relaxing and enjoying himself. We moved on to bigger places with dance floors where the girls outnumbered the men ten to one. He couldn't understand why so many were coming up to him and talking to him while their friends giggled and watched.

'What does she want?' he said.

'She wants to go home with you.'

He kept laughing while dancing, sharing his beers and handing out cigarettes. He had stopped asking me to translate.

By 4.00am, I had had enough but Peter wanted to carry on partying. I got him to drive me back to the hotel, pointing out all the landmarks I could. We agreed to meet for breakfast at 9.00am and I bade him farewell. I sat on the veranda with a cold beer when, unannounced, Miss Lipstick arrived in a taxi with a pretty young thing I had not met before for us both to play with.

Peter knocked for me as agreed and I left the girls still comatose to join him for breakfast; he had obviously just got back and was a little unsteady. He looked at me wide-eyed and with a grin from ear to ear. He told me that, after dropping me, he had got lost and drove around until he saw a sign saying 'American Bar'. He had gone in and was entertained by a really nice Moroccan girl behind the bar who spoke English. He said that quite a few pretty girls joined him and he spent a fortune on drinks. I told him that 'American Bar' was a French euphemism for brothel and he replied that he had pretty much worked that out by the morning. It was only a mile or two away and we planned a visit that evening to check it out.

We met again for a late lunch by the pool. I returned Jean Marc's car, leaving the keys with the houseboy, and we went in search of Peter's American Bar on the Honda. After a few false starts, up and down some dusty unmetalled residential streets, a pointed arm and triumphant shout of recognition from Peter let me know that we had found what we were looking for.

Quite a large two-storey building, it stood at the end of a street of similar-sized houses, surrounded by a high wall and some tall trees. The frontage was open to the road and set back enough to allow parking without obscuring the sign. We were met by a guard obviously happy to see Peter, who ushered us into a long bar, freshly cleaned and empty. Within a couple of minutes, a dark-haired girl appeared, kissed Peter three times on the cheek and, in turn, rather formally shook my hand. She apologised for the lack of girls who were still mostly sleeping but, if we were in no hurry, we could chill out with a couple of drinks and wait.

She poured us a couple of cold beers. We sat at the bar chatting and watching the pretty manager pass to and fro doing this and that in preparation for the night ahead. A couple of fans lazily rotated over the bar at just enough speed to circulate the air and sabotage our attempts to use the ashtrays.

The girl came back and joined us with a smile; I remember her deep black eyes. Peter had already told her that he was a newly qualified surveyor come to join me to prepare a feasibility study on a piece of resort development land, sparing me the need to explain in any depth what I did. In any event, it was not the kind of establishment which required a proposer and seconder.

The girls began to filter in about an hour later, all of whom came to greet Peter and meet me. They were all North African, pretty and sleepily friendly, as they slowly got themselves ready for the night shift. We chatted for a while and they all laughed about Peter's misinterpretation of the bar's name. Peter asked if he could roll a joint and was asked to do it outside.

He and I walked out to the bike and used it as a stand on which to build a spliff. When he lit up, a couple of girls came out to join us. We had decided by then that this was to become our local, which we would name The Dog and Duck. None of the girls spoke good enough English to understand Cockney rhyming slang, and it somehow lost its meaning when translated into French.

We were standing around the bike chatting and smiling when, all of a sudden, a repeated shrieking sound started from an area at the side of the building.

'What's that?' I asked.

'That's Tarzan trying to fuck the guard dogs,' replied one of the girls.

She explained that Tarzan was a chimpanzee who lived in the grounds. 'Go and see him and give him a beer.'

Peter went to get three fresh beers and he and I walked down to a gate at the end of the building. As we approached, the noise from the yard became ever louder and we opened the gate to see a fully grown male chimp attached to a long chain chasing a couple of very worried-looking Alsatian dogs round and round the dusty yard.

Tarzan spotted us, immediately calmed down and loped towards us with an arm outstretched towards a bottle of beer. Peter gave him the beer and we all sat on the conveniently placed branches of the large tree to which was attached the other end of Tarzan's chain. Peter lit a cigarette and it was immediately obvious that Tarzan had already been introduced to nicotine.

We watched in amazement while Tarzan leaned against his tree, beer in one hand and cigarette in the other. We were like three mates in a pub. We stayed for a while longer, shook hands with Tarzan, who handed me his empty beer bottle, and returned to the bar.

Apparently, Tarzan belonged to the proprietor who was Lebanese and seldom came to Abidjan. The chimp was, thought the Moroccan manager, about ten years old and had been there longer than her. The girls complained that his screeching disturbed their customers and put them off their stroke. They were fed up with being woken up early in the morning after a hard night's work. We stayed a while, paid an exorbitant bill and waved goodbye to the girls, promising to return. We could hear Tarzan calling to us as we made a noisy departure.

Peter was what we needed. Somehow, the extra pair of hands lessened everybody's load and, after a hard night's work, we could see that, all things being equal, we would make the deadline with enough time for plenty of fun. Lamine came by early and told us that the two porters were back at work after a night in custody.

A pensive moment.

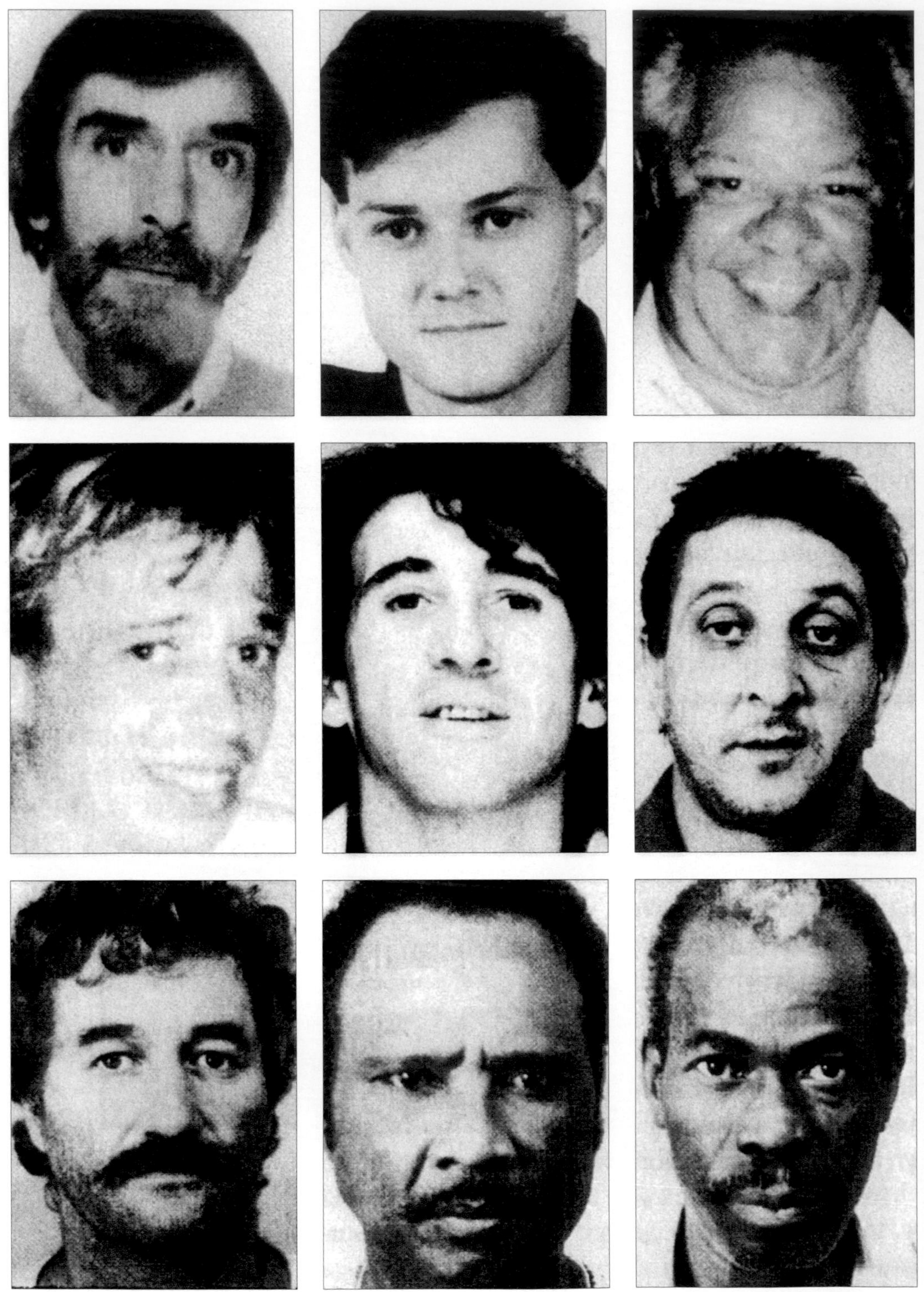

My co-conspirators:

Top: John Upton, David Evans and Roy Crack.

Middle: Peter Lambert, Michael Bateson and Jean-Marc Devaine.

Bottom: Marc Piquet, Albert Kokou and Lamine Fadika.

Top: The consignment which led to my arrest.

Bottom left and right: Some of the grass that was taken from the warehouse.

My mother and father in the mid-1990s.

Emily and my granddaughter Fifi in the early 1990s while I was away.

With my wife in 2000.

Riding pillion on the scooter with me in Jodhpur are my daughters Charlotte and Emily around 2003/4.

My granddaughter, then 14, and I in 2003.

Apparently, the reason for their arrest was because they had no papers and, no doubt, the border guards saw the opportunity of an unexpected bonus.

A large stockpile had been brought to the other side of the border and a lorry was being loaded for Lamine to escort into town some time the following night. Peter couldn't wait to visit his new mate at The Dog and Duck again and spoke about him constantly.

We were a little later than the day before and arrived to find the bar in full swing. Tarzan recognised the sound of the bike and we could hear him screeching excitedly as we approached. There were a couple of cars parked in front of the building and an equal number of girls were missing from the bar. Peter took a beer to Tarzan and I stayed chatting to the manager. She explained that the girls would usually come on a three- or six-month tour of duty. Each had her own room from which she worked and their air fare was paid by the house.

The clientele in Abidjan seemed mostly to be French ex-pats and Lebanese businessmen. The girls could make enough money to go home at the end of their tour of duty with enough money to live well until the next.

One of the girls offered to show me her room. It was comfortable and homely with plenty of evidence of her own personal possessions. I was amused to see a manual credit card machine beside the bed. The procedure for such transactions was that the girl would ring down to the bar for the voucher to be collected and no activity was permitted until telephone authorisation had been obtained. In the Ivory Coast, this could take some time.

Peter had not returned, so I took some beers to find him and Tarzan sharing a joint. We stayed for quite a while and, this time, Tarzan was clearly sorry to see us go. We both had come out without any cash and were told it would be easier to run an account, which we could settle from time to time. We arrived at work where Peter animatedly explained to the others that he had found heaven – a pub staffed by crumpet, a drinking mate who understood him and all on a monthly account. We all agreed to work hard that night and take a break the following day.

We were just getting started with the physical work when Lamine came in followed by Harry Appiah and a blonde. The lorry was outside and two men I had not seen before brought in the contents. The blocks of grass varied in size from the rough equivalent of a house brick to something about four times larger.

Harry and the blonde had flown into Accra and gone into the bush where her presence would have caused ripples over a fair distance. He had supervised the pressing of the grass, which was done manually with big wind-out lorry jacks. They were lightly wrapped in cellophane and then swathed in wide brown sticky tape. The load weighed in at about 600 kilos. Harry and I went to the office where I expressed concern about his lack of discretion and he gave me some bullshit in reply.

He told me that there was about another tonne-and-a-half which he would bring in two or three loads over the course of the next week. I gave him some money and he tried hard for more. Harry and the blonde left in the lorry with the two workers sitting on the open back. Lamine left in his car.

Peter was a much greater authority than I was in judging the quality of our Ghanaian crop and we split a couple of packages. One was bright green and fresh with a much more pungent odour than the other, which was dry and crumbled more easily. They smoked as expected. When we were arranging the packages in the name of another member of the Royal Family, we noticed that about half-a-dozen were heavier than they should be. Inspection revealed that some large metal nuts and bolts had been pressed inside them. The farmers were paid by weight.

The shipping usually took about a month plus another week at the docks for processing the paperwork. Often, the ships took an unexpected detour and sometimes we had a delay of nearly two months from dock to dock. This always caused a deterioration in quality.

The individual packages had to be sealed as well as possible in order to keep the smell in and the elements out. If the grass started life fresh and moist, there was a danger of it becoming mouldy during the long hot journey. Often, dry packages would become dryer still and, inevitably, it would lose a noticeable degree of potency. There was only a certain amount the British market could take at any one time and a large importation would take some time to sell. Often, as we got near to the end, prices would fall dramatically.

I remember taking some time to go to sleep that morning. The logistics of each operation were always tortuous and, not wishing to write anything down, I had a lot to keep in my head. I used to smoke, too, which often served to befuddle my mental diary.

I was woken by a light, urgently repeated tapping on my door and I knew that I had not slept for long. Mme Diplomat walked in, pushed the door closed behind her and kissed me.

She was wearing a light summer dress under which she wore a bra but no knickers. I had always admired her firm and pampered 30-something body. She fucked me with a sense of aggression that smelled of revenge.

We shared a glass of water and a cigarette after which she left hurriedly to return to her children by the pool in the charge of their nanny. I wouldn't sleep again and showered before walking to the pool. As I passed her lying on a sun bed, she looked up, smiled and averted her eyes.

I was surprised to see Peter sitting with a drink and looking out to sea; it wasn't yet midday. Although we had known each other for some years, there had been little social contact. He had bought himself out of the army which he hated, and had then married and fathered a succession of children. He was easy company and we chatted for quite a while. By the time we were ready to eat, it had already become a late lunch. He told me that he would love to take Tarzan home to his kids and look after him. I replied that he would cost a fortune in beer and cigarettes.

When the conspiracy 'came on top' a couple of years later, Peter, too, was caught in the net. He was to die tragically from a melanoma shortly after his release from jail; he was in his early thirties.

We had arranged to meet Lamine and the others for dinner. When I got back to my bungalow, I found a 'diplomatic note' from Mme Diplomat, inviting me the next day to a garden party at the Russian embassy. She had written in longhand in perfect English with a map drawn on the back.

Peter and I had agreed to meet Lamine at a restaurant which I knew. It was a large shack built in wood and thatch by the side of the sea and served only chicken or lobster barbecued, served with a fiery sauce and brought to your table by scantily clad young girls. They would dance on stage at the end of the evening to an accompaniment of loud and wild drumming.

Food would keep coming to your table until you said stop. Chez Kakpo had been around for many years and was a favourite of the ex-pat and diplomatic community. We had already begun when Lamine arrived. I told them of Tarzan and Peter's desire to take him home.

'*Pas de problème*,' replied a serious-looking Chief of Police.

Nothing was a problem if you had money and influence. A friend of Jean Marc's, whom I met several times while out drinking, had been convicted of killing his business partner. Sentenced to a long prison term, he came to an arrangement with the prison Governor requiring him only to attend once a week for roll-call.

The party continued to The Dog and Duck, where we all met Tarzan. Jean Marc took two of the Moroccan girls off for some exercise. Later, Lamine, who had drunk a lot of brandy, was deep in conversation with the girl behind the bar. She told us that, although he would be missed, Tarzan was beginning to be a problem and was not good for business. He was free to go to a good home.

Lamine made an arrangement to meet Peter and me there the next day at 2.00pm and left. The girl said that, although they were not open at that time, she would be there to let us in. Jean Marc had been gone for some time but returned to say that he wanted to take both of the girls home with him. Before they left, they had another drink with us.

'The girls want to know why you don't fuck them,' Jean Marc said.

I replied that I enjoyed the scene better as it was, and saw The Dog and Duck as a refuge from sexual excesses.

Peter and I prepared to leave and invited the girls to join us later in

Treichville. They were shocked to hear that we ever came out of there alive and had heard tales of kidnap, murder and sales directly into the slave trade. They were all curious and said that, if Lamine was with us, they would close one night and join us on a visit into hell.

It had once been known for The Dog and Duck to close for a month by arrangement with a famous movie director who was in Abidjan to make a movie on the beach. The girls were shipped to the Intercontinental where wild parties were staged nightly in the suites of the film personnel. Apparently, the coke budget was astronomical, too, and a couple of the girls who were there told me that the crew were so spangled that they were mostly incapable of sex.

My recollection of the rest of the night is hazy, but I knew it was mad and debauched. I was beginning to think that life might be calmer if I sought the company of a busty necrophiliac.

We could not fathom what it was that made Lamine ask us to meet him at The Dog and Duck at 2.00pm but we were soon to find out. We arrived to be offered a refreshing drink of tea before Lamine turned up a few minutes later with a man in tow toting a camera. Lamine asked the girl to pass him an airline captain's hat which hung on a hook behind the bar and explained to us that Ivorian law forbade the export of chimpanzees and, in his opinion, the only way for Tarzan to leave was with us on the aeroplane. We were more than somewhat amused at this suggestion but we had been sampling some of our new crop since lunch and it didn't sound impossible.

We took Tarzan his usual refreshments. He refused to pose in the hat without his beer and cigarette. The photographer was eventually satisfied and he sped off with Lamine who explained that it would probably take a couple of days. Tarzan was getting a passport.

We went back to the bar to some fresh tea. I had some money on me and asked to settle our tab. Jean Marc had forgotten to pay for his pleasures and we had consumed rather more than I thought the previous evening.

The girls all agreed to take a night off and close the place on Sunday and we agreed to lead the motorcade for a night on the town. I think after settling a bill of film-budget proportions, the girls took pity and insisted that we would all go Dutch on the works outing. Be warned, dear reader, never run a tab in a brothel.

Peter did not want to go to the Russian reception with me so we arranged for him to take a taxi to work where we would meet later. I allowed enough time to be sure to arrive a little late so that enough people had already arrived ahead of me to make my entrance less conspicuous.

With the help of a map, I found myself in an area nowhere near the other embassies and arrived at a large colonial residence. The roof was bristling with aerials.

Security was evidently somewhat slack and I walked through the building to the garden where the hubbub of conversation nearly drowned a balalaika and two fine Russian voices. I took a drink and began to circulate. This was a first for me and I immediately sensed that, although some formal dress and a couple of fine uniforms were on view, the atmosphere was decidedly more party than business. I made small talk and met many Russians who, happy to speak English, fitted well into my preconceptions of KGB. They were a jolly lot and, within a short while, vodka, tossed back as if going into battle, became the order of the day. The English lady I had met at the French embassy some days earlier spotted me from a small huddle of Brits and waved with a brief smile.

I felt relaxed and chatted to a young man who explained that he was a languages graduate from Kiev and had been in the diplomatic service for about five years, working as an interpreter. He had been in Abidjan for two years and, although the embassy staff were discouraged from going out except in groups, he had found ways to enjoy the place. He explained that they often made their own entertainment and many of the staff had a classical musical training.

Mme Diplomat came over. I remember my Ukrainian friend raising an eyebrow at the passionate way she embraced me. Hubby must have been watching. She whispered that she would see me at lunch the next day. She left to join some others and I made my excuses as I had to go to work.

Another lorryload was being delivered as I arrived. Appiah had come on his own this time. I gave him more money and, after he left, we had a weigh-in. We ascertained that the total would probably be about three-and-a-half tonnes.

Jean Marc was in fine spirits. 'I like ze Maroccaines,' he said in his comic French accent many times through the night.

I told him to pay for his own fucking whores in future. He promised to reimburse me but never did. It was a good night's work and we could see that we had less work ahead of us than we had already done.

Somehow, Mme Diplomat's children, driver and nanny had been directed elsewhere for the afternoon and we enjoyed a much more relaxed tempo to perform our duets. She had a sexy, husky voice and I insisted she spoke English to me. She had announced to hubby that she was having an affair. He seemed too preoccupied with his own philandering to take any notice. She was educated and cultured and I liked her company. She left in the late afternoon. I had given Peter the bike for the day and I enjoyed some time alone listening to music before taking a cab to The Dog and Duck.

I went to the bar where Peter met me. In a state of excitement, he took me outside and, when we were alone, handed me a passport, which Lamine had delivered to him earlier. Tarzan Lambert, Peter's family name, had become a 20-year-old pilot and now had his very own Ivory Coast passport. We laughed so much that night, my sides hurt now at the memory of it.

I awoke the next morning to find that not all was right down below. I had caught a dose. I found a doctor within the hour who, with a Gallic shrug, took blood and skewered me with a needle full of antibiotics. He told me to call him in a couple of days, during which time I should abstain from sex and reduce my alcohol intake.

I was in a state of panic but the doctor was nearly 100 per cent sure that it was nothing nasty. AIDS had begun to rear its ugly head in Africa and I had accordingly been very cautious. There was one exception – Mme Diplomat. She wasn't at the pool that day. I told Peter the story and he reacted, as I expected, in the same way as we had to Tarzan's passport.

That night, Harry arrived with the final lorryload. He was responsible for supervising the preparation and delivery of almost exactly two tonnes. I was pleased. We wrangled a bit in the office after I had challenged him to show me a hotel in the bush which cost more than the Intercontinental. He pretended to be disappointed with his payout. He was returning to Ghana to spend a week or two with relatives and would make contact with our distribution team when he got back to London.

We resolved to try to pack the final boxes by Saturday. We had our 'works outing' planned for Sunday and the load could go down to the docks early the following week in readiness for shipping.

Strangely, I was becoming concerned for Mme Diplomat. I felt sorry for her in a funny sort of way. I spotted her the following morning and, from the way she smiled, I knew that I had news for her. She followed me to my bungalow veranda and, when I told her, she burst into tears. I comforted her and told her to calm down. After she had sent the children home with the nanny, I took her to the same doctor who had good news for me and a syringe for her. Although we were sure her husband was to blame, I told her that it could have been different. I kissed her and she promised to return the next day after a confrontation.

We arranged the works outing at The Dog and Duck. The trip was to begin at midday with a 50-mile journey to a wonderful part of the coast. Tarzan was happy. Peter and I, with the benefit of occasional lucidity, began to appreciate that, even if Lamine with his influence could insinuate Tarzan beside us in a first-class seat back to Paris, we were likely to be rumbled upon arrival, if not many hours before. It was a story one of us would have to write about some time in the future.

The next day, I had a visit to confirm that hubby was indeed the culprit. She had told him that her story about an affair was just to make him jealous and he begged forgiveness. I was sure that that was the end of his fucking around for at least three days.

Jean Marc had nicknamed me Michelin Man because of my use of rubber and I often encountered incredulity and laughter at my caution. About six months after I was arrested, we received news that Jean Marc had died of an AIDS-related illness in Abidjan.

We met our target by breakfast on Sunday morning and went to rest, promising not to be late at The Dog and Duck. Nobody was. Amazingly, the girls were ready, dolled up in high heels, flimsy bits and pieces and a selection of very good shades. They brought drinks in coolers and the ten of them fitted into three waiting taxis. I left the bike there and climbed in with some of the girls. Peter sat in the front skinning up for 50 miles, pulling over from time to time to distribute his spliffs evenly between the cars.

There was an atmosphere of great excitement and we arrived to find that the beach was almost entirely our own. All of the girls stripped to the waist and, after our first swim, only Jean Marc insisted on keeping his shorts on. We all got stoned, happy and drunk and, as we got ready to leave, one of the girls burst out crying. 'This is the happiest day of my life,' she sobbed.

We ate some fish cooked on the beach by a fisherman's wife and left for Abidjan. I had a bet with Jean Marc and drove his Peugeot all the way back, steering only with my knees. This time he paid.

Back at The Dog and Duck, the party continued. I went to shower in the boss's girlfriend's small ground-floor apartment. She told me that she was one of his first workers and had arrived from Morocco at the age of 16. By the end of the tour of duty, she had established the relationship, which they both found convenient. She had run the place like a benign mother superior ever since. They spent what time they could together whenever he could get away from his wife. He was a jealous man and would not have approved of what she did with the English resort developer that Sunday evening.

Funnily enough, Lamine had not shown his face all day and the girls happily got ready to go to Treichville with us, forgetting that, within hours, they might all be abducted and have every ounce of blood drained from their bodies before being tossed to the vultures. We left again in convoy and had a riot dancing, drinking, laughing and snogging until dawn. We bought breakfast of omelettes and fruit by the roadside and returned to The Dog and Duck. I fell into bed with one of the girls where we slept until late, naked but unaroused, tenderly sharing a mutual release from excess.

Peter left on the Tuesday flight to Paris. Tears rolled down his cheeks as he bade farewell to Tarzan. I stayed on while the consignment was taken to the docks. Jean Marc and I supervised the total cleaning of the warehouse and machinery, while we waited for the bills of lading and shipping documents, which I would take to London.

Before I left, I was happy to spend a long day with Ami who arrived with another new girlfriend. That evening, I took Mme Diplomat to dinner. And, before leaving, I bade farewell to Tarzan. I am sure I left an unpaid bill at The Dog and Duck.

25

A WARNING

The consignment arrived around October. It was the largest amount of timber we had ever imported at any one time and it took up more space than we expected. Dave continued to supply the market with iroko but the demand was small. In any event, rough-sawn planks of quality hardwood with nail holes were more than somewhat irregular and could arouse suspicion. In due course, large amounts of this beautiful timber were sawn up and given away for fireworks parties. The bookkeeping was well managed by Dave and his VAT returns were engineered so that we made a small payment every quarter.

Moving that amount of grass was bound to take a long time and there was nothing we could do to halt the deterioration in quality. After breaking down the bales, the cannabis was moved to a series of stashes from where it was distributed. Despite all the usual problems, it was still bringing in a great deal of money.

Kwame, true to form, monopolised the incoming calls on my telephone. We had never screwed him out of a penny, but still he persisted. He was paranoid and judged others by his own standards.

Jean Marc finally left Air Afrique. He had made a lot of money from our 'joint activities' and took a well-earned break. He returned to France for a long holiday where it was also much easier to collect his share of the proceeds as the money rolled in. I enjoyed our regular meetings.

Emily would be 17 in March 1987 when she would become eligible for a licence to race cars. We decided that this was the route to take and I came to an arrangement with a team run by David Sears. A Formula Ford car was prepared for Emily's use and we spent the winter months practising mostly at Snetterton in Norfolk. The opening race in the championship was to be at Silverstone the day after Emily's birthday.

It did not take long before Emily began to turn in competitive times. The car was a very different animal to a kart and had much less grip. The gearbox was also new to her but, with the help of some of the best expertise available, she was ready for the new season.

One winter's evening at Snetterton, shortly before the end of practice, Emily's car took longer than usual to come into view. Word soon came through that there had been an accident at the end of the long straight. I was in the pits at the time. I jumped in my car to get to the accident and arrived to find Emily already standing unhurt beside the wreckage of her racing car.

It transpired that, as the light began to fade, ice had begun to form on the track. At over 130mph, Emily hit the brakes at the usual point at the end of the straight. The car hit the banking and proceeded to roll, disintegrating as it gradually came to a halt. We all had to come to terms with the fact that this was part of a normal day's work for a racing driver.

As the season approached, more and more drivers began to appear for practice sessions. Cars were being bought, teams were hiring mechanics and budgets were being scratched together for the annual spendfest of the hopelessly addicted.

I had been a keen shot for most of my life. During the time I had the lease of the grouse moor, I had formed some good connections and, with a combination of invitations and as a paying member of a syndicate, I continued to shoot quite regularly every winter.

I had joined a syndicate on a shoot near to the estate where the mad bad Earl of Dashwood ran his 'Hellfire Club' near High Wycombe. Apart from an elderly but ramrod-straight retired brigadier and a myopic farmer who seemed to miss everything except owls, most of the 'guns' were successful London-based businessmen. It was a good shoot, the birds were plentiful and well presented by a well-selected band of keepers. The shoot had quite a number of white pheasants, an albino mutant which was very rare.

There was a tradition that anyone who shot one of these beautiful birds would have to pay for a case of Glenfiddich malt whisky by way of a fine. The misfortune would occur from time to time in the heat of the moment as 'flushes' of large quantities of birds would fly towards the guns. One day, as we were driven back to lunch, we noticed that our farmer was missing. A search party found him trying to bury a white pheasant with his hands. He paid a double fine.

The day would always end with a game of poker. Playing late into the night, the usual suspects, with more money than sense, would more often than not provide me with a weekly pension. I remember one time driving away with several thousand pounds stuffed into my pockets. My oldest daughter, Lucy, who often came with me, spent most of the journey home counting the winnings and laughing as she found money in every possible opening in my jacket.

Oscar continued to do well. He had come second in his class at the British Championships. The weather was often wet at that time of the year and he was always at his best in adverse conditions. His spectacular control and daring overtaking manoeuvres always attracted a crowd of admiring spectators.

I was beginning to tire of our business from the Ivory Coast. I was concerned that, like throwing a pebble in a pond, as the business got bigger and bigger, more and more people got to know about it. None of my friends knew what I was up to, but I was increasingly concerned that my associates were not as discreet or careful.

Lamine came to London. He had never been out of Africa before and I was happy to do my best to make his stay enjoyable. I installed him in a comfortable central London hotel, gave him a tour of the sights and took him to lunch. We spoke at length about the divide between the African way and the need in the UK to view the authorities with more trepidation. I thought that I was getting through for a short while but eventually realised that it was a hopeless cause. He had been good to us and gave us enough assistance to make the Ivory Coast user-friendly for what we had to do. From my experience, the commodity was not important. Without local help and influence, even the most innocent of activities in Africa were doomed to failure.

The racing season occupied a great deal of time. With one or two practice days a week as well as a race meeting, we were always on the road. Emily was doing well. She would always qualify on the front three rows of the grid and put in a fighting performance. I was not there to see her first win of the season at Brands Hatch in the Easter of 1987. I was with Oscar at a championship kart meeting in the Lake District where he won his class, narrowly beating David Coulthard in the final. We drove back south to witness Emily winning again on the Easter Monday at Castle Coombe, as well as walking away with the driver of the day award.

The Managing Director of Brands Hatch, John Webb, approached me. His wife Angela was very much a champion of women in motor sport and Emily's talent was being noticed. The net result was that we landed a sponsor with money, race tracks and, best of all, influence. Emily had free testing at all the group circuits and access to Brands Hatch for a couple of hours in the evenings. She was given the best of engines and equipment and the PR department made regular use of their pretty young protégée. We were given invitations to trackside hospitality suites and the run of the facilities. Emily, already accustomed to television appearances, was in demand and it looked like her future was secure. She received two *Blue Peter* badges and taught the lovely Caron Keating, who later tragically died of breast cancer, to drive a racing car.

One day I received a strange telephone call. 'Is that Paul Newman?'

'Yes... who's calling?'

'Let's just say I'm a friend. Can we meet?'

'Can you tell me what it's in connection with?'

'I'd rather see you face to face.'

I was intrigued. 'Where are you?'

'In a call box at the bottom of your road.'

The Dutch House, a big old roadhouse on the A20 half-a-mile from Norlesden House, had a telephone box at the entrance to the car park. I drove down and a man of similar vintage to myself climbed in.

'Where can we go to talk privately?' he asked.

I took him to the house and we sat in the study with some coffee that I'd made on the way through the kitchen. 'Now you know who I am and where I live,' I said. 'Who are you?'

'I'm not going to tell you, but, believe me, I have come as a friend. I don't want money and I have travelled quite a way to be here, so please take what I have to say very seriously indeed.'

He proceeded to warn me about Jim Kavanagh. He knew that we had been working together. He told me that he had been harmed by Kavanagh and did not want to see it happen to anybody else. He would not elaborate. I told him that I had not seen Kavanagh for a long time and heard that he had been arrested. The man insisted that Kavanagh was intent on doing me harm and to heed his warnings. I could not get the man to give me any more information but thanked him for his concern. I drove him to a nearby station and shook his hand. I never found out who he was and never saw him again.

I was spooked by this encounter. I had a very fast car and was always vigilant, using my rear-view mirror all the time. I would take different routes and vary my speed dramatically to expose or shake off any tails that might have been following me. On my way to Roy's house, I stepped up the procedure. Accelerating at stages from 60mph to 160mph, I took a circuitous route and arrived, certain that I had not been followed. My visitor was smart and well spoken; he could have been ex-army or a serving policeman. My mind was racing.

Roy pointed out that we had not had an import for several months. I replied that there was still a lot of cannabis around and a great deal of sales activity. I failed to make him see that my visit was something to be seriously considered. He pointed out quite rightly that Kavanagh had disappeared a long time before. He dismissed my visitor almost as a figment of my imagination.

I had heard enough. We already had one man nicked from not heeding a friendly warning, and I knew that the money I had would not last for ever. I would need to work either legitimately or otherwise, but I knew at that moment that it would never again be with Roy.

26

ON TOP

As the year progressed, income from the last delivery was drying up. We still had quite a lot of stock but I was told that sales were negligible. I was already spending a good deal more money than I was receiving.

I had seen John a few times since he had announced his retirement to go racing but our paths had moved in different directions. Towards the end of the year, John had become a regular visitor to the house again.

It came as no surprise to learn that he had been back working in Ghana. I knew that he had been paid quite well to run a couple of drivers in his F3 team but the income had been inconsistent. Ross Cheever had been very successful with wins in Belgium and France, but I knew that he had brought little money into the team. It did not take a genius to work out that John must have been subsidising the high costs from somewhere.

He had not been completely successful either. Apparently, a delivery which had successfully cleared Customs had recently 'come on top' – in other words, been discovered by the authorities. The timber arrived at his warehouse and needed to be taken off the lorry. The warehouse manager, a genuine 'straight-goer', could not start the forklift. The one that he borrowed from a neighbour to do the job was not man enough, so, undaunted, he decided to break the bands and remove the stacks of timber piecemeal. As soon as he began to split the first bale, he found the packages of cannabis. Unable to call his boss, he contacted Customs to explain that he must have received the wrong delivery.

John and I both agreed that we wanted out. Both of us wanted to make enough to be able to retire and agreed to pool our resources for one very large, last importation combining the best of our contacts and suppliers. Michael Bateson, a friend of John's, would form an entirely new company for the delivery.

We had never lost a delivery from the Ivory Coast and I was happy with my contacts there. We were all of the opinion that Ghanaian quality was no longer the best in the marketplace. I was reluctant to go to Nigeria but Kwame's grass was the best we had ever received. It sold quickly and at a very high price.

I would have to change my telephone number. If we were relying on Nigeria alone, we should maintain a presence there for as long as the work was under way and supervise the packing of the container ourselves. I had already established that we could not trust to promises or chance. We estimated that we could each clear a little over £1 million if all went to plan.

It was a few days before Christmas and we were already well into planning our retirement importation when John delivered a bombshell. A delivery of his had just arrived and, for three days, he had been unable to get a reply from his warehouse manager. John feared the worst. Their warehouse was on a trading estate in north London and John wanted to drive there and find out for himself. I managed to persuade him that it was a crazy plan; if the delivery had been rumbled, John would certainly be nicked.

We deliberated for a long time. Eventually, I agreed to drive to the warehouse with John. I had no connection and the warehouseman would not recognise me. I could take a sniff around and see if I could spot any unusual activity. John parked a little way away and I got out of the car, making sure once more that John would wait for me until I came out.

As I approached the trading estate, I saw a board advertising vacant units. I walked in and made my way to the estate office. The manager told me that there were two units available and offered to show me round. We walked to one with a board outside. He opened the padlock and I took a look at the building, asking all the right questions.

I could see no sign of any surveillance operation and asked the manager about the second unit. He pointed to another warehouse on a corner. When I asked to see it, he told me that it was not possible to view for a few days because there was something going on he couldn't talk about. That was all I needed to hear. Rapidly winding up the conversation, I prepared to leave to give John the bad news. At that moment, I could see John driving into the estate. Obviously fed up with waiting, he decided to see for himself. He drove straight into a trap. I hurried away as quickly as I possibly could, expecting to have my collar felt at any moment.

John was nicked. I don't know how much difference, if any, his impatience made on that day. It turned out that my house had been under surveillance by Customs and Excise for some time anyway and I had been observed at various meetings. My telephone was tapped but John never called me on it. It may well be that, if John had not gone there, they would have had difficulty connecting him to the conspiracy. As far as I knew, Westbury had never met John and I knew that Appiah didn't know who he was.

I had got away. I had no idea if I had been seen or if I was being followed. I just knew that I had to get as far away as I could and get the news to Michael. I didn't want to go home in case they were waiting for me. I needed time to gather my thoughts. I thought about disappearing for a while but I had no car, no passport and little money with me.

I walked as quickly as I could. A girl I knew was having a party that night and I decided to make for her place in town. I could make a call from there.

I walked for a long time. I hopped on a bus as it was pulling up at a stop; I had no idea where it was heading. After a few stops, I got off, made for a Tube station, took a train to the West End and hailed a taxi to my destination.

I made my call. I was not really in the mood to enjoy the party. I drank a lot, smoked a lot of dope and cursed John for his madness. The party was a long time breaking up but eventually we went to bed. By the time I woke up, I knew what I had to do. Little did I know that this was to be the last time I would make love for many years.

I owed it to Roy to warn him about what had happened; he had no connection with John.

I took a taxi back home to Norlesden House. I had no idea what I might be walking into but decided that I was better keeping cool and facing any music that might come my way. I figured that the only evidence against me was by association and circumstantial.

I got word to Roy. We agreed for him to keep away for a while and give the dealing a break. I didn't feel good. Every day I expected a visit but, as each day passed, I began to loosen up. Christmas went by and then New Year.

A few days in to 1988, on a Sunday, I arrived home to hear that Roy had been looking for me. It was late but I gave him a call.

'I'm on my way over,' was all he said to me.

He lived about an hour's drive away but, after 45 minutes, his car pulled in to my drive. Roy and Peter came in the kitchen door. In the sitting room, Peter told me that Dave Evans had called him early in the day. He was very anxious and wanted to meet urgently. We had been betrayed.

Kavanagh had approached Dave and Steve behind my back and asked them to use our company and warehouse to import a consignment of cannabis from South Africa. He offered them £50,000 each and insisted that nobody, especially me, was to be told about it. They both accepted his offer.

The delivery had arrived the day before and Customs were swarming all over the warehouse. Dave thought that Kavanagh and an accomplice had been nicked at the scene.

I was very shocked by this news. I knew Dave very well and believed him to be totally trustworthy. He knew Kavanagh from karting but his loyalties lay with me. I would have expected Dave to come to me as soon as he had been approached, but he had not. However, we had no alternative but to be realistic.

We talked for a while and agreed to make sure that we had no evidence around to incriminate any of us. Roy and Peter left. I was panic-stricken. I took the car and went to town for a while thinking about 'doing a runner', but eventually decided to go home and wait for what I was sure was the inevitable.

The next morning, before daylight, the front doorbell was answered by my youngest daughter Charlotte.

I was nicked.

27

CHARGED

Two men came into my bedroom. I was sleeping in my underpants and, before I was able to dress, each article of clothing was checked. The house was teeming with people. Most, in plain clothes, split into groups and headed for separate rooms. I picked up a couple of unread books from beside the bed and was led downstairs. Some uniformed policemen, evidently seconded to assist with a thorough search, were in the hall.

A police sergeant said something like, 'It's been a long time coming, Newman, and now the game's up.'

I remember the words so well; they were straight out of *Dixon of Dock Green*. It turned out that he was from the local police station at Chislehurst.

I said nothing. I was told that I had been arrested and was being taken for questioning. I was led out to an unmarked car and sat in the back seat, handcuffed to a plain-clothes Customs officer. The driver placed a magnetic blue rotating light on to the roof of the car and we sped up the road with the siren blaring.

I can't remember exactly what my feelings were but I was deeply concerned for the welfare of my family. The sequence of events leading up to that morning left me fearing the inevitable. Customs closed the house down for the day. No telephone calls were permitted and each of the children was subjected to exhaustive questioning. Only one of them was 18.

I asked where we were going which was met with a non-committal response. I decided to remain silent. I noticed that the door handles in the back of the car had been removed. We sped towards the West End. The car drove through a gate and parked in a courtyard in a building I had not noticed before somewhere near Fleet Street.

I was led up a couple of flights of stairs into a room in which there was a desk and a couple of chairs. On a table beside the desk was a tape recorder. The handcuffs were removed. I was offered breakfast by a well-spoken man who told me that he wanted to speak to me as soon as possible. I refused food but accepted a coffee, which was brought to me by the man to whom I'd been handcuffed. He and the other man sat down and tried gently to persuade me to answer some questions.

'Look, the sooner you co-operate, the sooner you can leave.'

I asked to call my solicitor.

'Who is your solicitor?'

I told him.

'That won't be possible for the moment. Look, all you need to do is answer a couple of questions.'

The tape recorder was switched on. The senior officer recorded a preamble.

'I want to speak to my solicitor.'

'Look, Mr Newman, we just want to clear up a few things. Would you like another coffee?'

I declined. 'Why can I not speak to my solicitor?'

There was a hesitation. 'We have not finished our morning operations.'

Obviously, this was how the police liked to describe 'a series of dawn raids', and they had not nicked everybody yet.

'Besides, we believe there may be a conflict of interest with your solicitor.'

I didn't understand.

Eventually, I confirmed my name and address. I responded to every other question that I would not answer any more questions until I had seen my solicitor. The tape was turned off. I had learned my lesson a few years before – co-operate and be damned.

During the next couple of hours, I was offered sandwiches, cakes, coffee and cooked food. Each time, an attempt was made to get me to talk to them. I was shown a couple of photographs. Black-and-white and grainy, they had been taken from a distance. It became obvious that I had been under surveillance. I didn't relish the thought of having to explain away some of these photos. Some showed me with my African visitors. This was not going to be easy.

On a couple of occasions, I was warned that it might not be wise or possible to use my solicitor and friend of many years, Chris Johnson. Eventually, I was handed the phone. I got through to Chris, who told me that a young partner, Colin Lewis, whom I had come to know quite well, was best qualified to do the job. He would send him straight away but warned me not to answer any questions.

'Just say "No comment",' he advised. He wished me luck and rang off.

It would be quite a wait; Sevenoaks was a bit of a trek. They left me alone with the door open but, each time I picked up a book, one of them would come in, sometimes offering refreshments, at other times trying to engage me in pleasant conversation. I began to realise that these guys were professionals. God, how I wished I had been nicked by the drug squad. Customs had a reputation for being better educated, better trained and more intelligent.

Each time I wanted the lavatory, I was accompanied. On the floor I was on, there were two or three more rooms and I tried to see if I could make out who they had in them. I thought I heard Roy's voice on one occasion. My suspicions were confirmed shortly afterwards when one of the men came in and told me that Roy had been describing his yacht.

I made it clear that I wanted to wait for Colin before I said anything. I was left alone for a while to read.

At lunch, I was hungry and I accepted a sandwich. Another quite stocky man sat with me while I ate. He soon told me that he was a rugby player. I did not ignore him but answered in such a way as to show that I had no intention of engaging him in conversation.

After a while, he asked, 'Tell me, Mr Newman... does the light at the front of your house come on automatically when somebody walks up the drive?'

Any fool knew what a movement-sensitive light was. He was trying to spook me by letting me know that my house had been watched. I made a point of returning to my book, pretending that I had not heard the question.

Colin arrived, looking harassed. He asked me if I had said anything and was pleased to hear that I had not. He was not hopeful about my chances of going home that night and confirmed that Roy and Peter were indeed my neighbours. He said that Customs officers had been to his offices and demanded to have any files that they might have on me and Roy. I had recently introduced Roy to the practice. Chris had refused their demands. Recently, Roy had been taking money to Colin to put on a client account for him, explaining that it was takings from his pubs and clubs.

Colin urged me to allow him to instruct another solicitor on my behalf who specialised in criminal law. He had spoken to one earlier who would be happy to take the case on and to do so on legal aid.

The two men came into the room. Colin confirmed that we were ready for them and the tape was switched on once more. I can't remember what questions they asked me but I replied 'No comment' to them all, even refusing this time to acknowledge my name or address. After several minutes, they got the message, acting quite hurt that, despite all their hospitality, I had chosen to reject their advances.

Colin asked to be alone with me for a while and asked me to consider seriously the wisdom of engaging a criminal specialist. When he left me, it was after dark on that January evening. For the first time that day, I felt alone and vulnerable.

I was taken to a small police station near the Elephant and Castle. None of the others was there. I was checked in, searched, given something to eat and a hot drink and locked in a cell. I had a small argument with the police sergeant into whose custody I had been handed and was given back my lighter. One of the Customs officers had bought me cigarettes earlier with the cash I had in my pockets.

I couldn't remember when I last had such a good night's sleep. The resilient, thin mattress and coarse grey blanket did nothing to impede my rest. I was woken by the key in the lock at breakfast. Police cells had lavatories, but, from that morning on, I was destined to slop out in every prison I went to until I reached Downview four years later.

My interrogators collected me after I had showered and we returned to where we had been the day before. They had not given up but were far less persistent and left me to read for most of the day.

By the end of the afternoon, I was on the move again. Down the stairs there was a Black Maria and, for the first time, I knew who else had been arrested – Roy, Peter, Steve, Dave, Westbury and John's cousin Bill Mollett were either in or waiting to be loaded into the transport. There was no sign of Kavanagh.

'Where's Jeremy Beadle?' I asked, which broke the ice.

The van pulled out of the yard and, within a few hundred yards, Dave spoke up. He related what he had done with Kavanagh and, now sobbing, begged our forgiveness. Nobody was in a retributive mood and Roy took advantage of the moment to tell us that he had omitted to hide the book with which he kept a record of our dealings. It had been found on his kitchen table. Furthermore, when he was searched, Customs found a key to one of our stashes in his tracksuit trousers.

I had already reached my conclusions. Kavanagh had been nicked with our grass or, worse still, he was a Customs plant from the beginning. He had traded us in exchange for getting clean away. Customs had helped him stage the importation from South Africa and he had buried us by making Dave and Steve an offer they couldn't refuse.

Nobody would tell us where we were heading and, when the van arrived at the M3, we were all in a state of total confusion. Our destination was Southampton Police Station. In the cellar of this huge building, which also housed the Magistrates Court, was an underground labyrinth of white-ceramic-tile-lined cells. At the end of these was an ablutions area with two rows of sinks, open-doored lavatory cubicles and two large showers. The whole place smelled of piss and Old Holborn tobacco.

The lengthy process of photographs, fingerprinting, weighing and measuring took us into the early hours. By this time, a selection of local drunks was making such a noise kicking, screaming and vomiting that we had to shout to be heard.

At the very last, we were all charged with conspiracy to import cannabis. I was charged with Kavanagh's piece of work from South Africa, too. It reminded me of the wonderful film *Kind Hearts and Coronets* where the central character played by Alec Guinness, having killed off several members of his own family to inherit a fortune, was eventually convicted of the only murder he had not committed.

It was not a good night's sleep, banged up three to a cell and serenaded by the inebriates of Southampton. The policeman who opened my door to take me handcuffed up the stairs to the courtroom said that the local radio had already made us famous. I offered an autograph.

In the large room was a gaggle of bewigged young barristers, mostly only having been given a dock brief the night before. A few solicitors sat behind them and both press benches were filled to bursting. The magistrates entered and, immediately, one of the barristers got to his feet, complaining that they had not been given access to their clients. There followed an adjournment, during which we were marched down the stairs again and popped back in the cells.

Within a couple of minutes, I was brought to an interview room. My young barrister had come from London on the early train. I asked him what was likely to happen. I naively expected to get bail and was concerned whether sureties could be arranged at short notice; I need not have worried.

The prosecution barrister outlined the foiled importation from

South Africa, which had arrived at Southampton Docks. Now I knew why we had been taken to this God-forsaken hole. He explained that they expected to uncover a massive operation run by international organised crime. When pressed to substantiate his claims by a daring young brief, he sideswiped the issue deftly, by saying that it would be unwise to give details publicly of an ongoing operation. 'Clap them in irons...' 'Take them down...' 'Lock them away...' There was to be no sympathy for any bail applications on that morning.

We were bundled back in the stinking cells until the court business was finished for the day, and we were then whisked off in another van to Winchester Prison.

28

ABANDON HOPE ALL YE WHO ENTER HERE

Winchester Prison is unusually central in the ancient Roman city. Just past the towering cathedral and down a short road, the massive wooden double doors swung back to swallow the prison van. Like Jonah in the belly of the whale, I was a captive; incommunicado in a totally alien environment. For the first time in 40 years, I felt emasculated.

One of the oldest prisons in the country, this brick-and-stone edifice harboured two centuries of human misery and degradation. The gates rolled shut behind us. For a while, we were trapped inside the gatehouse until the galvanised-steel internal gates, swathed in razor wire, opened inwards. The van drove on no more than another hundred yards and parked in front of the 'reception' building.

Handcuffed two by two, we were led in. The screws, blue-sweatered, beetle-booted and behatted, were an entirely different animal. More military than anything else I had encountered before, they were there to let you know who was in charge. For them, humour was not on the agenda. The keys that each of them wore like a badge of office served as a constant reminder that I was no longer master of my own liberty.

In prison, all the work is done by the cons. The all-powerful screws sit and issue instructions and do nothing. They sign forms, provide escort from place to place, they turn keys.... otherwise, they do nothing.

Uncuffed, I was made to stand in front of a screw behind a high desk; my property, noted item by item, was sealed inside a polythene bag and signed for. My money, counted and put inside a cash box, was signed for, too. Divested of my belongings, I progressed further along the well-trodden path of dehumanisation. I became a number – XB 0091. In future, if the screws had to refer to me, it would be by my family name and at Sergeant Major volume.

The whole area was manned by the cons. Reception was a coveted job where property and possessions crossed desks and tables all day long. Occasional gifts of cigarettes, tobacco and valuable toiletries were currency on the wing; these were the semi-barons, the quartermaster's boys.

We were already famous. Regular news updates on local and national radio had sealed our celebrity status. Crimes of this magnitude were rare in local provincial prisons and the coverage did us no harm. Blue plastic mugs of hot sticky tea were pressed into our hands and the store men ensured that we had the pick of the sheets, towels and uniforms. As a remand prisoner, I was allowed my cigarettes and left behind presents of Benson and Hedges with the grateful cons at reception. The euro is restricted to only a few European countries; the 'Bennie' could have taken over the world.

Laden with bedding, plastic piss-pot and a free letter to send home, I was escorted on to the remand wing, which had already been locked down for the night. The four floors, iron walkways and stairs, so familiar to all, echoed to the steel-heeled footsteps of the marching screw. At the end of the wing, a massive, cathedral-like arched window spanned the whole height of the building.

I was given no choice. A cell door was opened and shut noisily behind me. I was to share my first night with Jimmy, an Irish alcoholic vagrant so institutionalised that, within days of release, he would smash shop windows to get back inside. As a regular guest, he gave me a run-down of the dos and don'ts. I was a quick learner and needed as much information as I could get.

Woken regularly by the footsteps of the screws in the night, I had a fitful night's sleep. The cell door was opened at about 7.00am to a cacophony of action. I walked to the sluice for my first slop-out. The stench of that synchronised emptying of buckets assaulted me and will never leave my memory. Then there was the walk down the stairs to breakfast served by the cons under the watchful eyes of the screws, and back to the cell to eat it with plastic on plastic behind a locked door.

Unlocked later in the morning for exercise, I rushed to the SO's (Senior Officer) office and bumped into Bill Mollett, intent on the same mission. Our request to transfer together in order to prepare our cases was granted. I spent the first ten minutes of exercise transferring my bedding and bucket into Bill's cell. Outside, we spent the next 50 minutes marching anti-clockwise around a metal-fenced enclosure topped with rolls of razor wire. Roy approached me. Fully recovered from his short spell of humility in the van on the way to Southampton, he was getting his temper back.

'What the fuck's wrong with me then... ain't I good enough for you?'

The thought of being banged up with Roy filled me with horror. Peter, his son-in-law, felt the same. He had paired up with Steve, leaving Roy to share a cell with his manager Westbury.

'Tell the old cunt to go fuck himself,' was Bill's reaction.

Up in the razor wire, an occasional trainer swung by a lace in the wind. All along the ground beneath the cell windows lay shit parcels wrapped in newspaper and posted through the bars during the night. The atmosphere was friendly enough and the exercise ground was full of men keen to share their notoriety with the London celebs. I was certainly an 'A-list' convict.

Straight after exercise, we were filed past the lunch offerings. It all looked pretty horrendous and I remember Bill and I choosing to be locked up with nothing to eat. We both expected our first visits that afternoon. For the first two weeks, we were able to take advantage of an old rule which entitled unconvicted prisoners food brought in to them on visits. Even a half-bottle of wine was permitted daily. By February, the old tradition was to end and prison food was the only sustenance on offer.

I had met Bill only a couple of times before but I liked him. We both shared the same politics and outlook on life and he had a wicked sense of humour. He had done a short spell in prison before and knew the ropes. A Cockney ducker and diver, he was a resourceful man, able to manipulate his lot to his best advantage.

Over that lunch break, I soon learned that, although we had cigarettes, it was tobacco and cannabis that would give us a trading edge. He had managed to smuggle a little puff in with him and we shared a joint blowing the smoke out of the window.

I received a 15-minute visit from my family. They had driven from London, queued for an hour and had been treated as sub-humans by the staff. During that quarter-of-an-hour, the other cons pointed me out to their visitors as the local radio celebrity. We were all still shell-shocked from the events of the previous few days. My wife and I had been going through a bad patch prior to my arrest, and it was far too early to sort out our respective emotions.

Bill had recently split up from his wife and had moved in with a very sexy young woman. She drove from Hastings to see him. Both lots of visitors had brought generous supplies of food and tobacco.

The hiding of contraband in prison has occupied the minds of millions over the years. There are no hiding places in prison cells. Surprise visits at any time of the day or night were made by 'the burglars' – the security screws. You never knew when the key might turn in the lock and it would be your turn. After a strip-search, you had to stand outside the cell door while your 'peter' was subjected to a 'spin'. Nothing would be left unturned, unread, unopened or untouched. It did not take long before I got used to this regular violation.

Bill and I had obtained an ounce of cannabis resin. We split it and I soon learned how to clamp the stuff firmly between the cheeks of my arse. Later, at Brixton, where strip-searches included a quick squat, I was never to let go of that clingfilm-covered comforter.

God, we got stoned that night. I don't know if it was bravado, the puff, the jokes or anything else but we spent the whole night laughing. Like naughty schoolboys, we would dissolve into fits of giggles at the slightest thing. I was happy to have the company of a kindred spirit.

The next day, anxious to hear what was happening with representation and a bail application, I was permitted to call my solicitor. My first attempt to make contact failed; there was no reply. The procedure was that a screw would make the call and only hand you the telephone when he had established that a connection had been made to the right party. I did not believe the screw's report that this large legal firm did not answer their phone. He persevered and eventually managed to get through to a receptionist. Once I'd been handed the phone, I eventually ascertained that my call had interrupted a full-scale raid by Customs.

The next morning, after a night in the cells in Southampton, my solicitor Colin Lewis arrived on the wing. This was not how I wanted to see my 'brief'. He would spend a week in prison before he got bail and several months before all charges were dropped against him. While he was at Winchester, I did what I could to console him. I knew that he was totally innocent and had no idea where the money he had handled came from, but I was helpless.

The routine continued. At night, Bill and I would talk, smoke and joke but, after Colin arrived, I began to see a more sinister side to my predicament. I knew that Customs powers were almost limitless and, all the time I was behind bars, there was nothing I could do to influence my fate. Sometimes, assisted by paranoia from puffing, I would panic that I might still be under surveillance, filmed and recorded from afar, even through my cell window.

On my first Sunday, the door was opened to the gruff words 'TV'. We came out to see the ground floor of the wing laid out with chairs in front of a big television. When Bill and I found out that the whole wing was about to watch the Omnibus edition of *EastEnders*, we asked to be locked back in our cell. It was with total incredulity that the screw met our request to refuse the weekly cultural experience.

We had all agreed to opt for our right to weekly remand hearings at Southampton Magistrates Court. Our main motive was to cause the maximum possible inconvenience to the prosecution and hopefully keep more up to date with developments.

The day before our first remand hearing, I was brought from my cell to the legal visiting area of the prison to meet my new solicitor, Tom McGoldrick. Of similar age to me, he shook my hand firmly. Out of a carrier bag came cigarettes, sandwiches and biscuits. I was to discover the next day that, on his way to see me, he had stopped at a local newsagent, ordered and paid for a month's supply of the *Guardian* to be delivered to the prison every day.

Tom never received a penny from me; I had little left to give him. He worked on Legal Aid alone and looked after me as if I were his most valued client. He visited me more often than needed, spent hours longer with me than necessary, gave me hope support and encouragement and never arrived empty-handed. A true friend and ally, I shall remain eternally grateful to him 'til the day I die.

He gave it to me straight; he would do everything he could to get me bail but held out little hope. He warned me not to trust anybody and to expect, if it had not already happened, many of my co-defendants to be looking for a back to climb over. He confirmed that, even if the Customs had only a flimsy case for a conspiracy conviction, they could take as long as they wanted to gather and put together a case. They would, he said, be looking for weak links and try to persuade them to turn against us. He painted a bleak picture.

My deepest regret was that Emily's career was in tatters. The story of my arrest had hit the headlines and there were photographs of Emily everywhere. The day after I was arrested, Emily was at Silverstone testing the Formula Three car that she was due to drive that season with serious sponsorship from Brands Hatch and others that John Webb had co-ordinated.

In no time, everybody was running for cover. I am still able to spot a motor-sporting talent and there is no doubt in my mind that Emily was the only female driver I ever saw with the ability, technical understanding and stamina to make it competitively in a Formula One car. Another season and things might have been very different. I shall never know.

The day after I met Tom, we were all back in court. The place was milling with Customs men and the general atmosphere could only be described as smug. Tom had arrived with a different young barrister.

He pressed the prosecution to substantiate any of their allegations and met with the same response as before with the vociferous support of the Bench. My barrister, not satisfied with condemnation by innuendo, remonstrated but was silenced almost before he rose to his feet.

I am of the opinion that the British legal system is a sham hiding behind a façade of respectability. I have done jury service and my impression was that the jurors were more concerned with the charisma and performance of the barristers than justice. So many appalling miscarriages of justice are brought to light with monotonous regularity thanks to the untiring efforts of great men like Paul Foot. However, magistrates and judges continue to refuse to countenance accusations of irregularities by the police. As long as justice is seen to be done, the rest is irrelevant.

Back in the van to Winchester. More hot tea at reception and banged back up behind the door. At least poor Colin got bail.

I had been at Winchester for several days before John arrived. He had been in custody in London and charged with the delivery that failed in north London. Now, he had been drawn into the net, charged with conspiracy and kicked in the bollocks like the rest of us with Kavanagh's bit of work. He was in good spirits and I was pleased to see him. A seasoned campaigner, he had elected to attend remand hearings once a month, not counting on bail.

Michael Bateson had fucked off to Spain when John got nicked but, on a trip back, met with a reception committee at Heathrow and a free ride to Southampton in a police car. He always had a wry smile and a funny comment. He shared a cell with John.

The monotonous daily routine continued. Essentially, the only time I had out of the cell was one hour's exercise each day. Most of the men on the remand wing were local to Winchester and awaiting trial for relatively minor offences. Many could not read or write, had addiction problems and were totally dysfunctional. Most were keen to tell their stories; others were passing through for one reason or another, but one or two had interesting stories to tell.

A German guy was in a cell a few doors away from me. He had

been at Winchester for some months. Resident in Marbella, he had a business ferrying cannabis from Morocco in fast boats on to the Spanish beaches under cover of darkness. He had been making a very good living for some years and was well enough connected to ensure his liberty. He had photos of his spectacular villa and a few rather grainy ones of his yacht. These he told me, had been taken by satellite and formed part of the surveillance evidence against him. He made his money from transport services only, but had allowed himself to accept an offer to get involved in a big operation with a British 'firm'. Told to come to England to get his money for his part of the successful operation, he had been nicked in a sophisticated Customs 'sting'. The evidence against him was quite flimsy and eventually he was returned to Spain to face the music with evidence provided by British Customs to the Spanish authorities.

I helped a lot of men less fortunate than me to write letters home. Many had difficulty grasping the basic realities of the cases against them and I did what I could to assist. Some worked in the kitchens, others in the stores and I would receive the odd present – a lump of cheese, some coffee, an extra pillow. It all came in handy.

Westbury began to befriend me on exercise. I really do believe that he was ex-SAS. I saw enough memorabilia and photographs to convince me. When he was arrested, he had an armoury of weapons in his flat, all legitimately licensed to him. He must have satisfied the police that he was a fit and proper person to own semi-automatic rifles. I can't for the life of me understand what it is that attracts people to this kind of collecting but I do firmly believe that there is some direct negative correlation with performance in the sack.

He told me spine-chilling stories of active service undercover in Ireland. He related tales of being in the initial invasion party at Goose Green in the Falklands war. He talked of a turkey shoot of hundreds of starving and terrified young Argentinean soldiers trying to surrender and orders to take no prisoners.

I was genuinely shocked at his stories. I don't know why he told me, because he knew me well enough to know that I would be anything but impressed. I wanted to write it all down and expose these brutalities. Already jaundiced about the ability of the authorities to manipulate justice, Westbury's revelations did little to inspire confidence in my own chances.

At the first remand hearing, each of the defendants was served with a small bundle of evidence. This was to be a weekly event and, like a legal soap, the plot became increasingly dramatic. The first bundle included a copy of Roy's dealing book, which was to prove to be an insurmountable obstacle. Roy, desperate to find an explanation, tried to use it as proof that the dealings referred to gold. It just did not add up.

Tom McGoldrick was right. Within days, hostilities began to emerge. There were suspicions about legal visits that might have been meetings with Customs; suspicions that statements had been made after the arrests. Every top London criminal specialist solicitor was involved representing us individually and the atmosphere became distinctly competitive.

Tom came again. I had said nothing during my custody interview and had declined to be led into friendly conversation. There was no doubt that I had been under surveillance and my phone had been tapped. Nothing had been found to incriminate me at my house but my passport had been found during the raid on my solicitor's office. They had photographs of me with Lamine and Kwame in London. There were numerous stamps in my passport that had to be explained. However, not one single importation from the Ivory Coast had been discovered.

A case would have to be proved against both Kwame and Lamine to incriminate me and I knew that the chances of bringing them before a British court were slim indeed.

Tom thought that, as things stood, I had a fighting chance but he warned me that Customs would be hard at work to piece the jigsaw together and bury us all. I had already been described in court as the ringleader and I was their number-one target. I spent a long time at night in discussion with Bill.

There was very little to hold Bill, some circumstantial and association evidence only, and that was flimsy. He arranged with his solicitor that, at the third weekly remand hearing, he would make a bail application. He held out high hopes.

One afternoon, two days before the hearing, a screw came to the cell and announced that Bill had a legal visit. He looked surprised. He returned two hours later and told me that this unexpected arrival was from Customs. He told me that they had informed him that they would not object to bail but, if he helped them with information, they would also drop the charges against him. He told them to fuck off.

On the day of the hearing, Bill gave me his radio, nearly an ounce of puff and a few very rude nude photographs of his girlfriend. Bill's application was the first item of business. I have never seen him since.

Within months, charges were dropped against him. His naughty girlfriend wrote to me regularly and sent me more rude photos and always a message of encouragement from Bill. He never needed to tell me that he had received a visit from Customs and I would never have known.

After Bill's departure, we were led into the dock once more. Unexpectedly, my barrister got to his feet and addressed the court: 'So far, the prosecution in this case has failed to bring before this court any concrete evidence whatsoever against my client. Already several weeks have elapsed in this matter. There is no more against my client than there is against Mr Mollett, who has just left the court a free man. We therefore request that Mr Newman be granted bail.'

I was shocked.

The prosecution barrister called the leader of the Customs team to the dock. 'Mr Newman has been under surveillance for several months; his telephone has been tapped and he speaks fluent French and Italian... we believe that he is a central figure in international organised crime and that granting him bail would seriously damage our preparation of the case against him and others.'

The magistrates were all ears.

'We intend to make investigations on a worldwide scale and to make more arrests of key figures in the conspiracy,' he continued.

Would I get bail? I had more chance of seeing the Lord.

Michael Bateson got bail on that day. Customs were playing a shrewd and well-rehearsed game; by appearing to be reasonable and letting some of the minnows back into the river, they could increase the focus on those they wanted badly. The minnows could always be netted again later. As things go, Michael broke the conditions of his bail within two weeks and swam his own way back into the keep net of Winchester Prison.

In the van on the way back, I reflected that I had lost my cellmate. I need not have worried. As soon as I returned to the wing, the SO told me that I had been moved upstairs to a cell of my own. I had been made a 'Double Category A Prisoner' – a threat to national security. I had been 'kicked upstairs' into the midst of the criminal aristocracy.

29

ON THE BOOK

That night, the puff remained firmly clenched between my cheeks. I needed a clear head to think. There had to be some mistake. I saw myself as not much more than a bootlegger, a purveyor of contraband. Surely Customs knew that what they said in court was a load of bollocks. According to Tom, they could keep me where I was for a good deal longer. It was patently obvious that the prosecution had the magistrates eating out of their hands. If they had alleged I was the devil incarnate, the Bench would have believed them.

I began to explore the deeper, darker recesses of my mind. Was Westbury a plant? Had he told them that he had told me too much? Was I about to be quietly disposed of? I might only be on the first floor now, but could I be several thousand feet above Hampshire tomorrow. A final freefall, a dive in the dark. What the fuck was going on? Who could I appeal to? What could I do? Where could I go?

I already knew the answers – I decided to go on hunger-strike.

The next morning, unlocked for breakfast, things were different. This time, only a handful of doors were unlocked and half-a-dozen of us filed down two flights of stairs to the hotplate. Four of my new colleagues were in 'patches'. This is the very distinctive yellow and blue uniform, not even vaguely sartorially elegant, that identifies the escapees – the E Cats. Nods were exchanged all round. I did not take my plate and made a point of refusing everything on offer.

The screw at the end of the line, hardly looking up, said, 'Refusing food, Newman?'

'Yes.'

'I'll make a report,' he said in a bored sort of way.

Not more than five minutes after being banged back up, the key turned in the lock. In came the SO of the day, a small gruff Welshman, not known for his conversation. In his hand was a plate of bacon and eggs. He sprung the lock and pulled the door to behind him.

'They don't give a fuck if you live or die,' he said offering the plate.

'Why should you bother to do this?' I said.

He didn't reply.

'Why have I been made Cat A?'

'You'll have to apply to see the Governor and ask him. I don't know and, if I did, I wouldn't tell you.'

I asked him to put me on the Governor's list, took the plate and thanked him.

I sat at the table. I was alone. It was an unusual experience for me and I was not sure if I would ever come to terms with it. From a practical point of view, it had its advantages. From the first day, I had only ever pissed in the bucket, using the lavatory on the wing in the mornings. That was how I intended to carry on. I would not have to share another man's personal habits. I only liked to listen to classical music and would have to make no compromises. I could have a wank whenever the urge took me. If only I could find a way of getting used to the solitude, I could at least become master of my own tiny environment.

The SO came to get me for Governor's 'parade'. It was common practice for the 'cons' to call the screws 'Guv'nor' or just plain 'Guv'. I never did, it just wasn't in my vocabulary. I was lucky to have an expensive education and I am well spoken. I never pretended to be anything else and could not and would not bring myself to talk like a Cockney sparrer. As far as I was concerned, the Governor was the man I was brought in to see.

He was seated behind the SO's desk. In army fashion, the SO stood beside me. This was a young assistant Governor. One seldom saw the engine driver.

'Governor, why have I been made Cat A?'

'It's not a decision made by the prison,' he replied. 'Your security status has been decided by the Home Office.'

'Then why has it taken three weeks before I have been considered a threat to national security?'

'I can't answer that.' His body language let everybody in the room know that the interview was over.

In the cell next to the SO's office, the con whose job it was to distribute household items slipped me a box of tissues as I passed.

A and E Cat exercise had just begun and I was escorted to a different yard through another wing. This little enclosed area was used by condemned prisoners awaiting execution in an adjoining cell not so many years before. Their remains lay in unmarked graves near by.

A couple of the guys in patches had vaulted the dock in the local Magistrates Court and been picked up at 'mum's' or the 'girlfriend's' later, real professional criminals. My other Cat A colleagues were murderers awaiting trial. This was not a prison that catered for maximum-security prisoners. There are local Crown Courts just as capable of trying serious crimes as the London show courts and, usually, the place of the crime dictates the place of trial. Once convicted, Cat A prisoners would be moved out of the local prisons and into others designed to accommodate them.

We stopped at the library on the way back to the wing. I was surprised to see a really fine selection of reading matter and a representative from the local library service more than happy to help. There were so many classics I wanted to reread having rejected out of hand any that might have been recommended by my teachers, whom I despised. Any set books I had to read in order to pass exams were grudgingly speed read and discarded as soon as possible. I chose two by Thomas Hardy – *Tess of the d'Urbervilles* and *Jude the Obscure*. I took a couple more and reckoned that I had enough to digest until the next week's visit.

Not permitted to carry any money whatsoever, spending at the weekly visit to the canteen was restricted to wages earned from prison work. Those who did not work or, like Cat As, were not allowed to, received a bare minimum of, I think, £1.20 a week. The maximum wage for workers in the most responsible jobs was no more than six or seven pounds. Everything barring batteries and newspapers had to be purchased from this weekly pittance. It was certainly not enough for habitual smokers and the situation was therefore biased towards the resourceful. If a half-ounce of Old Holborn was borrowed one week, you had to return three-quarters the next. A 16th-of-an-ounce of cannabis was worth two ounces of tobacco.

The class structure in prison encompasses many layers, rather like the Indian caste system, from the 'Barons' at the top to the untouchable 'paraffin' (paraffin lamp – tramp) 'swooping' for discarded dog-ends at the bottom. Like Indian society, it was not an entirely commercially dictated hierarchy. The wise men like the Brahmins and the Rajput aristocrats often received gifts and privileges in recognition of their status.

Anyone setting up shop in prison had to be sure to be able to enforce the repayment of debts. These were non-negotiable and due on the nail. Hard-luck stories or extended promises were a waste of breath. Any sign of weakness would precipitate an avalanche of piss-taking and enforcement had to be seen to be done. There were more stabbings and beatings over a half-ounce of tobacco than for any other reason.

Sex offenders, grasses and convicted policemen all fall into the Rule 43 category, established for the protection of certain classes of prisoner from the rest. Often, a cell door could be heard opening during lunchtime bang-up of a con unable to pay his debts who, fearing retribution, had 'gone on the numbers'. Some might resurface on the wing at another establishment but would often pay the price, having been recognised by somebody who knew his story.

On remand, I didn't need to be trading. I was able to receive cigarettes and toiletries from my family. I used to give the odd gift in exchange for the few extras that I received but didn't want it known that I had organised a regular supply of puff.

I decided to settle in as best I could. I was effectively in solitary; apart from an hour a day rotating in a prison yard, I was locked up alone.

I rang the bell. After a while, a screw came to the door and slid aside the peephole. 'What do you want?'

'I'd like to clean out my cell.'

I don't remember how long I had to wait before my request was granted but, at some time during the day, I was able to spend a good hour sweeping and scrubbing until my 10 foot by 8 foot domain was clean. I arranged the space as best I could and, with some Blu Tack, stuck some photographs on the wall.

Cat A security status is normally reserved for terrorists, senior Mafiosi, non-domestic murderers, household names and the cream of serious criminals. Described inside as 'On the Book', each Cat A has a book into which every movement has to be written by an obligatory uniformed escort. Some of the heaviest criminals who never achieve a lower-security status on the day of their release have written 'escort to gate' as a final entry.

Visitors to Cat A prisoners have to be screened and approved by Special Branch to whom a written request has to be sent. It is a rigorous process.

A very good friend of mine, who is an airline pilot, duly applied for approval to visit me. He received a visit from a very courteous plain-clothes officer who, having asked a few questions, indicated that it should be a formality for him to be added to the list of my visitors. A couple of days later, he had an overnight stopover in Amsterdam. He left his hotel to go to dinner and returned to find that his attaché case was missing from his room. When he went down to reception, he was handed the case and told that it had been given in a few minutes earlier by a well-spoken Englishman. In due course, he received visiting approval and remains convinced to this day that dark forces were at work in the Netherlands.

My friends were followed, their telephones were tapped and they were stopped at the roadside and questioned. My son was stopped and searched almost every time he went out at night. If the whole procedure was designed to spook me, they had succeeded.

Tom McGoldrick was shocked when I called him with the news. Not wanting to discuss the matter on the telephone, he told me that he would come to see me again the day before the next remand hearing. He gave me words of encouragement and, together, we resolved to fight all the harder.

On the second day, we were joined by Greg, another young chap in patches. Awaiting trial for armed robbery, he had made a run for it through the Magistrates Court and got away. He managed to avoid capture for several weeks but it had been hard sometimes living rough. He was eventually caught at a friend's house where he had gone to get fresh clothes and some money. He said that he wanted to get back to a London prison and hated Winchester. One of the Cat A remand prisoners, he told me, was a 'nonce', a sex offender who had raped and killed a child. Greg planned to get him in the showers after exercise.

The ensuing scene in the showers had a Keystone Cops element. True to his word, Greg steamed into the man. He smashed his head against the white-tiled wall of the communal showers. The nonce slid to the floor with his blood streaming down the wall and coursing down the plughole in the middle of the floor. Hearing the commotion but allowing enough time to elapse for the nonce to get badly hurt, two screws eventually tried to bring the incident to an end.

Greg was not ready to comply with shouted orders to stop and the screws had no option but to come to the rescue. Rubber-soled, beetle-crusher boots and slippery wet ceramic floors don't make a grippy combination. Like a pair of drunken skaters on the ice for the first time, the screws spent more time on the floor getting soaked under the still running shower than upright. The net result was that we never saw the nonce again. Convicted of crimes that make my stomach turn, he remains in prison where I hope he stays for the rest of his life, unable to inflict his evil on another poor victim. Greg failed to get his transfer to London out of it and received a perfunctory penalty for his assault from the Governor. One of the screws took his dousing in good spirits and was regularly offered shampoo when on shower duty.

I remember getting a 'spin' a day after I had spent so long putting my cell in shape. The burglars walked in on me just after lunch. I had managed to acquire an extra pillow and mattress as a result of looking after a couple of the right workers on the wing. One of the screws seemed to be in favour of relieving me of them but it came to nothing. It took me a while to put everything back in place; the one thing I had plenty of was time.

The *Guardian* became my constant friend and companion. One of the things you are allowed to buy outside of your prison earnings is a daily newspaper. Batteries, too, could be purchased from 'private spends' which was kept in a second account for each prisoner. Newspapers could either be ordered from within the prison or by visitors outside. On occasions during my time 'away', my patience would be tested. Missing newspapers, letters and misplaced VOs (visiting orders) were a favourite weapon.

I read the daily paper from cover to cover and, at Winchester, began to take an interest in the crossword. I set about learning the ropes back to front, looking at the answers and working out the logic of the cryptic questions from the clues of the day before. It was a gradual process but, after about three months, I successfully completed my first. The warm glow from picking up my daily *Guardian* stays with me to this day.

By the time Tom came, I was beginning to calm down about my new security status. Tom warned me that it would affect my already slim chances of getting bail in the Magistrates Court. The procedure was that I got one shot at bail before the Bench and then another before a High Court judge. Tom was of the opinion that we should choose our timing wisely, ideally at the critical point where the prosecution would be seen to have had enough time to gather evidence and had little to show for it. He thought that another week or even two would be right for the first application and to move straight ahead with the second immediately thereafter. Tom was more concerned about trying to get the case transferred to a London Crown Court, where juries were more diverse. This would mean moving to a London prison, too.

The next morning was a revelation. Handcuffed to a screw on the journey to reception, I was led to a very different vehicle to take me to court. The Cat A van awaited me in the yard. A large armoured truck, it contained six tiny separate compartments with just enough room inside each to sit down. With my wrists now cuffed together, I was locked into one of the compartments. We drove out of the prison yard.

Next to my seat was a blackened one-way window from which I could see quite well. As the great wooden doors of the prison opened, I saw our escort. A line of four police cars and motorbikes were already waiting in line outside. The police in the rear were flak-jacketed and carried small sub-machine guns. They all wore dark-blue beanie hats and a selection of killer sunglasses.

Sirens blaring, the motorcade moved off, stopping vehicles along the way through town in their tracks. Above, a police helicopter led the way, the staccato stutter of the blades clearly audible from within the van.

The M27 motorway had been closed for the journey to Southampton and the police escort took up their position straddling the road two ahead and two behind. This Mafioso motorcade, this Palermo Popemobile far beyond the imaginations of Kafka and Magritte combined, traversed the Hampshire countryside in my honour.

Arriving at court in Southampton in record time, I glanced upwards as I was led from the vehicle to see several armed police on surrounding rooftops pointing their weapons straight at me.

My barrister, another new dock brief, was visibly impressed. Tom told me that everybody entering the court had been searched and bags inspected. In all his years as a criminal specialist, he had never seen such a spectacle. Each central character, basking in the reflective glory of this Hollywood blockbuster, seemed to be enjoying the experience. The magistrates, cloth-eared to any pleas for reason, committed me down the dock stairs back into the bowels of the Earth.

This lunacy must have cost the taxpayer more in one day than I earned in six years. I resolutely determined from that day to continue to insist upon my right to be brought every week before the Southampton Bench for remand.

Increasingly, as the case attracted more and more London legal expertise, the pressure mounted for the case to be transferred. Many of the defendants were already securing the services of top QCs but still there was no sight whatsoever of a timescale. The prosecution were in a cosy position with the case remaining in Southampton. The magistrates were a pushover, satisfied on each occasion by the slightest suggestion that this was a matter of national importance and that international investigations took a great deal of time.

The Rule of Law flew out of the window and was used as a weapon against us. On one occasion, after the prosecution had alleged that they were on the trail of deposits of millions of pounds in banks all over the world, my barrister succeeded in pressing them to quantify their case. The response was that, because, despite the massed investigative forces of the combined expertise of Customs, they had found nothing, it proved that I was even more of a mastermind than first alleged.

We continued to be served weekly with new items of evidence. A piece of paper was found in the company office in my handwriting, which I had given to Dave. On it was the wording requesting prices for timber and shipping details. At the time, I had told Dave to dispose of it when the fax had been typed and sent.

The warehouse had been found in Abidjan with bales of timber in the yard. Some evidence had been found to indicate that wood had been sawn and nailed. Each individual item was circumstantial and had been brought together cleverly to show a general picture that supported the charges.

Despite pressure from an increasing array of wigged and gowned barristers, no dates were even suggested for committal hearings. The Bench continued to indulge the prosecution in every way. And so the charade continued. My mad transport arrangements were repeated weekly and Tom held out no hope that they would be changed.

The routine at Winchester had no surprises in store for me. I was lonely frequently enough. Time, without human contact, sometimes dragged as if holding one's breath under water. I was alive; I kept my brain exercised; I wrote endless letters; I read my paper, worked at the crossword and I had my music.

One evening, deep into Hardy's *Tess*, I came upon a description of the arrival of Tess for execution at Winchester Prison. As if haunted by a ghostly manifestation, the hairs on the back of my neck rose chilled as I followed the detailed description of the very edifice in which I was sitting. This had been written from the perspective of the high ground I could see daily from the exercise yard. Each turret, wall and window unmoved and unchanged bleakly described by the author who must have sat with pen in hand sketching the scene in words.

One day, another arrival appeared in the exercise yard. About ten years my senior, this quietly spoken man joined us on our daily march to nowhere. Eddie Richardson, his reputation already gone before him, had been charged with a conspiracy to import. Like us, because the alleged importation had arrived via Southampton, he had been brought to Winchester Prison. Softly spoken, informed and well read, Eddie knew the ropes and had trodden this well-worn path before. He had an incredibly retentive memory, knew everybody and could converse on pretty much any subject. Circulating the little exercise yard, we discussed our respective cases and many other subjects besides.

We shared the same 'manor' in south London where he had run a series of very successful businesses. We both belonged to the same squash club in Blackheath but our paths had never crossed before. His case was transferred to London and he moved on to Brixton where we were to meet again. He was convicted on the flimsiest of evidence and received a savage sentence, twice as long as it would have been had his name been anything other than Eddie Richardson.

Week after week, the prosecution succeeded in resisting pressure to agree a date for the committal hearing. There was agreement that we would opt for what was called an 'old-style committal', which would take the form of a mini-trial. The advantage from our point of view was that the prosecution would have to show their evidence or at least as much as would guarantee that the case would be set down for trial. The disadvantage was that the defence would have to show a large enough part of their case to show that there was insufficient evidence to allow the case to continue. It was estimated that the proceedings would take at least two weeks.

Customs arrived in the Ivory Coast and returned with a folder of photographs and a statement from Jean Marc who, they said, was in custody. I didn't believe them. Two weeks later, we were told that he had died. I had no idea that he had been ill. It had been not that long before I was arrested that we had met for the last time in Paris for a couple of days and he had been in good spirits. I mourned his death, privately remembering the Gallic rebel with the comic French accent when he spoke the few words he knew of English. He was 'may freeyend'.

Finally, a date was set aside for the committal which would take place at Southampton Crown Court before a London Stipendiary Magistrate sitting alone as a qualified judge. It was to take place ten months after I had been originally charged, an inordinately long time.

During the intervening period, I was refused bail at the Magistrates Court, where I was present, and, one week later, before a High Court judge, where I was not. The Welsh SO came to my cell one afternoon to tell me the news.

Tom told me that at one time during the application he really thought I was going to succeed. It was not to be.

Greg, my friend in patches, escaped once more, this time from the prison bus taking him to court. He had slipped his handcuffs, overpowered one screw and frightened another enough to unlock the door and set Greg free. He was to receive an extra sentence for his trouble but spent some time on the run before recapture. He was not brought back to Winchester.

Tom came down to see me more frequently as the committal hearing loomed closer. I was to be represented by a QC and a highly respected junior barrister for the event. He came to Winchester a few times with Tom. My barrister was hopeful that the evidence against me was circumstantial. He believed that, in the absence of more evidence, I stood a good chance of an acquittal before a jury but, considering the evidence against the rest of the defendants, we would stand little chance of the case being thrown out of court at committal. He believed that the trial would be transferred to London, maybe to the Old Bailey, especially because the magistrate had been sent from London.

My escort never changed. My barrister was concerned that, because of my security status, the prosecution would be asking for a 'minded' jury throughout the trial. The trial would take several months and he told me that the prosecution would have a great advantage if each juror had a police or Customs 'minder' able to influence them against us on a daily basis. I would also be at mercy of the 'no smoke without fire' argument. I could just see it – 'Why would they spend all that money and effort putting him on the Cat A list and guarding the jury from threats and bribes if they thought he was innocent?'

On the morning of the first day of the committal hearing, we were all served with a long and detailed statement by Harry Appiah. We had been betrayed. The court, full of irate barristers, granted a half-day adjournment to consult with their clients.

Appiah, now in prison himself, convicted of an unrelated charge, had sung like a fucking canary. His detailed statement told everything – our meetings in London with the politicians and Kwame; our activities in Abidjan. He had spilled the lot, even naming the others in Africa and offering a detailed description of the warehouse. He told how he had organised the carrying of the cannabis over the border and how, with Tundi and his brother, it had been brought to the warehouse for packing. He gave details of the sales of the stuff in London and mentioned by name everyone involved in distribution.

My QC was shocked but not daunted. Appiah had been described as a police informant and would, no doubt, have negotiated a deal, especially as he was serving a sentence on another matter. It might be possible to show that he had been led by the officers asking the questions and words put into his mouth. If that could be done, his evidence could be discredited.

Appiah gave evidence for several days. A few minutes after he had entered the witness box, there was a commotion. One of the Customs men in court reported that Roy had been observed drawing his hand across his neck at Appiah. I did not see it and Roy strenuously denied ever having done it, but it had the desired effect for the prosecution. The magistrate warned us all that, if another similar incident occurred, he would clear the dock and continue without us all. From that point on, Appiah had the sympathy of the court.

Each barrister skilfully tried to establish that Appiah's statement had been manufactured for him and that he had been schooled repeatedly as to its contents. Initially, the court was told that Appiah's statement had been made during two visits. A stroke of genius by one of the barristers subpoenaed the prison official visits record which showed that, in fact, he had been visited five times more, but it was to no avail.

Appiah did not crack. There were inconsistencies in his evidence and he admitted that his 'memory had been jogged' while making the statement but, on the whole, he made a good witness for the prosecution. The chances of my case being thrown out at committal had flown out of the window.

After two weeks of evidence, argument, vitriol and betrayal, the case was committed for trial at the Old Bailey. Already packed, I was collected from my cell two days later for the journey in my Popemobile to Brixton.

30

BRIXTON – THE CHAPS

My family had never missed a visit. For the first couple of weeks after my arrival at Winchester, they had come every day. Quite apart from the expense, it was a hell of a distance and all of it for half-an-hour's hurried conversation. Emily came to see me on her 18th birthday, but she could not contain her emotions and left the visiting room after five minutes in tears. The pressure was now relieved with my transfer to London. Although our relationship had been strained before my arrest, my wife stood by and provided me with every support.

It was an odd feeling. Already ten months behind bars, I had begun to get used to my own company and it wasn't that bad after all. Sometimes, days on end of 'inclement' weather would see the exercise hour cancelled and, apart from short trips to the hotplate, I would have no human contact. Writing, reading voraciously, keeping up with the news and labouring over the crossword helped me to maintain my sanity.

Unlike so many prisoners consumed by hatred, I harboured no anger for those who had put me behind bars. I knew the risks I was taking and had enjoyed the rewards. I recognised that it was now the role of Customs to make a case and make it stick. Already a cynic, I was not shocked at the manipulative tactics used against me but I could not help the feeling of surrealism at my situation and, in particular, my security status.

Several years at a British public school had served as a good apprenticeship for prison. From an early age, I learned that you never snitch on your colleagues. You decide if and when you face up to your own music but never take others with you. I learned a code of honour and pride during my childhood, which I have adhered to all my life. It did shock me to see how many conspiracies were torpedoed by grasses, willing to sink to any depths to gain even a small personal advantage.

I harboured a hatred for Appiah and still, to this day, despise him for what he did. I should have known better for trusting everybody around me and I should have been stronger, insisting that there would be no deviations from a 'need to know' policy.

I was a realist. The prosecution had won the first round and we had not put a single point on the scoreboard. What more might they have in store for us?

Around the time I was arrested, a new law had been introduced which entailed the confiscation of convicted prisoners' assets. No longer up to the prosecution to prove that these assets had been acquired from the proceeds of crime, the tables had been turned. It was now the defendant who had to prove that the confiscated goods and money were purchased with legitimate income if he wanted to keep them. The maximum sentence for the importation of cannabis was 14 years but the courts could impose up to an extra ten for non-compliance with confiscation orders.

Apart from a little money, I had spent what I had earned and, but for a few possessions, there was little left to show for it. Because the law was new and untested, we did not know how it could be applied and, for some time, my legal team and I feared that I could be looking at a total sentence of 24 years.

Whatever the sentence, apart from life tariffs, there is an automatic discount of one-third for good behaviour. That third can be diluted in varying amounts by misdemeanours committed in prison. Penalties under the new law in lieu of confiscation specifically excluded time off. I calculated that I could theoretically be made to serve 19 years behind bars.

These kinds of thoughts were destructive. I had to find a way of pushing them out of my mind and thinking positively. Sometimes, all alone, it was hard – very hard – but I never wavered even for a moment from my principles.

Another reception, another prison. After the usual process of induction, I was taken on quite a long walk by my Cat A escort to a special unit called A Seg. Effectively a prison within a prison, this part of the building had been constructed exclusively for Cat A inmates. Accessed at the end of a normal wing, a large heavy door opened to reveal a space on two floors with about 40 cells. It had its own exercise yard and staff and there was no contact at all with the rest of the prison population.

I had heard about this unit and, as soon as I arrived, I could feel a difference. It was quite late and the wing was locked up after the evening meal. I was allocated a cell on the upper floor and given a few minutes to sweep the area out and install my possessions.

After about an hour, I could hear some activity. It sounded like the cell doors were being opened one at a time and, after a while, it was my turn. The screw told me to take a plate and mug to the kitchen; I could smell toast. At the end of the landing on the same level as my new home was a small kitchen area not much larger than a single cell. Inside was a con making toast. He shook my hand and looked closely at me; we recognised each other.

'I'm Jimmy Rose,' he said. 'I know you from the squash club.'

I placed him immediately. Jimmy, a little older than me, was a very fit man. Slight and agile, he was a force to be reckoned with on the squash court. He had been in the senior Kent team and had won the senior championship at our club many times. We spent a little time chatting but the toast was piling up and others had to be catered for.

'I'll see you in the morning,' he said, as I walked back to my cell with a couple of pieces of buttered toast and a jug of hot water.

Jimmy and his son Richard had been arrested on a charge of importing a large quantity of puff from Afghanistan. It was around this time that the Cold War between Russia and America was beginning to come to a close. Jimmy and Richard fell foul of a new co-operation between Russian and British Customs and Intelligence, and the train on which the goods were travelling as freight was tracked all the way from the Russian border and transhipped to the UK under close surveillance.

Richard had been nicked as soon as the consignment 'came on top', but Jimmy managed to evade arrest for several weeks. With prisons full to bursting point at that time, Richard had been kept at a south London police station for quite some time. After his arrest, Jimmy, already a wealthy man from shrewd business activities, had a big problem with the new confiscation legislation. His case set a precedent for others that followed as he had to go through the laborious task of proving that his assets had been purchased legitimately.

The breakfast hotplate was on the downstairs landing. Allowed out for a few minutes to see to ablutions and get some food, I shook hands with several men who welcomed me into what was very obviously a much more relaxed atmosphere to the one I had been used to. Eddie Richardson was among them.

Within minutes of being locked away with my breakfast, my door opened. A brace of burly burglars were here to welcome me. Standing outside on the landing while they spun my cell, I could see another con below me undergoing a similar experience. In nothing more than a pair of boxer shorts, Dennis Campbell was dancing and singing to one of the burglars who had stayed outside his cell with him. Entertaining the troops with his particularly camp interpretation of the Village People's song, Dennis made all the right movements when he got to the chorus of 'YMCA'. I could see that his 'young man' audience was not amused.

I continued laughing long after I had been unceremoniously locked back in my overly trashed cell. Dennis was facing a long time away on armed robbery charges and, like Richard and Jimmy, was another south London 'face'.

Unlocked a few minutes later, the cheerful throng led the way into our private yard where an energetic game of football took place.

Some joined in and others, preferring to walk, circled the vociferous opposing teams. Unlike at Winchester, we were not locked away immediately after the precise elapse of an hour but allowed to circulate, visit, chat and play backgammon. Meals were always taken behind the door and the period afterwards gave time for newspaper, reflection, sleep or imagination.

Many of the inmates were deep into their trials. Whisked away early and returned late, it was only at the weekends that they could associate with their mates on the wing.

A Seg was a difficult club to get into and only the elite of the British criminal fraternity were on the guest list. Unlike Winchester, there were no nonces; they had a separate wing. Most of the club members were known by name and the rest received enough press coverage to identify them as falling within the necessary parameters to be accepted.

I remember during the first couple of weeks four cheerful turbaned Sikh fundamentalists being taken to court daily during the closing period of their trial for a sectarian murder which had taken place inside a temple. They would chant loudly in Hindi and celebrate vociferously on their way to the inevitable conclusion.

There was a very well-educated American who everybody called 'The Dude'. He had spent a long time fighting extradition back to the States to face trial where he fully expected to be sentenced to 'ride the lightning' for murdering his girlfriend's parents. The couple had absconded after the deed with a selection of stolen credit cards and were followed to their arrest from the trail of plastic transactions. The girlfriend had returned voluntarily to give State's Evidence and eventually The Dude flew back to face the music after assurances had been received that he would not face the death penalty.

I can't remember all who came and went when during the ten months I spent between committal and trial but many remain in my memory. Some of them I was to bump into again along the road and others I was destined never to see again. A tiny minority won an acquittal.

Ronnie Easterbrook was on trial as I hit Brixton. He had a

notorious past and knew that, if convicted, he was unlikely to see the light of day again. Like all the Cat A prisoners, he had the same transport arrangements as me to and from court. The trial was coming to a close and, fearing the worst, he planned to try to blast his way to freedom on the last day. Already a captive within the tiny compartment, he decided to try to blow a hole in the roof of the Cat A van with a charge of high explosive he had been accumulating for some time. It failed to work. Ronnie had crouched down and covered his head to try to protect himself from the explosion just above his head. Otherwise uninjured, he was to remain deafened by the blast for a very long time.

As a result of this attempt at freedom, the whole wing was shut down for a day. Visits were cancelled and nothing could come in or go out. The burglars were 'mob handed' and took the wing apart. A dreadlocked Rasta called Steppa, who had a club in Brixton and was on remand with four other Jamaican guys, was caught that day with a little personal puff and taken to the punishment block for adjudication by the Governor the following morning. Nobody considered cannabis particularly serious and many within the prison service thought life was easier for them when a prisoner was stoned and mellow. The usual result was a short loss of remission, which could be claimed back after a period of good behaviour.

Steppa, Bunny and Brian had been on a 'blag' at a big London post office. Ambushed by police, there ensued a shoot-out, OK Corral style, which resulted in nothing more than a couple of small flesh wounds and some very long prison sentences. Labelled as 'Yardies', they were to be joined in the dock by another friend, Andrew, who was picked up later. His accent was so strong that nobody could understand what he was saying. He had served quite a long term in prison in Kingston, Jamaica, and apparently narrowly avoided the gallows, still in use as a leftover reminder of British imperialism.

Brian, a mad cricket fan, and I wrote several letters to the late Brian Johnson who was commentating on Radio 3 during the West Indian tour of 1988. The letters were all read out on air during the lunchtime breaks.

I was to meet John Gorman at Brixton who did not fare quite as well as Steppa's band of merry men. Also on a blag, he had been caught in a hail of gunfire during which his colleague was shot dead and he sustained two gunshot wounds. Both John and his accomplice had dropped their sawn-off shotguns without firing a shot when they realised it was on top.

John, a big tall man with bottle spectacles and an ever-present roll-up in his mouth, became a good friend. He was fearless, did not give a fuck about anything and had a wicked sense of humour, which was accentuated by a stutter. He had been nicknamed 'Gorgeous' at Parkhurst, where we were later to spend quite a long time together, and he was an avid horticulturalist, supplying the wing there with fresh fruit and vegetables. By no means a good-looking man, he used to try to juggle his two rather pretty girlfriends so that his visits were alternated. The only time I ever saw him frightened was when his plans went very wrong and he was attacked by both ladies who had arrived on the Isle of Wight to see him on the same day.

We were also to spend some time at Wandsworth together, where he hatched a plan to get a very large quantity of cannabis into the prison. Very carefully concealed inside a radio, nearly 11 ounces of puff were sent to him by post. He never found out how it had come to be discovered by the Wandsworth screws but, as he denied all knowledge, the case had to be dropped for want of the identity of the sender. He ended up with a 14-year sentence. After his eventual release, John died from a massive heart-attack while on holiday; he was in his mid-sixties. John loved a drink and smoked like a chimney to the last.

We had a short guest appearance by Freddie Foreman who has been dubbed the enforcer for the Kray Twins. He was passing through on an extradition matter and was not at Brixton for long. Described as deadly enemies, the Krays and Richardsons seemed to have buried the hatchet, if indeed there was ever one to be buried, a long time ago. From what I could observe, what was left was a genuine mutual respect for those who had remained true to their principles.

One such person was Mad Frankie Fraser, whom I met while he

was on a visit to Tommy Wisbey, the Great Train Robber. Tommy was to become Frankie's father-in-law when he married his daughter Marilyn. Everybody had a great deal of respect for Frank. Brave beyond belief, he took on the most brutal prison regimes at a time when screws could and did get away with murder. He would never stand for injustice, resisted bullying and fought for his beliefs in spite of numerous beatings and injuries.

Mad he may be, but I take off my hat to the man to whom prisoners everywhere should be grateful, for it takes massive resistance and courage like his to effect even small changes in regimes. Frank, ever dapper and well turned out, can always be relied upon for a comment and opinion. Well reasoned and ever articulate, he has been a good friend and ally to many but, I am sure, even now, could be an enemy to be reckoned with.

I am still friends with Graham Petherick. Half of a pair of identical twins, he and Geoffrey have been an example to many. When we first met at Brixton, Graham was facing charges relating to ringing cars which the prosecution said were for use in armed robberies. Highly intelligent, well read and staunchly left, he and I immediately hit it off. The self-educated Graham and I would have a daily race to finish the *Guardian* crossword, the winner shouting triumphantly so loud across the landing during lunchtime bang-up as to wake the poor souls in unmarked graves within the prison walls.

He was more concerned with seeing his brother, who was well into an 18-year sentence at Parkhurst for armed robbery, than with his own fate. Both intensely competitive, Geoffrey and Graham, not always talking to each other, share a mutual love beyond words. It has been a privilege to count them both among my friends.

Graham ended up with a sentence of four-and-a-half years. His barrister, aptly named Robin Banks, got into deep trouble with the trial judge when he asked the jury if his angelic-looking client looked like an armed robber. It was not the first time Graham had seen the inside of a dock.

Another man who achieved a remarkable result was my friend Mark Rothermel. Mark, who had acquired the title 'The Colonel', was a senior member of an organisation which provided doormen and security services. He was facing a serious murder charge and had been grassed up by a colleague called Pierre Saint Ange. Mark, another adventurer with a good education like myself, was looking at a very long sentence if everything went against him. However, the jury were satisfied that, at the very most, he had assisted in the disposal of a body. He received six years for his trouble.

Our paths were also destined to cross at Wandsworth and, later, at Parkhurst. Mark is the sort of man you can trust and depend upon implicitly. He is fearless and nothing in prison gave him cause for concern. Even at Wandsworth, where sympathy and understanding were two words missing from the establishment's vocabulary, the screws soon gave up trying to taunt and annoy him. Called for a visit, you would often hear him shout, 'You'll never take me alive, copper.'

There were many others, all of whom had a story to tell. Humour was paramount and I honestly cannot recall a single incident while I was in A Seg. I fitted in well, met some very interesting people and did my best to help with measured advice or assistance wherever I could. The contacts I made at Brixton stood me in good stead for the rest of my time in prison and I always knew someone wherever I landed.

I occasionally meet people who update me on the comings, goings and whereabouts of many of my former acquaintances, and the news is usually depressing. Many whom I had come to know are now dead, several by their own hand. A good deal have been back and that's where some will stay.

The screws left us alone, did everything to avoid confrontation and, as a result, had little to do. We policed ourselves.

One day, playing football in the yard, I collapsed on the ground. I felt that I had been shot in the back of my leg and was unable to get up again. The pain was excruciating. I had snapped an Achilles tendon. I was taken on quite a long walk to the hospital wing the next day and an appointment was made for a physiotherapist to see me. I was given a pair of crutches and a Tubigrip. The physio took one look at my injury and announced to my Cat A double escort that I needed to go to a hospital where the tendon could be repaired under anaesthetic. I had no chance. I saw the Governor, who refused point blank to consider letting me be taken to an outside hospital and Tom McGoldrick made representations on my behalf to the Home Office. Eventually, the physio disappeared and so did any record of my injury. I had to let it heal on its own.

After committal, remand hearings came to an end. Although the case had been committed to the Old Bailey, the prosecution were procrastinating. After six months, we were no nearer to getting a date for trial than we had been at Winchester. The prosecution, still maintaining that they were gathering evidence, would not accede to a date until they were forced to do so.

Apart from the usual frustrations of the situation, there was the added problem that our barristers were much in demand. Everybody knew that the trial would take many months and our QCs could not commit themselves to being available without firm dates. It was a serious dilemma, which Customs must have relished. The case was becoming ever more complex and a new barrister would need a lot of time to get up to speed with the facts and circumstances.

Because the unit at Brixton was so secure, it was possible for the authorities to give us more latitude while we were safely locked inside. However, as soon as it was necessary to go through that door, security was more than somewhat evident. Cat A visits were in a special section at the other end of the prison and the rigmarole, whenever our lawyers or family came, was involved to say the least.

Two security screws would come to the wing where, before leaving, you were subjected to a search. After we were escorted to the visiting area, we were taken to a room opposite where we were strip-searched. Social visits took place under the watchful eye of a screw sitting within sight and earshot and legal visits were with a screw outside but viewing through glass. Before returning to the wing, another strip-search standing on a raised box involved dropping pants and trousers and a squat. On occasions, I would receive both a legal and social visit on the same day. With such high levels of security, it kind of made you feel all the more triumphant when in possession of contraband.

Weeks turned into months. I would see Tom every week and, as at Winchester, he never failed to bring a supply of cigarettes and some treats to eat. After seven or eight months at Brixton, during which time every single legal team was putting pressure on the prosecution, they finally began to indicate that they had finished investigations and were ready to go to trial. It was estimated that the trial would last six or seven months.

Finally, we got a date. The trial would begin almost exactly 20 months after we had been first arrested. Barrister's diaries were co-ordinated, legal teams selected and finalised and notes and depositions reread in preparation for the trial. There were one or two notable changes in personnel, one of whom was my QC; Tom hurriedly found another, an elderly somewhat theatrical man who was halfway to becoming a judge. He came to Brixton a couple of times to see me and I was deeply impressed with the speed with which he had grasped the intricacies and complexities of the case.

He was quite encouraging about Appiah. Confident that it would not be difficult to prove that Customs had on many occasions put words into his mouth, he indicated that it might even be possible to obtain a ruling that Appiah's evidence was inadmissible.

My QC would not be led when I tried to press him as to his opinion of my chances, but I could tell that, given the choice, he might have opted to climb Everest. He did say that, in view of the fact that we had all spent a lot of time on remand already, and the astronomical cost of the trial, it might have been wiser to consider all of us negotiating a much reduced penalty in exchange for a guilty plea.

A week before the trial was due to commence, we had to go to the Old Bailey to formally plead: back in the Cat A van and a short trip to court with traffic stopped along the way by a police car ahead of the convoy. From the courtyard to the Cat A holding cells in the newly refurbished building was quite a walk. Tom was there already and, as soon as I was uncuffed, I was taken to see him. From the look on his face, I could see that all was not well.

Having just been served with the statement a few minutes before, Tom told me that Westbury had turned Queen's Evidence. Together, we looked at his lengthy and detailed account. He had buried us all except John and Michael, whom he did not know. In the court, the barristers were furious, which only seemed to please the army of gathered Customs officers all the more. To say that their expressions were triumphant would be the understatement of the year.

The judge, too, expressed his displeasure that a lot of time had been wasted in not serving the Westbury statement before we all had a chance to discuss it and consider its implications. Back to Brixton for another week.

'It will take a jury of 12 certifiable anarchists to acquit you,' were the words of my QC when next I saw him a couple of days later. He told me that the case had been like fighting a terminal illness. This time, the complications were fatal. There was no doubt in his mind that I would receive the maximum possible sentence – 14 years – but, if I pleaded guilty at this stage, I would receive a reduction. When I asked him, he was not able to quantify but promised to approach the judge for an indication.

Still unconvinced, I asked him to see if he could find out what I was facing if indeed I did change my mind. The barristers left. Tom stayed for another hour chatting. He and I had both been looking forward to our day in court and spent a lot of time preparing. Neither of us believed it would be easy, but realistically rated our chances if we were lucky enough to have a jury in which there were some who had a jaundiced view of British justice.

The decision was one that I would have to make on my own. I would not know the outcome of my QC's discussion with the judge until the morning of the day for pleas. He had refused my QC an audience without the prosecution QC being present, too.

If I held my hands up, I would not be in court for the trial and that would almost certainly mean a transfer from Brixton to what was called a dispersal prison, almost certainly Wandsworth, the darkest prison in London with a reputation for a brutal regime. I would not be considered for transfer until after I had been sentenced and that could not be before the trial had ended. I was in a quandary.

Back at the Old Bailey, I spent some time in the holding cells before I was taken to see my QC. In the legal visits area, the whole team was gathered. The judge had refused to be specific and would not place a number on the likely sentence I would receive for a guilty plea. He would go no further than to say that, if I were to plead, I would receive a substantial discount for saving court time and being honest. My QC told me that he was unable to do more but the tradition was that at least 25 per cent would be deducted for a guilty plea. He promised me that, if it turned out not to be the case, he would appeal the sentence free of charge. Deal or no deal? I made my decision.

I stood in the dock. 'Guilty,' I said loudly.

The judge said that my honesty would be taken into consideration when it came to sentencing and I was returned to the cells.

About an hour later, I was brought into the legal visits area. Tom and my QC were there to greet me. 'There is no doubt whatsoever in my mind that you have done the right thing,' he began. 'I have to ask you this,' he continued. 'After your guilty plea, the prosecution QC approached me to ask if you would give evidence for them.'

I stopped him then. 'Tell the prosecution to stick it up their arse.'

'I thought you might say that,' replied my QC.

31

WANDSWORTH

It was late by the time the Cat A van drove through the massive doors of Wandsworth Prison. Inside the big reception area, only one con was at work. Two screws formed my reception committee and neither was in any hurry. I was given a coffee by the con and offered the dregs of the food on the hotplate, left over from the day, which I refused. The lunches at the Bailey were not half bad and Tom had kept me topped up with M&S sandwiches.

I showered and was given the best of what the con could find in the way of prison clothing. The prison-issue shoes were hideously uncomfortable and I asked one of the screws if I could keep my soft black slip-on shoes. He took a long look at my personal shoes and, much to my surprise, handed them back to me.

I had accumulated quite a bit of personal property in nearly two years in prison; letters, books, photographs, along with the bedding and clothing issued at reception, it was all quite a burden to carry on to the wing.

Built like the Starship Enterprise, Wandsworth Prison is made up of a series of massive wings connected to an enormous circular hub rising like some ecclesiastical edifice four storeys skywards. For some reason, the central part of the floor, like consecrated ground, is sacred and only crossed by an inmate not engaged in cleaning and polishing under pain of death. It served as a kind of pagan delineation between the Gods and Mortals.

The atmosphere in this place was entirely different. It was my first night as a convicted prisoner. I was now in an establishment full of others in the same situation. Gone was the hope of 'a result', an acquittal, a retrial. We had all lost our liberty to the system.

I was tired, it had been a long day and full of emotion. A cell was opened for me on the ground floor, not far from the dreaded centre. The dingy central light revealed that it had not been painted for a long time. The brick walls, initially a kind of magnolia yellow, had been stained from years of nicotine and were scratched and flaked in places, with a few scribblings in pencil here and there.

The door shut behind me. As I watched it close, I saw a note on the wall beside it. Somebody had drawn a cross at the head of a grave with an epitaph, which read: 'RIP Mickey Peterson... a good man'. Beneath it were two dates, which I took to be birth and death. It had been written recently.

I was to learn the next morning as I went on exercise that the previous occupant of my cell was Charles Bronson. Now in the punishment block, which is where he usually elected to be, he had written the epitaph as a tribute to himself. His real name was Mickey Peterson and the date beneath was when Charles had elected to change his identity at the beginning of his current sentence.

I saw Charlie for the first time in the block exercise cage. A bull of a man, his strength legendary, he sported an upwardly trained moustache, which, along with his shaven head, made him look like a Victorian strongman.

Charlie had originally received a seven-year sentence for robbery. Rebellious and fearless, he was constantly in trouble and it did not take long for the screws to find out that it took several strong and brave men to subdue him. They ground Charlie down, in and out of punishment blocks, taunted, transported and mistreated; they played games with his head until Charlie was in a constant state of siege.

With remission, a seven-year sentence usually equates to not much more than four years' loss of liberty. Charlie did not see the light of day for 13 years. In the course of that first sentence, he had spent most of the time in solitary and was eventually sectioned off under the Mental Health Act, which rendered his release indeterminate.

Eventually, after a short spell at liberty, during which he became a prize fighter with whom nobody would climb into the ring, he committed another robbery. It was not long before he was once again behind bars. He spoke very respectfully of a police sergeant who arrested him after a punch so hard as to knock him 'spark' out.

Ever on the prison merry-go-round, Charlie was never allowed to settle. Then began a series of hostage-taking, culminating in a spectacular incident when he took the Governor of Frankland Prison over his shoulder and barricaded him in his cell. Charlie's demands of a helicopter to take him to Libya were not met.

Charlie ran for Mayor of London. I rated his chances, especially against Jeffrey Archer. He proposed Nick Leeson who had single-handedly brought a massive bank to its knees, as his Chancellor of the Exchequer. Poet, artist, humorist and would-be politician, I thank goodness that in this often dull world exist brave eccentrics like Charlie. *Vive la révolution*!

The nights in prison were never quiet. Banging, shouting and kicking, it was often difficult to get to sleep. On that first night, I had no such problem.

Once the cell was opened in the morning for slop-out, I recognised many familiar faces. Several people I had come to know at Brixton shook my hand and cheerfully welcomed me to Hell on Earth.

The screws here were different animals to the ones I had encountered before. Red-faced, ex-army bully boys, with the peaks of their hats over their eyes sergeant major-style, ruled sadistically and often got away with murder.

Expecting an early spin, I had left my possessions in a box. I was not to be disappointed. Like a first mugging in Rio, it is quite a relief to get it over with. After the spin, I began to unpack and prepare for a long siege.

The Colonel and Gorgeous greeted me for exercise and together we circled the big area of yard like automata, treading constantly the same path every lap. Both already sentenced, they were there awaiting allocation to a long-term establishment equipped to house maximum-security prisoners. Some were lucky to find a place in a few short months and others would have to stay a year before moving on. All three of us were destined to be sent to Parkhurst but they were both to get there a long time before me.

Cat A prisons were spread all over the country, from the Isle of Wight to Durham, and no consideration was given to the distance visitors had to travel. Some prisoners would elect to save their visit allocation up and transfer for a few weeks to London to take them all together. As a convicted prisoner, visits were restricted to once a month with one or two discretionary extras per year. Those who worked in jobs where they looked after the screws like their personal batmen found themselves able to get a visit more or less whenever they wanted. I did not work and did not want to.

Now that I was convicted, letter writing was restricted, too. I could buy extra letters from the canteen from my £1.20 a week but, as a smoker, I would have to see to my tobacco needs, too. Knowing that I was likely to come to Wandsworth, I brought as much tobacco with me as I could. Permitted no more than two ounces, I had stuffed an extra ounce-and-a-half into a pouch of Old Holborn and had been sure to bring a supply of Rizlas. Economy was the order of the day. Some split matches four ways, while others made lighters using mop strands as dry wicks.

I had managed to bring a good supply of puff, stored where the sun doesn't shine, and would have to set about doing a bit of trading soon. I estimated that I could get by on two ounces of tobacco a week, which would have cost me five times my weekly wages. I had time to establish whom to deal with and who could be relied on not to mess me about.

It was to take me two weeks for my private cash to be transferred. Although Tom had seen to arranging a daily *Guardian* for me the day after I hit Wandsworth, it would be two weeks before they began to filter through. My letters out and in went missing. I had been warned that every newcomer was subjected to wind-ups and mind games. It is difficult to describe how in solitary you come to rely upon the newspaper and radio, which, beside your right hand, are your only source of comfort. Knowing that your patience is being tested, it is frustration that puts you permanently on edge and makes you ever close to anger.

Some were easily broken. Quick to anger, many were easily goaded into losing their tempers before being dragged kicking down to the block and mercilessly beaten up by the sadistic screws. The ex-army bastards held sway and I heard that any screws arriving with even a modicum of humanitarianism were also subjected to bullying.

I am proud to have known one dissenter – a newly arrived young Catholic priest. Father Tom introduced himself to me one day. He knew that I came from a different religious background and would be unlikely to be persuaded away from agnosticism. We became friends. He tried to arrange discussion groups in order to get the Cat A prisoners out of their cells. He succeeded for a week or two but, eventually, his plans were thwarted by 'shortages of escort staff'.

One day, another friend from Brixton, Kevin Brown, hatched an escape plan. Inside the perimeter wall was a high metal fence topped with the usual razor wire. After Ronnie Biggs's vault to freedom back in the Sixties, security had been tightened a great deal. In no-man's-land, a large JCB digger had been doing earthworks for a couple of weeks. Kevin figured that, if he could get a key to the inner fence, the boom of the JCB could be used as a perfect means to straddle the outside wall.

A young Irish guy, game and keen to go along, said that he had driven all sorts of construction vehicles and had been weaned on JCBs. A few others were invited to join and it was planned that the break would be made at the very beginning of exercise on a particular day. I had to decline. I was still limping from my Achilles injury and would not have been able to keep up.

It went like clockwork. Kevin jumped a screw and took his key. The men dashed to the fence and, in seconds, had pulled the driver from the digger. The Irishman took the controls and it was soon horribly obvious that he had no idea what to do. By the time the legs of the machine were eventually down, the screws had gathered in large numbers and were able to thwart the escape.

The aspiring escapees were dragged down the block. Tradition dictated that they would be subjected to a series of beatings, but it was not to be. Father Tom demanded to visit the men in the block and, for a while, his requests met with procrastination. Eventually, after remonstrating with the Governor, Tom had his way. The men had been initially roughed up, but Tom warned that if they were harmed any further he would take the matter beyond the prison. Each of the men had an extra month added to their sentences but, thanks to Father Tom, they were not subjected to any more violence. Even a Catholic priest has to sign the Official Secrets Act before becoming part of the prison system and, within a month, Tom was transferred elsewhere.

The visits at Wandsworth were dire. The Cat A visiting room was situated beside the large main area for the rest of the prisoners. There were frequent occasions when screws would rugby tackle a poor wife or girlfriend to the ground seen passing something illicit. Some would end up serving a year's sentence in Holloway for their trouble.

Each time the screws came for me, I would be referred to by my family name, 'Newman, you've got a visit,' or 'Newman, exercise,' always in a regimental, sergeant-major bark.

One day, I hatched a plan. Tom, my solicitor never forgot me. Even after conviction, I received visits from him whenever he could come. We were preparing an appeal and that was his official reason for seeing me. I asked Tom how much it would cost to change my name to Paul Sir. When I explained to him that the screws would then have to refer to me by my new family name, he was so amused that he offered to do it for nothing. 'You've got a visit, Sir... exercise, Sir...' I couldn't wait.

True to his word, Tom changed my name by deed poll. He brought me the papers and suggested that I serve them on the Governor with an official request for a change of name. I had been waiting for this moment with baited breath and, if it worked, several of my mates were going to follow – My Lord, Your Grace, Archbishop, Your Highness were some of the names we bandied about.

I applied to see the Governor. The next day, I saw an assistant who, obviously amused but trying hard not to show it, told me that she would come back to me the following day, but could not see any reason why my request would be turned down. It took two days before she returned to tell me triumphantly that you are known throughout your sentence by the name you give when first arriving at prison. Charlie Bronson had set that precedent. I don't think I ever changed my name back.

I had got a system going for my tobacco. Gorgeous and I had a source and, along with our puff, we even got a half-bottle of brandy on a couple of occasions. A con who worked on the wing used to deal a little for us and we were never out of tobacco.

A neighbour of mine who had a story to tell from his years of criminal activity in Jamaica was writing a book. I often had requests for letter writing slid under my door and I was happy to provide him with editing services. A non-smoker, he paid me an ounce of tobacco a week for my trouble.

One day, Gorgeous and I were walking around the exercise yard with Dogan Arif who had newly arrived. His daughter was at school with my youngest. He had a successful club in the Old Kent Road and we became friends. We had barely completed two laps when four Africans came rushing over, lined up in front of me and, in full view of everybody, they stood to attention military style and saluted. It took me a while to recognise them. Four soldiers from Ghana who had worked for us packing and delivering had been caught on a little free enterprise of their own. Referring to me always as 'Missa Paul', they told me that they quite liked the food at Wandsworth and found their quarters very much to their liking.

I was to spend two Christmases at Wandsworth. A depressing day for all, it was made worse by being unlocked to be given a paper bag containing an apple, an orange and a couple of spoons of sugar. That first freezing year on exercise, a lot of people approached to shake my hand with a word of thanks for helping with this or that. I put whatever was passed to me in those handshakes into my duffel-coat pocket. Back in my cell, I inspected what Santa had brought me; it was like a pharmacist's dream. I decided to take a Christmas trip.

Within minutes, I was under siege. On a shelf above my bed was a packet of cornflakes; the chicken on the side began to eye me up very aggressively. Sat on a chair, I had no escape as the fucking thing got bigger and bigger and, as it puffed up its feathers, I knew it was planning to eat me. I spent the whole of that Christmas afternoon scared shitless waiting to be devoured by the lurid bird.

We did get to the gym for an hour a week where the senior screw was Gary Taylor, later to become the World's Strongest Man. Greg, my escapee friend from Winchester, had joined the throng, by this time having been captured and convicted. He was still in patches. We had been assembled at the end of the wing under a blackboard where The Colonel had written, 'What is the difference between SO Smith and Tom and Jerry? Answer: one is a hunt with a cat.'

SO Smith, a particularly nasty piece of work, was incandescent with rage. Intent upon retribution, he demanded that the perpetrator own up. We all put our hands up.

Again, the library was excellent. I devoured books on a daily basis and relished my weekly journey to pick up what had been ordered or recommended by the librarian. Music and my newspaper kept me sane but I must confess to feelings of deep depression from time to time. I maintained my resistance and, to a large extent, the screws stopped trying to goad me. They never saw me lose my temper and I always had a quiet way of answering a jibe with a sarcastic put-down.

Time rolled by slowly. People came and went and I was gradually becoming the longest-serving Wandsworth inmate. Eventually, after ten months, the trial came to a close. Tom came to see me. Everybody had been convicted except one of the accused. Sentencing had been deferred for a while pending some confiscation enquiries and I would not be considered for transfer until afterwards.

Tom explained that, after I put my hands up, most of my co-defendants took advantage of the open goal I had left behind. I was portrayed as the evil enforcer who tricked others into cannabis smuggling, thinking it to be another commodity entirely. He warned me that the judge was not likely to treat me as an old friend. Tom showed me a letter from a journalist who worked on *GQ* magazine. He was going to do an article on the conspiracy and invited me to take part by responding to some questions. He would not have a chance of being approved for visits by Special Branch and Tom said that effectively I had nothing to lose. The article was going to be printed anyway and I might as well put my side of the story.

He sent me a long list of questions, many of which I ignored, but I did reply to one saying, 'The only way one can be harmed by cannabis is to be run over by a lorryload of the stuff.' It was used to headline an otherwise wholly sensationalistic piece of journalism.

Eventually, we were called to court for sentencing. The judge looked at me with hatred in his eye. He regretfully acknowledged that recognition had to be shown for my guilty plea and, having calculated a 25 per cent discount from the maximum, he sentenced me to ten-and-a-half years. He then told me that, despite the combined efforts of the best investigative officers who had found virtually nothing, he was convinced that I had millions stashed away in accounts all over the world. He angrily proceeded to fine me an extra half-million pounds or to serve another five years in prison.

The court was in chaos. My barrister was beaten to his feet by the prosecution QC and, before either of them could speak, they were ordered to sit down. The judge would have his day in court.

Back in the cells, I added my name to the list of men who had written their fate on the wall. I wrote: 'Paul Newman, got ten-and-a-half years, expected a knighthood.'

Afterwards, my barrister told me that the judge was completely incorrect and even the prosecution were adamant that only fines could be imposed relating to assets that had been discovered and the judge could not sentence on supposition. Two weeks later, I was brought back to the Old Bailey where the additional sentence was grudgingly removed by the still furious judge.

At last, I could now look forward to moving from the hell-hole.

Gorgeous had already been sent to Parkhurst from where he sent me a letter: 'For fuck's sake, get yourself down here.'

It took another four months. The screw in charge of allocations who had his office beside the condemned cell and gallows asked me where I would like to go.

'Parkhurst,' I replied, worried that in true Wandsworth fashion I would get just the opposite of what I wanted.

'Then that's where you'll go,' he said.

It was the first and last gesture of kindness I was to receive at Wandsworth Prison.

32

PARKHURST

Three weeks later, I was crossing a very choppy Solent chained into the van. The Isle of Wight was clearly visible through the blustery rain. Nearly three years had passed since I had enjoyed freedom. I felt nervous; I knew that I would be among friends and, from the tone of Gorgeous's letter, I was about to experience an entirely new regime.

The drive from the ferry did not take long. We passed Albany Prison and a short way further on I could see the massive wall which delineated the secure boundary of Parkhurst. Into the modern reception area and there was an entirely different atmosphere to anything I had experienced so far. The screws were referring to their workers by their first names. I was welcomed and given a cup of coffee. Nobody was in a rush and, after collecting everything I needed, I was taken to a small room in the old part of the big old jail. On the wall were hundreds of old Victorian photographs of previous inmates.

The screw who took my picture happily chatted about the identity of some of the more notorious ex-inhabitants and gave me a brief history of the prison. Back at reception, I was offered help with my burden and escorted to the main prison building.

Gorgeous had told me to ask to be placed in M Wing, a small unit with about 40 cells. My request had been granted. I was welcomed by so many of the friends I had made along the way. Here, I was introduced to Geoffrey, Graham's identical twin brother. After sentencing, Graham had got his wish and been transferred to Parkhurst to be with his brother. Because he had already spent a long time on remand waiting for trial, he only had a few months left to serve and had recently been released. I was invited to join Geoffrey's group for dinner and sat at a table with him, his co-defendant Peter and Gorgeous. Geoff, a true master chef, had cooked spaghetti with meatballs. It had been so long since I had eaten anything decent that I relished each and every mouthful. Imagine my surprise when the meal was rounded off with a plate of ice cream. All through the meal, I was welcomed by a selection of old friends and new neighbours – Greg, my escapee friend, still in patches, The Colonel and so many others.

I was quite overwhelmed. Unused to conversation and having to rush for so long, I had lost the ability to relax in company. I was used to a few snatched sentences at slop-out or standing in line for breakfast, so I still felt a sense of urgency. The few strong draws on a pipe before dinner had not helped and I felt a strange sense of paranoia at the table. It would take a week or two to pass and my friends who had been through the same experience understood.

I was upstairs. All the cells on M Wing had tiny low doors. This had been the children's wing over 200 years before when the prison had been built. I would have to remember to duck a few inches to clear the lintel.

My neighbour, Steve Chandler, a double for Roger Daltry, helped me in with my stuff and made me feel welcome. We last met some time back at Brixton and got on well.

At 9.00pm, when the time came for the doors to be locked, I was exhausted. It had been a long day and the effort to make conversation had made things harder. I did a little unpacking but, after a cup of hot coffee, I fell into my freshly made bed and slept like a baby.

There was a pecking order in prison which, allied to an overwhelming atmosphere of paranoia, had to be adhered to religiously. Long-term incarceration sets people on edge. With too much time to think, no sexual release apart from masturbation and sardine-like accommodation, reason becomes distorted. There was always a ritual of acknowledgement when passing anybody or making eye contact. Those with whom one shared a friendship needed to have that friendship confirmed frequently; regular reassurances with a nod would do.

One day, I was in the large wing at Parkhurst just after morning unlock. The wing, which rose four floors, had white-painted walls. Watching the men emerging from their individual spaces, the whole sight unfolded like a cliff face and the men like a colony of seabirds. The noise, the busyness and the visible signs of recognition were all so similar.

Violence was not a daily occurrence, but the atmosphere of tension was always bubbling near the surface. When it flared up, it was always serious and immediate. Stabbings in the showers were not uncommon. At Parkhurst, we were generally left to police ourselves. Bullying was frowned upon by the inmates and, often, the weaker ones were given protection by those who held sway and influence. Debts aside, the main cause of trouble was paranoia. A missed hello, a forgotten acknowledgement, could be interpreted as a sudden disaffection and often ended in violence as a result of a decision to get in first.

Rational behaviour like a 'Have I done anything to upset you?' or the odd 'Are you all right?' was not much in evidence. It was a continually testing atmosphere and stress was never far from the surface. I remember on many occasions a feeling of unease because I may have misinterpreted a look from a friend.

Geoff welcomed me. I was unwilling to work but he persuaded me that I would be bored alone on the wing and urged me to join the work party in the laundry. More emphasis on party than work, the job consisted mostly of folding a few sheets and running a private business washing and ironing for a few mates. The chaps always got their laundry free and would repay the compliment with whatever they could do for you in return. Others paid in tobacco.

I had arrived from Wandsworth with practically nothing. I just managed to keep going for the time I was there and only remember running out of tobacco on one occasion. I was permitted to transfer enough personal money into my wages account as soon as I reached Parkhurst to enable me to get started with supplies. I had about two weeks' worth of dinner invitations from a lot of people who I knew.

Once a week at Parkhurst, we could go to the canteen where we could spend whatever we had in our wages account. If you had enough money for fillet steak, you could buy it, and whatever you ordered was delivered to you a couple of days later. There were fridges and freezers on the wing. The cooking facilities were quite adequate and sharing was negotiated in a civilised way. At about £7.00 a week, an individual was not likely to get very far and so began the commercial reality. Not everybody subscribed to self-catering, and regular prison food was available to all. Tobacco was always in demand and it paid to keep stocks for trading. Puff was the key trading commodity and a 16th-of-an-ounce sold for about £7.00 in wages. A 16th-of-an-ounce accompanied with a £7.00 shopping list to enough people ensured home cooking every day of the week.

In due course, I teamed up with Steve, The Colonel and later Dennis of the 'YMCA' dance at Brixton. I was not much of a chef but we had two Sicilian guys on the wing who would always cook at lunchtime and were ready and willing to help with recipes and advice. Geoff, too, possessed a fine array of cook books and was more than pleased to help.

Steve was a great guy. Soon we were spending a lot of our time planning our meals and considering recipes. Shopping lists were carefully considered and our menu was ever diverse.

Gorgeous, the wing horticulturalist, had an allotment in the large exercise area. He spent months lovingly digging it over and tending it as seeds of every kind were sown at various times of the year. He also constructed a greenhouse of sorts with scrap and polythene and spent a long time and a great deal of effort keeping it weatherproof. The net result was that we had a constant supply of vegetables, potatoes and soft fruit, along with a selection of fresh herbs to go with it. Having lost four stone on my way to Parkhurst, I was rapidly putting it all back on.

John Marriot, the Governor, was a good man. A humanitarian with a conscience, he viewed his role essentially as ensuring that those committed to his care were kept within the walls. He was happy to adopt a *laissez faire* policy, encouraging minimal staff intervention and self-policing. Parkhurst contained many prisoners who would never be allowed into the community again. It would make no difference to them if they committed murder inside, as some of them already had. The screws were ever mindful that this was the case. The result was an establishment containing a reasonable percentage of desperados who, on the whole, lived together harmoniously.

The Governor was later to be used as a convenient scapegoat after a successful escape. He was discredited and dismissed and driven to an early grave. Always approachable, the Governor was ready to consider any reasonable suggestion and, hearing that Charlie Bronson had arrived in the block, Geoff applied to him for an audience.

'Let him up on the wing, Governor, and we will do our best to look after him.' Arguing articulately, Geoff got a promise that his suggestion would receive serious consideration.

The next day, we were told that Charlie was happy to join us on M Wing and would arrive later in the day.

A young chap called Del who had not been on the wing for very long was often in the company of Vic Dark, a blagger with a great sense of humour. Del had been at a young offenders' institution on a burglary charge and, one day in a temper, he had attacked a screw. He ended up with a suspended sentence for the burglary but six years for the GBH. As soon as he was 18, he was sent to Parkhurst. Vic decided to set him up.

If any strangers arrived on the wing, it was normal procedure to ask to see their case depositions to confirm that they were bona fide. Charlie arrived during tea-time lock-up, so, before he had time to come out of his door, Vic told Del to check out 'the stranger'.

Del duly knocked and walked in. 'Excuse me,' he said.

'Yes, boy,' came the gruff reply.

'But...'

'Yes, boy.'

'Could I ask to see your depositions? We don't know who you are.'

Sensing a wind-up, Charlie put his nose up to Del's. 'I'm Charles Bronson.'

'Would you like a cup of tea, Mr Bronson?'

'That would be very nice, boy.'

Del emerged to find Vic at the door with a couple of mates doubled up laughing.

'You cunts... you fucking cunts,' shouted Del.

Charlie was great company. He did the rounds of the dinner-party circuit and settled in very quickly. Always ready with an anecdote, he had a wicked sense of humour and an infectious laugh. He had a cocktail of tablets he had to take regularly which, together, would anaesthetise a herd of mustangs. The general consensus of opinion was that these reacted rather badly with alcohol.

Graham Gooch (hooch) was a continuous game with the authorities. Small quantities of puff would secure quite large quantities of yeast stolen from the kitchens. With warm water, orange juice or liquid malt, the yeast would ferment and produce some pretty foul but effective alcoholic beverage. Made by the bucket load, the stuff had to ferment for about ten days and, as the fermentation process advanced, the smell increased. There was an unwritten law that, if we could avoid capture by the burglars, whatever was ready by Saturday night could be consumed uninterrupted.

Some ingenious hiding places were devised – behind walls, inside cupboards and, of course, under beds. Always locked up over lunch, the wing would be supervised by a single screw who sat inside a warm garden shed-like construction in view of the wing. One day, there was an almighty crash as ten bucketfuls of hooch which had been hidden on top of the shed crashed through the roof and drenched the man in sticky alcohol. The penalty for a captured bucket was usually a £2.00–£5.00 fine and, of course, the forfeiture of the alcohol.

One Saturday night, the wing was enjoying the benefits of a week of successful evasion from the alcohol burglars; nobody was sober. I used to drink out of defiance more than anything because it was never long before I threw up after night-time bang-up. Worse still was that feeling of the room spinning round and deciding whether to stay upright or lie down.

Sometime quite late one night, there was the sound of a bell going off, footsteps and the words, 'Oh my God, Charlie, what have you done?'

Radio contact was made with the hospital wing. Charlie had taken a razor blade and cut several vertical lines down his bald head. With blood everywhere, the two hospital screws opened Charlie's door. It was all he needed to make his escape on to the wing.

There followed a rampage that lasted two hours. The urinals were first to go, torn from the wall and tossed over the landing to the floor beneath; Charlie followed with the recently flooded screw's wooden shed, banisters, metal balustrades, tables and chairs. The destruction, like a single-handed hurricane, continued unabated. Above it all, from time to time, we could hear Charlie saying, 'We're going to die... we're all going to die...'

We tried to calm him and some of us shouted through our wooden doors at the man who had stayed with us on the wing with no problems for two months, the man the system could not tame. It took an army of riot screws with shields and batons to subdue Charlie and we never had the pleasure of his company again. I feel sure that the booze we served him that night, together with his medication, was one cocktail too far.

33

THE SCOURGE OF STAMFORD HILL

It was about midnight. I had felt uncomfortable for no reason for most of the evening before bang-up and now I began to sweat. The pain in my chest was becoming increasingly crushing and my pulse raced uncontrollably. I rang the bell. The night screw called the hospital staff and I was taken on a two-wheel stretcher to the hospital wing, banged up in a cell until morning and given nothing by way of medication. I survived and in the morning was given an ECG by the doctor. I was told that I had suffered a minor heart-attack. I knew from that moment that I had a better chance of support from my friends back on the wing and asked to be returned. I had to stay for five days.

That evening, a screw came and asked if I wanted to watch TV on the ward. I went with him and sat on a chair. Next to me sat an old wizened man with sunken eyes and the pallor of death. He looked across and nodded. He gestured to the others on their beds in the ward with the weak sweep of an unsteady arm. 'Don't talk to any of them cunts... they're all nonces.'

'I'm Paul Newman.'

'I know who you are,' he replied, his head nodding up and down almost uncontrollably.

I smiled. 'Who are you?'

He held out his cold claw-like hand and looked at me as I took it gently. 'I'm a doomed man,' he replied. I assumed that he was in the last stages of cancer. 'I'm John Hilton... I'm starving myself to death.'

John had been taken into care as a small boy but clearly remembered his mother whom he described as a well-dressed and elegant lady. She visited him a couple of times shortly after they were parted but, after a while, she vanished from his life for ever. From a young age, he began to be known by the police and mixed with street criminals where he served an apprenticeship in dipping and thieving. He was small and agile and, by the age of 16, had become a cat burglar with a rapidly growing reputation as a brave and skilful operator.

In a short time, no home in Tottenham and Stamford Hill was beyond his reach and, along with an accomplice, he soon developed a taste for stylish clothes and a luxurious lifestyle. He moved into a big flat and took up with a succession of pretty girls. It was not long before he graduated into the world of armed robbery and developed a penchant for guns.

A big robbery at a dairy in the early Sixties in Surrey ended in the fatal shooting of a 'have-a-go' security guard and, in a short time, John and his associates were arrested. After a trial at the Old Bailey, which attracted a great deal of publicity, all of the defendants were found guilty. John recounted the scene when the judge donned the black cap and pronounced the sentence of death upon his co-defendant, Thatcher, who had killed the guard, and life imprisonment on the rest.

They were all taken to Wandsworth Prison where Thatcher was removed to the condemned cell beside the gallows.

This section of the prison is still maintained in working order and the trap-door tested twice a year in case some lunatic succeeds in reintroducing capital punishment. During my time in prison, I met a few victims of miscarriages of justice and was there during the release of both the Birmingham Six and Guildford Four. It is a sobering thought that these ten, along with the Maguires, would all have undoubtedly hanged for crimes which everybody who was closely involved knew they had never committed. I am sure that, after execution, it would have been easier for the authorities to sweep the matter neatly under the sinful carpet of injustice.

I have no personal religious beliefs, but sometimes wish that a day of reckoning would have to be faced by those complicit in crimes against humanity while so cleverly hiding behind a façade of respectability. With the advent of DNA science, who is to say that the police cannot doctor the evidence when they have an eternity of experience on which to call. No matter what one's beliefs, the proof that one innocent person has been erroneously executed in the past is sufficient reason never even to discuss the reintroduction of such barbarity.

John told me of the regime in those days – the compulsory silence, sewing mailbags in the cells and no radios or papers. Each time Thatcher was moved, the screws would make way for him by shouting, 'Dead man coming through.' On the eve of his execution, his sentence was to be commuted to life imprisonment by the then Home Secretary. From time to time, I think of the ritual killing of Ruth Ellis, her head covered in a black bag, her hands cuffed behind her, dropping to her death through the open trap-door.

One of the great songs in the repertoire of the great Paul Robeson, which I love to sing, is an American worker song called 'Joe Hill' who, as leader of the copper workers' union who became an increasing embarrassment to his bosses, was fitted up on a murder charge and executed by firing squad. His last wish was to send a telegram to his union with the words: 'DON'T MOURN FOR ME; ORGANISE'.

John served 15 years and was finally allowed out primarily into a hostel on licence. Not long after getting his freedom, he and an accomplice set out upon a spate of armed robberies until one ended in him accidentally shooting his friend. He managed to drag him to the getaway car where, after a while, his accomplice died from loss of blood. John buried him in a railway cutting and his body was never discovered. When arrested, his life-sentence licence was revoked and a further sentence imposed.

John told me that his dream was to rob the jewellers Boucheron, who always boasted that each one of their four windows contained at least £1 million of gems. He devolved a plan to ram-raid the shop front with an intricately constructed truck, carefully modified to be able to do the job. The detailed planning occupied many a year, but he needed two essential ingredients – freedom, which looked unlikely, and working capital.

While at Kingston Prison near Portsmouth, John befriended a young chap due for release. Shortly after, John was sprung over the wall in an elaborate and well-planned escape. Not long after, the two of them were involved in a shoot-out at a jewellery shop in Brighton and arrested at the scene where they had hoped to raise enough to finance the big one. They were taken to Brixton, where John decided to do the right thing by his co-defendant.

He wrote at length about his violent past, especially when armed. He told for the first time of the whereabouts of the friend he had buried all those years before and explained that he had forced his co-defendant at gunpoint and with threats against his family to help him rob the shop in The Lanes in Brighton. He stated that this was his dying statement, gave a copy to his solicitor and left another to be found after his death. He then swallowed a cocktail of medication he had been gathering for the purpose and made his peace with his maker.

On the brink of death and with a faint heartbeat, he was discovered and eventually revived; it was touch and go. He was then transferred to the hospital wing at Parkhurst where he began the hunger-strike, which had reduced him to the six-stone walking corpse I first met.

I told John that, in my opinion, a posthumous statement would have much less impact than his appearance in the witness box to give evidence in person. I persuaded him to begin eating again and, eventually, to be taken to the main wing where he could be fed and looked after by his many friends.

John gave evidence at the trial and stated that he had indeed made his co-defendant commit the robbery under pain of death to him and his family. The jury disbelieved him and his friend was sentenced to 14 years. John is one of the prisoners on a Home Office list who have been told that they stand no chance of parole or early release and that they will die in prison.

My overriding memory of John is of a softly spoken, articulate, educated, humorous, well-mannered, elderly gentleman with a twinkle in his eye.

34

ESCARGOTS

The regime on the two normal wings at Parkhurst was very different indeed from that in the prison hospital. Parkhurst traditionally housed some notoriously monstrous individuals in parts of the prison inaccessible to the general population and under the control of the hospital staff. Here, the screws held the upper hand; they had at their disposal an armoury of weapons and wielded them with relish.

Electric shock treatment was still in use and was a sanction regularly meted out to those who would not conform. Padded cells and body belts were used with little provocation and just about everybody got their regular shots of Largactyl. This stuff, like a liquid cosh, would quell the unquellable and stop an elephant in its tracks.

Called the Largactyl Shuffle, every prison-hospital exercise yard was full of zombies who, like the living dead from a Michael Jackson video, dragged themselves along, unable to speak, argue or plead.

Parkhurst housed a mixture of people – all races, creeds, cultures and beliefs – and, yet, nobody harboured a hatred for anybody else. I met many Irishmen there, proud to be Republican, who regarded themselves as prisoners of war. Remaining true to their beliefs when they were almost guaranteed to remain incarcerated for the rest of their lives, these men inspired respect even from those with diametrically opposite views. We were all thrown together, we had time on our hands and we conversed and communicated. We were all painfully aware of the lengths to which the authorities were prepared to go in order to win and we respected those who resisted.

Livio, one of the Sicilians on our wing and a man to be reckoned with, played the guitar with great skill. He loved the music of Django Rhinehart. Sometimes, I would play some opera, which was guaranteed to reduce him to tears in moments.

On my birthday, having established from one of the cookery books on the wing that all snails were edible, The Colonel and Del spent a long time in the exercise area gathering a bucketful. After purging the snails on oats for a couple of days, it was time to cook them.

After dropping them one by one into a pot of boiling water, the three of us were busy discussing how we were going to serve them. Into the kitchen walked one of the inmates, a contract killer doing life. When he demanded to know what exactly we were doing, he called us all 'fucking murderers' and stormed out in disgust.

I didn't stay at the laundry for long. The active education department boasted a high level of success. It succeeded in helping a lot of inmates from basic literacy skills to Open University degrees. There was a dedicated staff, who really cared. I got involved and was soon recording children's stories on to tape cassettes for the local hospital.

I received a visit one day from the rabbi. He travelled once a week on the ferry from Portsmouth and we soon became friends. Within a short while, a few others joined in and we spent many a long hour discussing a wide variety of topics. A truly good man, I regret not having kept in touch with him.

I had been at Parkhurst now for a year. Already four years into my sentence, I began to see those around me moving on to lower-security establishments and nearer to freedom. I knew that I was never to be more comfortable than at Parkhurst but I, too, had to plan for the future.

I got on well with John Marriot but he always looked at me a little sideways. I made an application to the security department for a downgraded status but they laughed at me. I put down to see the Governor.

He always made himself available and, within 24 hours, I had my chance to put my case. He listened carefully. Refusing my application, he told me that he found me impossible to classify. He said that most who come to prison with an accent like mine kept themselves at a distance. He could see that I was socially active and mixed well with the most dangerous criminals. He concluded by saying that, because of this, I would remain at the higher level for the time being. I was trapped in a situation I could not argue my way out of.

A blagger called Tommy Hole, not far into a 15-year sentence, was with us on the wing. His son, also called Tommy and who had been in a prison near Durham, came down to Parkhurst for visits and to be near his father. He was three months away from release.

The visits area was modern and quite comfortable. We were encouraged to receive visitors whenever we liked, and they lasted the best part of two hours. Security was tight but, once in, the visitors could relax. Joint visits were quite common, too, and, sometimes, it would be possible to take a friend who did not see people of his own to join in and meet family or friends. My family continued to come to see me on a regular basis.

Young Tommy's family had come to stay on the island for a few days and plans were in place to celebrate his impending release. Tommy was tense and on edge, but it was to be expected. After a visit one day, Tommy accused Vic of planning to knife him. Paranoia was playing its ugly tricks. Tommy asked to be taken to the block but, after some persuasion, his father calmed the situation down. Young Tommy was in the cell next to mine.

The next morning, with the doors quietly opened and left ajar, Tom Sr went to make some tea. He brought a jug upstairs and pushed open his son's cell door. I shall never forget the howl of anguish when Tom found his son dead. He had hanged himself during the night by a wire suspended from the bars of his window.

Not long after Tom had finished his sentence, he was gunned down in a local pub while drinking with his mates.

I was allocated a probation officer. Jo first came to see me one afternoon, having travelled by train from Woolwich. A young woman with a strong social conscience, she and I hit it off immediately. She ended up staying chatting until the end of visits. After this, we corresponded from time to time and I told her how much I enjoyed writing. The next time she came, she presented me with a portable typewriter she had bought with her own money. Jo supported me, trusted me and made strong representations to the parole board on my behalf. After my release, I had to visit Jo from time to time as part of the conditions of parole; it was always a pleasure to see her. She left to get married and have a baby. I remember her fondly.

For some months, an escape was being hatched on my wing. The occupants of a line of four cells began to dig away the bricks behind their noticeboards piece by piece at night. The end cell on the corner of the building was occupied by The Colonel. He was coming to the end of his sentence and declined the offer to join the expedition. However, on the night of the escape, a hole would have to be made through the outside wall of his cell in addition to the one through his noticeboard.

One of the escapees fell and broke an ankle and the party was apprehended in the grounds. The Colonel, covered in rubble and his cell newly air-conditioned, remained in bed. When the screws came to get him, he took some time rubbing his eyes and expressing shock at the devastation; he claimed to be a very heavy sleeper. He was shipped out to finish his sentence at Albany where there was an unfortunate fire a few days before he left.

I finally persuaded John Marriot to allocate me to a Cat C prison and, after nearly 18 months at Parkhurst, I was taken, this time in an ordinary prison van, to Downview Prison, near Sutton in Surrey.

All seemed well at reception but, as soon as my medical record was handed over, my transfer was refused and I was sent back to Parkhurst. Because I had been ill, the doctor had classified me as unfit for work, which suited me well on the Isle of Wight. This was not acceptable at Downview. My mates laughed at my predicament when I was returned to Parkhurst to find my bedding divided up between them.

It took little time for me to persuade the doctor to alter my medical status and, two weeks later, I was on my way again.

35

DOWNVIEW

This time, everything was in order. I knew nobody at reception but, while I was there, I was given a cup of coffee and chatted for a while. A short walk away, the main building was approached past a large gym and football pitch set in well-tended grounds in which stood some fine mature trees.

I was allocated a cell overlooking the garden, on the first floor at the front of the building. More like a room with bars on the windows, it was enormous, at least three times the size of what I had become used to. For the first time since the police station over four years back, there was a lavatory.

While I was unpacking, a couple of guys I knew from Parkhurst came by to welcome me; they were not encouraging. There was no cooking at Downview and I would have to eat what was given to me. I was warned to never leave my cell open because the prison was full of scumbags. I had never encountered a cell thief before; it just did not happen. Most of the inmates were short-termers and there were a lot of convicted street criminals. If they had earned a living mugging the vulnerable, I could understand that they would think nothing of stealing from their fellow prisoners.

Downview was very much a carrot-and-stick regime. There was a lot of freedom within the prison. Everybody would get a taste of home leave but a single transgression of the rules could meet with draconian results. Those who fucked up were shipped out and often ended up at Wandsworth.

There was a fair percentage of long-termers within sight of the end of their sentences and a handful of lifers who had already spent a long time away. Two of these had been fighting for justice for years and both, eventually, had their convictions overturned. One had been in prison for over 20 years.

There was and still remains a catch-22 situation with parole and, in the case of lifers, release under licence. Basically, you will not be released until you show 'remorse' for your crimes. If you were innocent, you had a dilemma. As a consequence, many innocent lifers ended up doing much more time than they would have served if they had committed the crime for which they were convicted.

My arrest coincided with the introduction of confiscation of assets and a resolution by the then Home Secretary that violent criminals and convicted drug-traffickers would not be considered for parole. Time had moved on, however, and, with the prisons bursting at the seams, parole was once more becoming a very real possibility.

The day after my arrival, I had to attend an induction process. I was seen by the doctor who, concerned about my problem at Parkhurst, wanted to arrange a blood test.

I was told that many of the inmates were engaged in outside work in the community. Old ladies' gardens and manual assistance at the local hospitals was a favourite. The prison had a very strong association with Mencap and many of the inmates were engaged in working in local homes for the mentally disabled. Every week, a large number of residents in these homes would come to the prison and spend the morning in the gym, where they would be supervised and attended to by the inmates.

I opted for full-time education and was soon seconded to help with the reading and writing programme.

Several of the screws had a little business on the side and the first party I was invited to had a selection of half-bottles of spirits. I was glad to leave Graham Gooch behind at Parkhurst. When I began to skin up, I was warned that I should be very careful and make sure not to be caught. There were a lot of Nigerian prisoners at the jail and they had a reputation for mercilessly grassing up anybody they could.

I received a gypsy's warning from one of the screws one day – after smelling cannabis, two of the inmates had rushed to the wing office. 'I would like to report the grave matter that Mr Newman in cell 24 has been smoking cannabis,' said the first.

'No, no,' said the other, 'I saw him first.'

Within days of my arrival, I had a problem to deal with. The occupant of the cell next to me had his radio on full blast until the early hours. He would accompany the loud music with hoots and shouts and occasional banging on the wall. I went to see him. I knocked on his cell door, which had recently been opened for breakfast, to find him fast asleep in bed. I was none too pleased with him and decided to shake him awake. He was instantly very aggressive. I had tried during the previous evening to get him to turn the music down and all I had got was shouted abuse.

'Go fuck yourself and don't come in here fucking waking me up.'

I saw red. I picked up his radio and smashed it against the metal frame at the end of his bed. He leaped out of bed and came for me. I floored him with his chair. It was all over in seconds but the incident had created a lot of noise and I expected the troops to arrive at any moment. Fighting was, we had been told, very much a taboo at Downview.

It turned out that my neighbour was universally disliked. He moved to another cell later in the day and, a couple of weeks afterwards, was shipped out for mugging a guy for his tobacco.

I didn't mind the regime too much. I avoided contact with the scumbags and soon settled into life at Downview. I was not too busy in the education department and was able to help a few people. I went to the gym to see what was happening with the weekly Mencap visitors and stayed to help; it was fun and I could see that even the most severely disabled enjoyed themselves. I played badminton and pool and took advantage of another very good library.

About ten days after I arrived, I was called to reception. There, I was told that I had to go to the local hospital for my blood test.

'How are you getting down there?' asked the screw.

I was somewhat taken aback. 'I don't know.'

'Come on,' he said, 'we'll give you a lift.'

No handcuffs, no prison van, I walked out of the prison gate with two screws, into the car park and off in the back of a private car to the hospital. We pulled up outside and one of them said, 'You go off and get your blood test and we'll park the car. We'll see you in the café when you've finished.'

I got out of the car and stood for a while. I felt nervous and very alone. At that moment, I realised that, like it or not, I had become institutionalised. This would never do.

I strode off and did what I had to do. Back at the hospital café, I was treated to a coffee and a sandwich; my escort was in no hurry to return. I soon established that they knew very well that it was the first time in five years that I had been free of restrictions. I asked them if they had been worried that I might abscond and they explained that it was an occupational hazard at Downview. A lot of prisoners absconded on their first home leave but, because they were not considered a high-security risk any more, it became a low-priority problem. They were usually picked up after a few days, and the resultant loss of privileges usually made the exercise counterproductive.

I was beginning to pick up on what it was that occupied everybody's minds here. Freedom was so tantalisingly close and yet our fate was still very much in the hands of our captors. Most of the inmates were serving short sentences and had a release date close at hand. In the absence of parole, I would have at least another two years to serve. I determined to try to get it out of my head, but I never succeeded.

Visits were very pleasant and relaxed. Visitors could bring hot food and, if discreet, some alcohol. We were allowed to buy phone cards and use the many call boxes to keep in touch with the outside world.

The rabbi from Sutton would visit regularly and we would chat in the comfort of an office beside the Chapel. He had a very active local Jewish community for which he worked hard.

In due course, I applied for home leave and it was approved first time. Two weeks later, I walked out of the gate on Friday evening under strict orders to return on Sunday before 6.00pm. My beautiful Norlesden House was long gone but I was surprised to feel quite at home in a maisonette on a Kidbrooke council estate. My Staffordshire Bull Terrier, Spliffy, circled me uncertainly for a minute before recognising me, whereupon she jumped into my arms.

36

INSIDE WITH JOOLS HOLLAND

I had been thinking. I called my friend Jools Holland over the weekend and asked him if he would consider giving a concert at Downview for the inmates and the people from the Mencap homes. He readily agreed. I told him that I had not passed the idea in front of the Governor but I was sure he would go for it. We agreed to keep in touch.

By this time, Jools was very much in the ascendancy. With his own television show and constantly touring with his own band, he was a busy man. Highly respected internationally as a musician's musician, he could get almost anybody in the music world to make a guest appearance on his shows.

I went to see the wing SO. He was obviously excited at the idea and promised to take it to the Governor. The next day, not sure that what I was suggesting was genuine, I was asked to get Jools on the telephone. Two minutes later, an arrangement was made for him to come to the prison a week later during lunchtime.

The Governor was excited at the idea and handed the planning to me and the SO. We soon concluded that the large visits area was the only suitable place for a concert. Calls were made to ascertain how many Mencap guests would like to come and needed to be catered for.

On the day that Julian had arranged to visit, I had a stand-up row with the SO who, I discovered, planned to leave me locked up in my cell while he was entertaining my friend. I was furious but eventually won the day. We both greeted Jools who, having looked at the venue, was given lunch in the Governor's office. A date was fixed and Julian decided that the whole band would take part in the concert. They would just fit on the large raised stage at the end of the hall. Afterwards, Jools and I were left alone for an hour when I had the opportunity to thank him for his kindness.

The following day, I had a visit from my daughter Emily and her boyfriend Dave. Excited that Jools was doing a concert at the prison, Dave had called Mike, a cameraman friend of his who worked and lived locally and was a devoted fan. Mike asked if he could come to see me on a visit to discuss bringing a camera to the concert. I asked the SO, who let me call Mike straight away. Mike and Dave were there to see me the following afternoon. Mike worked at the head office of *Encyclopaedia Britannica* which was a couple of miles away in Sutton. There, they had a fully fitted-out TV studio which made promotional videos, largely for internal use. Mike's boss was very tolerant and had no problem with him borrowing anything he needed to film the concert. He had another cameraman friend and suggested that he could make a TV-quality film with three cameras. The third could be manned by Dave, which would be on a fixed pedestal at the back of the hall. He would need an assistant, and so it was that Emily, too, would be able to come to the show. We decided that we might just as well work towards making a whole programme. By the end of the visit, the three of us had decided to form a TV production company and Mike would speak to the Governor to see if I could be allowed out to run it.

The Governor was in complete support of the plan; his only requirement was that he would approve anything we proposed to include in the film first before it was screened. Jools, too, had no problem with the show being filmed and asked if I could spend a couple of days with him prior to the concert as co-ordinator.

Two days before the concert, I was allowed to set about dealing with the arrangements. I did a good job. I travelled back to Blackheath with Jools and arrived later with the band to introduce them on-stage.

Mike had done a wonderful job of setting up the film shoot. As the guests arrived, he was there with a camera and took some great footage.

It was a great show. The audience was treated to a fantastic performance and the whole band was in top form. Food was laid on by the prison and Jools was kept busy at the end signing autographs.

I helped Mike and Dave packing up the camera equipment and, with the Governor's permission, went to stay at Mike's flat after we had deposited everything in the studio at his work. It was already late and we talked long into the night.

Mike had a job to do but he had cleared it with his boss for me to come to the studio every day and prepare the film for editing. Nobody in the management of the company had been told who I was or what I was doing. Mike had kept my identity quiet.

The Governor was happy for me to be out on day release and, during the next few weeks, just a phone call from Mike sufficed to let me carry on working 'til late into the night. I soon learned how to log the footage and Mike was a good teacher. In the weeks that followed, I was gradually involved more and more in the day-to-day running of the studio and was often employed manning a camera or arranging lighting.

Once I had logged everything, Mike and I put together a short demo using bits of footage here and there. We made a few copies. We had secured the services of a top editor who was happy to work nights on a speculative basis and receive a fee if and when the film was sold.

We had a big problem, though. The camera fixed at the back of the room taking a long-shot of the show had been out of focus the whole shoot. It presented a permanent dilemma and we had to spend ages scrutinising every shot before agreeing the final edit.

I made a phone call to Channel 4 one day and was asked to send them a demo tape. Two days later, I got a call from Andrea Wonfor who was the Commissioning Editor for music. She was full of enthusiasm and asked if we could go to see her. I cleared it with the Governor who was most enthusiastic and, two days later, Mike, Dave and I were in her office.

She loved what we had sent her and was keen to see the finished programme. She asked us to give her an estimate of the production costs. We were not prepared for this eventuality so soon. We had so far done the whole thing very cheaply and with borrowed equipment and reckoned that after paying the editor the total budget would be no more than £600.

Andrea pressed us for an answer. 'Look, I really want to buy this but we are on a very short rein at the moment. Give me an idea.'

'We really don't know,' I said.

'What do you think... ten thousand, five thousand? Give me an idea.'

'We can do it for six thousand,' I said.

It was as simple as that. The only hard thing that day was giving myself up back at the prison gates.

We put the programme together and everybody was delighted with the result; it was shown several times. We had enough money to give Jools a contribution towards expenses, put some in the bank and make a large donation to Mencap.

Jools was really there for me when I most needed him, for which I shall be eternally grateful.

37

FREEDOM

One day, Mike told me that we had been rumbled. The boss of *Encyclopaedia Britannica* had found out who the new unpaid cameraman was. I was no longer welcome.

Our original project was finished and we had delivered the film. However, we had big plans and discussions had already begun to film a series of concerts in different prisons with a variety of bands.

Andrea Wonfor had expressed great excitement at the plan and I spent some time with the Governor at Downview who received word from the Home Office that I should be given every assistance.

We took a small office with a telephone in Sutton, which cost very little, and I commuted by bus every day to work. I was now in liaison with another SO and we got on very well. He had applied for promotion and warned me that, if he was successful, it would involve a move to Latchmere House, an open prison near Twickenham. He implied that it might not be a bad idea to apply for a transfer there myself.

We had travelled together to London to look at future locations and I had been given a guided tour of Holloway and Pentonville Prisons. Here I was, walking round Holloway, and only a year before I was still at Parkhurst, worrying John Marriot about my security status.

Pino Paladino, Jools's bass player, married to one of the 'Wealthy Tarts', had been helping to find bands for the concerts. We went together to the Albert Hall to see Eric Clapton, whom we wanted to persuade to play at a final concert at Wandsworth. We had secured the services of Ian Dury for Holloway and seemed to be on a roll. Most of the stars we approached were very much drawn to the idea of performing in prison.

I had been given a date for my second parole hearing and was to be interviewed on a Tuesday after another home-leave weekend. Preparing for my return behind bars, I had taken a bath. When I got out, I pulled my back so badly that I could not move. I was taken by ambulance in agony to Greenwich Hospital. There were no acceptable excuses for returning late from home leave but I could not move for 24 hours. The Governor had been informed by the hospital and my doctor. I hoped that it would not jeopardise my situation. The prison sent a car for me and nothing was said. Thankfully, my cell was now on the ground floor where I was laid up for several days.

The next day, the parole board came to me. When I was asked the inevitable question, I answered that I regretted wasting several years of my life and that I would not do it again. It was a satisfactory compromise. I tried to put parole out of my mind but was constantly reminded of some long-termers getting some very good results. One in particular went home three years earlier than expected.

I also received a visit from an Assistant Governor of Latchmere House; my application for transfer had been successful and I was expected the following Monday. Latchmere House, a big old country house, had been occupied by the Intelligence Services during the war. Used as a place to house German spies, many an enemy agent had been turned there into working for the allies. Most of those not selected for the purpose had been summarily executed and I assume that the extensive and private grounds surrounding the imposing building may have been as good a place as any for this task. Rudolf Hess had spent some time there during the war.

Given a lift there by my daughter, I could see when I arrived that inmates were coming and going pretty much as they pleased. More like a hotel when I checked in, I was given a key to my room and nobody searched my belongings. I can only assume that the fence which surrounded the place was there more to keep the locals out than the inmates in.

The rules stated that I was not permitted to go to work for two weeks, during which time I would be assessed. The Governor shortened this to a week in my case, and I was given access to a telephone to keep the business going. I was asked to let reception know if I was going out for a walk and to observe the rule not to drink to excess. On the first day, I went for a long walk by the Thames with a guy I knew, after which we spent a leisurely couple of hours in a local riverside pub.

During that first week, I was allowed to rehearse with a local opera company who were putting on a performance of *La Traviata* in English. There were some good voices but, for me, a good deal of the story was lost in translation.

After that first week, I was back in the office. I was permitted to use a car and the family had bought me an old yellow Ford Fiesta. We were near getting a date for the Holloway concert. I prepared a detailed list of what we required and, this time, we planned a four-camera shoot.

I got a call from Andrea and I went to see her the next day. She took me to lunch at an Italian restaurant in Charlotte Street across the road from her office and I could tell that she was uncomfortable. She told me that Channel 4 had pulled the plug on the project and their budgets had been slashed. She was bitterly disappointed.

We spent some time over lunch, during which I answered a few questions about how things were in prison. She gave me some ideas, leads and encouragement and promised to help with advice any time I needed it.

I reported back to Mike and Dave. None of us had any personal experience or contacts in the business that we could call on. We had been lucky to hit the jackpot first time with the Jools Holland concert. I was sure that we had a fantastic product but we had no idea where to go with it.

After six weeks at Latchmere, I returned one night to find a note on my pillow. It was from the prison social worker. After serving five-and-a-half years, I had been granted parole. My sentence had been shortened by just over a year.

Four days later, I walked out of the gate, got into my car and drove away.

EPILOGUE

There was no time or money for a party or a holiday; I had to earn a living. The prospect of making a success of the film production company with no working capital was too unrealistic. I came out to a very new environment – a council flat on the notorious Ferrier Estate. It took me a while to recognise that I had changed. I suppose that the first inkling was when I realised that my new environment was not such a shock as I would have expected. I did not want to stay there for ever, but the possessions and the grand lifestyle were no longer a big draw for me.

I had wasted many years behind bars and had had taken from me the one thing that I valued above all else. I was determined that I would not repeat the experience and risk my liberty once again.

Within a few months of gaining my freedom, Jo, my ever supportive probation officer, willingly agreed for me to apply for a new passport. With the support of my old friend Flaviano Preston, I was on my travels once again.

I spent many years designing and making glassware. My travels in this connection have taken me to Poland, Ukraine, Hungary, Germany and Iran. I achieved a high level of success and exhibited my wares at many international trade fairs.

I have travelled to China, Mexico and India, designing and making furniture.

I have sung in America, Poland, Spain and India. I have performed in a royal palace and two cathedrals. I have run the London Marathon.

I keep my love of motor sport alive, managing and 'mechanic-ing' for my grandsons, Jasper and Joseph, who race junior Moto X.

I have made many new friends.

Adventures? There have been so many.

But that's another story.